TED HUGHES: A Critical Study

TED HUGHES:
A Critical Study

TERRY GIFFORD and
NEIL ROBERTS

FABER AND FABER
London   Boston

First published in 1981
by Faber and Faber Limited
3 Queen Square London WC1N 3AU
Printed in Great Britain by
Fakenham Press Limited, Fakenham, Norfolk
All rights reserved

© *Terry Gifford and Neil Roberts 1981*

British Library Cataloguing in Publication Data

Gifford, Terry
  Ted Hughes.
  1. Hughes, Ted – Criticism and interpretation
  I. Roberts, Neil
  821'.9'14   PR6058.U37Z/

  ISBN 0–571–11701–5

For
Edna and Dennis
Christine, Paul and Amy

❧ Contents ❧

❧ Acknowledgements ❧

A shorter version of Chapter 4 was published in the *Dutch Quarterly Review of Anglo-American Letters*, vol. 8, no. 1, 1978. The first part of Chapter 8 appeared in Delta, 60, 1979. The book is also extensively indebted to a Sheffield University M.A. thesis by Terry Gifford, 'The Poetry of Ted Hughes'.

We are most grateful to Ted Hughes himself for his helpful answers to our letters, and to Olwyn Hughes for her generous co-operation. We are also indebted to Keith Sagar both for his published biographical work and for his generous personal help.

In addition we wish to thank Peter Redgrove for lending his tape of *The God of Glass* and for correspondence with Neil Roberts; David Craig for his discussion and correspondence with Terry Gifford; Hamish Hamilton for transcribing the broadcast of *Cave Birds*; Richard Kemp and Harriet Gilmour for their help with the bibliography; Marion Salvin for typing the manuscript; Gil Gilmore for researching material in the USA; Karen Wile and Ralph Grant of the Hobson Gallery, Cambridge, for allowing Terry Gifford to study material from their Baskin exhibition; Sheffield University Research Fund for financial help with typing.

We gratefully acknowledge permission by Olwyn Hughes to quote 'Light' and 'Bud-tipped twig' from the Rainbow Press edition of *Adam and the Sacred Nine*; by Routledge and Kegan Paul Ltd. to quote from 'On Losing One's Black Dog' by Peter Redgrove, published in *From Every Chink of the Ark*; and by Doubleday and

9

ACKNOWLEDGEMENTS

Company, Inc., for permission to quote 'At the Gate of the Valley' by Zbigniew Herbert from *Postwar Polish Poetry*, edited and translated by Czeslaw Milosz. Copyright © 1965 by Czeslaw Milosz.

January 1980

TERRY GIFFORD
NEIL ROBERTS

❧ 1 ❧

Introduction

This book is inspired by the belief that Ted Hughes is a great poet, in whose hands our language is both familiar and different from anything we had thought possible. He reminds us that we really do still speak the language of Shakespeare, that locked within the words we use is an instrument capable of registering the reality of things and of inner states. He is a prolific poet—much more so in the seventies than he seemed to be previously—and an uneven one, but his characteristic virtues can be seen in a remarkably large proportion of his work, and his failures are usually matters of excess, hardly ever of paucity. He is a poet who has developed—from an early reliance on external nature to a greater metaphysical assurance and the creation of a distinctive imaginative world—and there have inevitably been many critics who have regretted this development. We are not among them. While the passage of time has made such early poems as 'Wind', 'Pike' and 'View of a Pig' seem greater, not smaller achievements than when we first read them, Hughes's greatness for us is to have gone on from those and the best *Wodwo* poems to produce such work as 'Crow's Account of the Battle', 'Crow on the Beach', 'Crow Tyrannosaurus', Lumb's visions in *Gaudete* and, from *Cave Birds*, 'The executioner', 'The knight', 'Bride and groom' and 'The risen'.

What is perhaps most remarkable about this development is that it does not entail either a radical reorientation or a rejection of the imaginative heart of the earlier work, as was the case in different ways with Eliot after *The Waste Land* and Yeats from *Responsibilities* or (to take a contemporary example) Thom Gunn from *My Sad Captains*. Hughes has neither overturned his imaginative world

11

nor written himself out but has gone on finding new strategies for remaining true to a consistent inspiration.

Throughout our book we are concerned with language—most explicitly in Chapter 2 but in practice in every chapter—since we believe it is only through attention to language that a poet's reputation can be argued for. In this we differ from Keith Sagar's thorough and enthusiastic book *The Art of Ted Hughes* which, despite its title, is mainly interpretative and can, we feel, persuade only the converted. We do, of course, offer interpretations of the poetry, but we have tried to avoid allowing these to become divorced from critical judgement.

It is, of course, a part of our sense of Hughes's greatness that his poetry says something important. We have spoken of a 'consistent inspiration'. What is this inspiration? What is the main unifying perception in his work? In an interview with Egbert Faas, published in the *London Magazine* in January 1971, Hughes said:

> Any form of violence—any form of vehement activity—invokes the bigger energy, the elemental power circuit of the Universe. Once the contact has been made—it becomes difficult to control. Something from beyond ordinary human activity enters. When the wise men know how to create rituals and dogma, the energy can be contained. When the old rituals and dogma have lost credit and disintegrated, and no new ones have been formed, the energy cannot be contained, and so its effect is destructive—and that is the position with us. And that is why force of any kind frightens our rationalist, humanist style of outlook. In the old world God and divine power were invoked at any cost—life seemed worthless without them. In the present world we dare not invoke them—we wouldn't know how to use them or stop them destroying us. We have settled for the minimum practical energy and illumination—anything bigger introduces problems, the demons get hold of it. That is the psychological stupidity, the ineptitude, of the rigidly rationalist outlook—it's a form of hubris, and we're paying the traditional price. If you refuse the energy, you are living a kind of death. If you accept the energy, it destroys you. What is the alternative? To accept the energy, and find methods of turning it to good, of keeping it under control—rituals, the machinery of religion. The old method is the only one.

(pp. 9–10)

This gives us a map of the territory of most of his major work. It gives us, with remarkable completeness, the theme of *Gaudete*, and it gives us the spirit in which the early animal poems are written. The use of the term *hubris*, the tragic pride of trying to outmanoeuvre one's destiny or resist the processes at work in oneself and the nature of things, gives us a thread connecting 'Egg-Head' and 'Meeting' from *The Hawk in the Rain*, 'Revenge Fable' from *Crow* and 'The scream' from *Cave Birds*. It is of course in the poems that the inspiration finds its expression, and the purpose of quoting from an interview is not to explain the poems but to define their territory and, in fact, to point out some of the problems that occur when one attempts to translate into conceptual terms what has been apprehended in the language of the imagination.

The most obvious problem here—a notorious matter with Hughes—is the word 'violence'. He seems to equate violence with 'vehement activity'. Is the activity of an athlete breaking the pain barrier, then, or the dance of a dervish, 'violent'? Obviously not—or, if these things are violent, we need another word for a man beating another over the head with a rock. Hughes is certainly abusing language here—his hostile critics would say, in a symptomatic and sinister way. We prefer to take a more generous view. The very first words of the interviewer are, 'Critics have often described your poetry as the "poetry of violence"': Hughes has been confronted with the word throughout his career, and its use is characteristic of the 'civilized' attitudes against the grain of which his work so evidently runs. To reject it might well seem to him evasive; to accept it is to run the risk of confirming his critics' darkest suspicions. His touch was better, we feel, in an earlier interview (*Guardian*, 23 March 1965) when he said, 'My poems are not about violence but vitality. Animals are not violent, they're so much more completely controlled than men.' On the other hand this does not take account of a poem such as 'Second Glance at a Jaguar'. Really, the word 'violence' is very unhelpful, and we shall not be making much use of it. One only needs to ask the simple question, 'Do Hughes's poems suggest that it is a good thing for people to maim and torture each other?' The answer is that there are a couple of early poems, 'Law in the Country of the Cats' and 'The Ancient Heroes and the Bomber Pilot', which do give this impression, but that these are easily outweighed by poems that react with horror to human violence: 'Wilfred Owen's Photographs', 'Crow's Account of the Battle', 'Crow's Account of St George', the climax of *Gaudete*. Such a reaction is particularly prominent in *Crow*, supposedly Hughes's most anti-human book. The reason for the problem about 'violence' in Hughes's work is his determination to acknowledge the predatory, destructive character of nature, of which man is a part, and not to moralize about it. As we shall see, his work can be regarded as a prolonged confrontation with Manichaeism.

A look at his relation to Manichaeism will illuminate both his dealings with 'violence' and another problem raised in the passage we have quoted from the *London Magazine* interview, which concerns the references to God and 'the machinery of religion'. In the same interview Hughes uses the word 'materialist' in a distinctly negative sense and in general he talks and writes freely about 'the spirits'. One of the fundamental questions about his work, then, is, in what sense is he a religious poet, and does his work imply the existence of a reality other than our own in which the source of the 'divine power' lies?

Manichaean mythology, according to A. C. H. Smith, was a major influence on *Orghast*. The religion of Mani, which originated in Mesopotamia in the third century AD, posited a state of war between spirit and matter, light and darkness, good and evil. Its mythology explains the present mixed state of things as the result of a partially successful assault by the darkness on the light, and the whole duty of man is to restore the separation, largely by ascetic practices. A major figure in its mythology is Primaeval Man, a warrior of the forces of light, who

> clad himself in his armour and set forth to do battle with the cohorts of matter, of darkness, of evil. The armour consisted of his five light elements and in sum they constituted not merely his armour but his own being, his proper 'self', his 'soul'.
>
> (Geo Widengren, *Mani and Manichaeism*, pp. 49–50)

Hughes has used the figure of the Knight in two poems, the first of which is the third part of 'Gog', which begins:

Out through the dark archway of earth, under the ancient lintel
overwritten with roots,
Out between the granite jambs, gallops the hooded horseman of
iron.

Out of the wound-gash in the earth, the horseman mounts,
                              shaking his plumes clear of dark soil.
Out of the blood-dark womb, gallops bowed the horseman of
                                                        iron.

The blood-crossed Knight, the Holy Warrior, hooded with iron,
                              the seraph of the bleak edge.
Gallops along the world's ridge in moonlight.

Through slits of iron his eyes search for the softness of the throat,
                              the navel, the armpit, the groin.
Bring him clear of the flung web and the coil that vaults from the
                                                        dust.

The poem is somewhat laboured and repetitive, but it does communicate quite powerfully a grim self-sufficiency and hatred of
material nature. Whether Hughes was already familiar with
Manichaeism when he wrote this poem is unimportant, but there is a
clear resemblance to Primaeval Man. The 'blood-crossed Knight' is
also obviously St George, whom Hughes has described as 'this
innocent, virginal being inside this mechanized protective, aggressive, defensive case' ('Myth and Education', *Children's Literature in
Education*, 1, p. 65). St George is the Christian equivalent of the
Manichaean hero. Throughout Hughes's work we find a rejection of
the self-sufficient ego, in the guise of spirit, or of intellect, or of
heroic endeavour, and of the embattled, suppressive attitude to
matter and darkness that is figured in the myths of Primaeval Man
and St George.
    The second poem about a knight is from *Cave Birds*.

The knight

Has conquered. He has surrendered everything.

Now he kneels. He is offering up his victory
And unlacing his steel.

In front of him are the common wild stones of the earth—

The first and last altar
Onto which he lowers his spoils.

15

And that is right. He has conquered in earth's name.
Committing these trophies

To the small madness of roots, to the mineral stasis
And to rain.

An unearthly cry goes up.
The Universes squabble over him—

Here a bone, there a rag.
His sacrifice is perfect. He reserves nothing.

Skylines tug him apart, winds drink him,
Earth itself unravels him from beneath—

His submission is flawless.

Blueflies lift off his beauty.
Beetles and ants officiate

Pestering him with instructions.
His patience grows only more vast.

His eyes darken bolder in their vigil
As the chapel crumbles.

His spine survives its religion,
The texts moulder—

The quaint courtly language
Of wingbones and talons.

And already
Nothing remains of the warrior but his weapons

And his gaze.
Blades, shafts, unstrung bows—and the skull's beauty

Wrapped in the rags of his banner.
He is himself his banner and its rags.

While hour by hour the sun
Strengthens its revelation.

The use of the figure of the Knight here is in a sense ironical: his
conquest and his surrender are one. Far from riding armoured into
battle against the material world he conquers by surrendering to his
reabsorption into it. The poem is a meditation on a decomposing
corpse, apparently of a bird, and its achievement is the harmonious
marriage of the picture of the knight, the solemn and courtly
language, with the material reality that it represents.

'The knight' has the solemn and reverential tone of a devotional
poem, and yet it would be hard to call it religious in any usually
understood sense of the word—

His spine survives its religion,
The texts moulder—

but it is just this combination of religious awe and surrender with a
refusal to look beyond the processes of material nature that constitutes the distinctive heart of Hughes's vision. He summarized the
theme of Part 1 of *Orghast* as 'the crime against material nature, the
Creatress, source of life and light, by the Violater, the mental tyrant
Holdfast, and her revenge' (Smith, *Orghast at Persepolis*, p. 132).

This central perception seems to be that the world of spirit and the
material world are the same; that the reality 'beyond' our life whose
beckoning prompts religious devotion and theology is that of
material objects and processes, of which we are objectively a part
but feel ourselves to be in some way outside. This does not negate
the search for a religious dimension but is its only complete satisfac-
tion: the state of oneness that the great religions in their various
ways posit as their *telos* is the recognition of a literal truth, but the
religious sense is always at the mercy of 'the mental tyrant Holdfast'
and his armed warrior.

A striking parallel to this perception can be found in Mircea
Eliade's interpretation of primitive religion, which can also give us a
clue to the nature of Hughes's own interest in anthropology and the
primitive:

The hardness, ruggedness and permanence of matter was
in itself a hierophany in the religious consciousness of the

17

primitive. And nothing was more direct and autonomous in the completeness of its strength, nothing more noble or more awe-inspiring, than a majestic rock, or a boldly-standing block of granite. Above all, stone *is*.

(*Patterns in Comparative Religion*, p. 216)

But just as the great religions are drama as well as dogma, so this central perception of Hughes's cannot be held fast in any formulation. Moreover, horror at the material creation and protest against man's place in it are frequently to be found in his poetry. His work is not a series of statements but of re-enacted encounters and adventures. The best of his earlier nature poetry depends for its effect on an awareness of the perceiver, and the drama inherent in that is further exploited in the narrative and mythical forms of the later work.

The presence of the horror and protest have led Peter Porter, for example, to see Hughes's work as itself Manichaean, and the imaginative world of *Crow*—with its stark opposition of darkness and light, its battle between Crow and Stone, its 'two Gods', and above all the myth of 'God's nightmare' that underlies the book—might seem to support such a view. We think it is mistaken, and that the character of the mythical world of *Crow* (and consequently of Hughes's whole imaginative world) can be clarified by comparing it with two real myths of the kind on which part of it is based. Joseph Campbell, in *The Masks of God: Primitive Mythology*, relates a pre-Christian and a Christianized version of the same basic myth. In the pre-Christian version the Great Spirit tells a waterfowl to dive into the water and bring up earth and clay. The bird does so, the Great Spirit uses it to create the land and blesses the bird. In the Christianized version it is Satan, challenged by God, who dives into the water. Christ blesses the morsel of mud that he comes up with and creates a flat, smooth earth out of it. But Satan has concealed some of the mud, and out of this the mountains are made. Campbell points out the obvious contrast between the innocence of the one version and the ethical dualism of the other, which assigns the rugged parts of nature to an evil creator. In the *Crow* narrative God has a nightmare in the form of a voice and a hand, which mocks his creation and which he challenges to do better. The nightmare plunges into matter and creates Crow. Hughes's version occupies an interesting place between the two 'genuine' myths.

There is a suggestion of the devil, of evil and mischief, about God's nightmare—there is none of the 'innocence' of the pre-Christian version—but the ethical dualism of the Christianized version is broken down. God is fallible and impotent, incapable of breathing life into his own creatures; the nightmare's creation, Crow, is equally capable of good and of evil. The reader is given room to manoeuvre and judge.

The myth that has most consistently inspired Hughes is the subject of Robert Graves's *The White Goddess*: the nature goddess in her three aspects of maiden, mother and crone (Persephone, Demeter and Hecate in the best-known version). This myth holds, in a single imaginative unit, the total, inescapable character of reality, both beneficent and destructive. It assists Hughes in extending the perception of Wordsworth to incorporate all that is terrifying and predatory, as well as comforting and nurturing, in nature. The goddess is implicit in his work from the beginning, but becomes increasingly prominent, in the 'mother' of several of the *Crow* poems, in the object of Lumb's devotion in *Gaudete*, and in the hero's victim and bride in *Cave Birds*. The rational and moral controlling consciousness's dealings with her are the theme of Hughes's synoptic interpretation of Shakespeare in *A Choice of Shakespeare's Verse*. The goddess is not separate from the world of things, and she is present also in the human unconscious, accessible to disciplined techniques of imagination, states of meditation, ecstasy, extremes of anguish or bliss.

Our account of Hughes's preoccupation with the 'goddess' would be misleading if we did not stress that it has its practical side. He wrote 'The Last Migration' for a book whose royalties were donated to the Fauna Preservation Society; he has written a knowledgeable review of Max Nicholson's *The Environmental Revolution* and a letter to *The Times Educational Supplement* suggesting that schools encourage children to plant trees. This practical engagement with the natural world comes to the forefront of his work in the farming poems of *Moortown*.

It is, however, with the relation of consciousness to the forces and processes that govern our material being that his major poetry is primarily concerned, and this is the context in which we should understand his interest in shamanism, which might at first seem bizarre and eccentric. 'Shaman' is the anthropologists' preferred term for what is more popularly called a sorcerer or witch-doctor, a

19

function found predominantly in herding societies. He or she is initiated into the profession of shamanism through a form of mental breakdown which may be spontaneous or self-induced by fasting, drugs or sleep-deprivation. In the course of this experience, ordinary reality ceases for him and he enters the world of the 'spirits', where he encounters beings whose form is usually determined by his particular culture. This experience is terrifying, and often entails dismemberment and the creation of a new body. Subsequently he is taught the techniques of shamanic practice. Although the shaman undoubtedly lets go of ordinary sanity during his initiation and his practice, he is never mistaken for a madman or neurotic by his own people. He is valued for his direct experience of 'other' worlds which the ordinary man knows of only through myth and ritual. This is believed to enable him, for example, to cure the sick by rescuing their souls from another world. The shaman's practice ('shamanizing') involves singing, dancing and recitation, often in a special poetic vocabulary which is several times larger than that of the ordinary language. He dresses in animal skins, and most particularly in birds' feathers since 'flight' is an important part of his function; his 'helping spirits' often have animal forms and he is believed to have a special affinity with the animal world, not altogether distinct from his affinity with the world of the spirits. In Mircea Eliade's words: 'Each time a shaman succeeds in sharing in the animal mode of being, he in a manner re-establishes the situation that existed *in illo tempore*, in mythical times, when the divorce between man and the animal world had not yet occurred' (*Shamanism*, p. 94). Since his visionary experiences also entail crossing the borderline between the living and the dead he is valued for his ability thus to 'die' and return: 'The unknown and terrifying world of death assumes form, is organized in accordance with particular patterns' (*Shamanism*, p. 509).

A distinguishing characteristic of shamanic experience is the exceptionally vivid, coherent and shared forms taken by the unconscious life. The shaman can thus be seen as a man who, having experienced and overcome terrifying inward experience, is no longer at the mercy of death, of his animal self, of his unconscious in general and who, through a kind of artistic performance, shares this mastery with the community. It is clearly impossible for a modern English poet to *be* a shaman, but equally clearly Hughes's preoccupations with the unconscious, with death, with the animal world and mythology show an affinity with the shaman's function. What a poet such as Hughes ultimately shares with the shaman is a concern for psychic equilibrium.

In discussing the imaginative context of Hughes's work one cannot avoid stressing—perhaps overstressing—the 'primitive'. But it should be made clear that as a trained anthropologist Hughes's interest in the primitive is not a rejection of culture but a concern *for* culture. He does, indeed, reject much of our own culture on the grounds that the consciousness it fosters rests on a dangerously narrow base, but he does not reject it in favour of an illusory ideal of unaccommodated man. He is interested in the sophistication of primitive cultures (and not only primitive cultures) in areas, particularly dealings with the inner life and the natural world, where our own is barbaric. The American anthropologist Clifford Geertz, in an essay on 'Religion as a Cultural System', writes:

> The extreme generality, diffuseness, and variability of man's innate (i.e. genetically programmed) response capacities means that without the assistance of cultural patterns he would be functionally incomplete, not merely a talented ape who had, like some under-privileged child, unfortunately been prevented from realizing his full potentialities, but a kind of formless monster with neither sense of direction nor power of self-control, a chaos of spasmodic impulses and vague emotions.
>
> (M. Banton (ed.), *Anthropological Approaches to the Study of Religion*, p. 13)

Fear of this 'formless monster' understandably stiffens resistance to wholesale attacks on our own culture, but Hughes sees the monster in characteristic products of our culture—the demented positivist 'St George', the 'almost a person' of 'A Bedtime Story', the photographer taking shots of a woman being mauled to death by a tiger in 'Myth and Education'. Although, at times, his view of the world we live in is a caricature ('the whole mass of the people, slumped every night in front of their sets ... in attitudes of total disengagement, a sort of anaesthetized unconcern', *London Magazine* interview, January 1971, p. 7) there is running throughout his work the serious and convincing fear that the 'cultural patterns' of our society do leave us 'functionally incomplete'.

None of Hughes's fairly large bulk of critical writing is devoted to promulgating or inaugurating a 'movement' or 'school'. The generous, though discriminating, catholicity of his taste in contemporary poetry is indicated by the range of poets whose work he uses in *Poetry in the Making*: Peter Redgrove, Charles Tomlinson, Philip Larkin, George Mackay Brown. At each stage in his development his originality has, rightly, been noticed more than his indebtedness. But his poetry is, of course, steeped in tradition. The influences on his early work of Hopkins, Lawrence, Yeats and Dylan Thomas are too obvious and well known to need labouring here. Of these perhaps only the late Yeats persists as far as *Crow*. Deeper and more abiding influences are more remote in time: Greek tragedy, medieval alliterative poetry, Shakespeare and the English Romantics, above all Blake and Wordsworth. He has indicated two kinds of influence, or at least kinship, to which he is receptive: in his interview with Egbert Faas, in which he speaks of the connection between the dialect of his childhood and the language of Middle English poetry (*London Magazine*, January 1971, pp. 11–12); and in his review of Mircea Eliade's *Shamanism*, where he says that the shaman's experience of being 'chosen by the spirits' with the consequence that he 'must shamanize or die' is 'the basic experience of the poetic temperament we call "romantic"'—he specifies *Venus and Adonis*, some of Keats's longer poems, *The Wanderings of Oisin* and *Ash Wednesday* as works which share this 'temperament' (*Listener*, 29 October 1964, p. 677).

Hughes is not an isolated individualist. The mutual influence between Sylvia Plath and himself contributed importantly to the development of both poets: it seems to us likely that the greater rhythmical freedom, compression and elliptical language of Hughes's poetry from *Wodwo* onwards owes something to the example of Sylvia Plath's later work. His collaborations with artists in other fields, notably Peter Brook, Gordon Crosse, Fay Godwin and Leonard Baskin, are a significant feature of his career. In the case of *Cave Birds*, the creative relationship with Baskin is almost symbiotic.

Hughes's relation to other contemporary poets is difficult to do justice to without lengthy and elaborate comparison. Good essays on aspects of this subject have been published by Seamus Heaney, Peter Abbs, Michael and Lawrence Kramer (see Bibliography). His influence has of course been considerable. It is

22

pervasively evident in the poetry magazines, in work that is by no means always weakly derivative, though it does tend to be 'nature poetry' in a more limiting sense than Hughes's own. The influence of the mythical devices of *Crow* on established writers whom one would not necessarily assume to be sympathetic to the spirit of that work can be seen in R. S. Thomas's *H'm* (compared with *Crow* by Peter Abbs), Alan Sillitoe's 'Snow on the North Side of Lucifer' and D. J. Enright's *Paradise Illustrated*.

It is perhaps significant that the most distinguished poet to have been obviously influenced by Hughes, Seamus Heaney, has moved away from that influence in his best and most recent work. The splendid early poem 'Death of a Naturalist', which describes how the poet was cured of collecting frogspawn by the terrifying sight and sound of the 'gross-bellied frogs', is recognizably akin to 'Pike' and 'The Bull Moses':

> The great slime kings
> Were gathered there for vengeance and I knew
> That if I dipped my hand the spawn would clutch it.

The poet capable of writing as good a Hughesian poem as this will, however, end up ploughing his own furrow, and the work in which Heaney is Hughes's peer, such as 'The Grauballe Man' and 'Punishment' (in *North*), shows no sign of influence. Heaney's major and most original work belongs, in a way Hughes's never has, to the cisatlantic modernist tradition that can be traced, crudely, from Yeats and Eliot through David Jones to Heaney and Geoffrey Hill.

It is now generally agreed that the supposed similarity between Ted Hughes and Thom Gunn was a matter of publicity, supported by the lack of other reference points for these two distinctive writers in the England of the 1950s, and by the fact that many readers found them both threatening. As Alan Bold puts it, 'Thom Gunn and Ted Hughes had some things in common. Their names were mono-syllabic and, more significantly, alphabetically consecutive so that they were seldom apart in alphabetically arranged anthologies' (*Thom Gunn and Ted Hughes*, p. 1). The celebration of the will and the self-sufficient individual in Gunn's early poetry is, in fact, diametrically opposed to Hughes's vision, as a comparison of the conclusion of 'The Unsettled Motorcyclist's Vision of his Death' with any of Hughes's writing about death makes clear:

23

And though the tubers, once I rot,
Reflesh my bones with pallid knot,
Till swelling out my clothes they feign
This dummy is a man again,
It is as servants they insist,
Without volition that they twist;
And habit does not leave them tired,
By men laboriously acquired.
Cell after cell the plants convert
My special richness in the dirt:
All that they get, they get by chance.

And multiply in ignorance.

The characteristic Marvellian elegance of these lines is also, of course, utterly unlike Hughes. Furthermore, the older Gunn's rejection of the spirit of his early work contrasts with the consistency of Hughes's inspiration.

A more suitable Cambridge-contemporary 'twin' for Hughes would have been Peter Redgrove. Redgrove, like Hughes, is centrally concerned with the imagination as an instrument for re-establishing the continuity with the material world supposedly broken by Christianity and the ensuing rational-scientific ethos. Mythology, witchcraft, Graves's *White Goddess* and the literature of shamanism define part of the territory of both poets. It is probably not relevant to speak of influence, though, because Redgrove's voice is utterly distinctive, as in this beautiful poem from the sequence 'On Losing One's Black Dog', collected in *From Every Chink of the Ark*:

We opened the bungalow.
The sea-sound was stronger in the rooms than on the beach.
Sand had quiffed through the seams of the veranda-windows.
The stars were sewn thicker than salt through the window
Cracked with one black star. A map of Ireland
Had dripped through the roof on to the counterpane
But it was dry. There was no tea in the tin caddy,
Quite bright and heartless with odorous specks.
There was a great hawk-moth in the lavatory pan.
Our bed was the gondola for black maths, and our
Breakfast-table never had brighter marmalade nor browner toast.
Two ladies in a seaside bungalow, our dresses

24

Thundered round us in the manless sea-wind.
Her day-dress: the throat sonata in the rainbow pavilion.
We kiss like hawk-moths.

The invasion of the everyday by the elemental is reminiscent of Hughes, but the consequence is an enhancing, not an undermining, of the domestic. Such an effect, very characteristic of Redgrove, is rare in Hughes, though one could cite 'Full Moon and Little Frieda' in *Wodwo* and 'Football at Slack' in *Remains of Elmet*. This harmony is perhaps the reason why Redgrove is more congenial than Hughes to such critics as Peter Porter and Philip Hobsbaum. Another important point is that the peculiar eroticism of this poem is exclusively feminine. Hughes, like Redgrove, is a critic of the masculine consciousness and a worshipper of the nature goddess, but most of his poetry is characterized by an aggressive, distinctly masculine energy. This has led Geoffrey Thurley to remark perceptively that 'Hughes, like Lawrence . . . can never bring himself to submit to the law of the feminine' (*The Ironic Harvest*, p. 188). This submission is precisely what characterizes Redgrove's work, both his individual writing and his collaborations with Penelope Shuttle.

Perhaps Hughes's most important affinity is with the post-war poets of Eastern Europe, such as Vasko Popa, Zbigniew Herbert, Miroslaw Holub and Janos Pilinszky. Edwin Morgan, introducing a study of the first three poets named, has indicated some of the reasons why their work has preoccupied many British writers. Having asked the question, 'Why should we read them?', he says:

> One broad answer might be that they have had to produce their work under extremely testing social and political circumstances, and that this has given their poetry an edge, a clear-eyed quality not quite like anything we are familiar with in our own poetry. Another answer might lay stress on the theme of survival which in fact they do share with many Western poets but which they deal with in fresh and urgent ways because they see it from a different background, a different angle. Or from a third viewpoint, we might say that there is something to be learned from their attitude to language, from their pared-down, sinewy, anti-florid expression.
>
> (*East European Poets*, p. 7)

Hughes has collaborated on a translation of Pilinszky, and introduced a selection of Popa's work. His affinity with these writers, aspects of which will be examined in a little more detail in our chapter on *Crow*, can be seen in the way, when speaking of them, he seems often to be speaking of the measures by which his own work should be judged: 'Though the Christian culture has been stripped off so brutally, and the true condition of the animal exposed in its ugliness, and words have lost their meaning—yet out of that rise the poems, whose words are manifestly crammed with meaning' (Pilinszky, *Selected Poems*, p. 12).

The plan of the rest of this book falls into two sections. Chapters 2 to 4 concentrate, from different points of view, on poems in *The Hawk in the Rain*, *Lupercal* and *Wodwo*, extending their scope to cover later work when relevant. Because of the unified character of Hughes's books from *Crow* onwards, these books are considered individually in the later chapters. The earlier chapters establish themes which continue to predominate in the later ones.

2

Finding a Voice

A Utility General-purpose Style

It is a language for the whole mind, at its most wakeful, and in
all situations. A utility general-purpose style, as, for instance,
Shakespeare's was that combines a colloquial prose readiness
with poetic breadth, a ritual intensity and music of an exceed-
ingly high order with clear direct feeling, and yet in the end
nothing but casual speech.

(Keith Douglas, Selected Poems, p. 14)

That is Ted Hughes speaking of Keith Douglas. The best way to
start our discussion of Hughes's language is to demonstrate that his
own most characteristic style is 'a language for the whole mind, at its
most wakeful'. His most characteristic style is not, in other words, a
symptom either of obsession or of intellectual surrender. It combines, to a remarkable degree, receptiveness and control.

Here, from *The Hawk in the Rain*, are the opening lines of 'The
Horses':

> I climbed through woods in the hour-before-dawn dark.
> Evil air, a frost-making stillness,
>
> Not a leaf, not a bird,—
> A world cast in frost. I came out above the wood
>
> Where my breath left tortuous statues in the iron light.
> But the valleys were draining the darkness

Till the moorline—blackening dregs of the brightening grey—
Halved the sky ahead.

The deployment of rhythm, simple diction and sound-effects to evoke the freezing stillness is expert but not unusual. The characteristic Hughes note is in the way perception is anchored by a bold conceit—'the valleys were draining the darkness'—and, not content with the neatness of the conceit, he brings in a potentially disruptive detail: the moors are seen as the 'dregs' left by the draining. What might, by its excessive and domestic concreteness, have exploded the conceit, is actually its triumph: the clever perceptual idea of 'draining' is connected up with the spiritless bleakness of the before-dawn world, which pervades the early part of the poem.

This example is Parnassian restraint, however, compared with some of Hughes's later metaphorical extravagances. We take the opportunity of quoting from a superb poem so far collected only in the limited edition *Recklings* (1966), but deserving to be known as a Hughes classic. (It is reprinted in Michael Morpurgo's *All Around the Year*.) The poem, quite a long one, is called 'Stealing Trout on a May Morning' and this passage describes wading upstream:

Soon I deepen. And now I meet the piling mob
Of voices and hurriers coming towards me
And tumbling past me. I press through a panic—
This headlong army of river is a rout
Of tumbrils and gun-carriages, rags and metal,
All the funeral woe-drag from some overnight disaster
Mixed with planets, electrical storms and darkness
On a mapless moorland of granite,
Trailing past me with all its frights, its eyes
With what they have seen and still see,
They drag the flag off my head, a dark insistence
Tearing the spirits from my mind's edge and from under . . .

Again the poet disdains to leave the metaphor general and safe. He brings in all the particular details, in a deliberate jumble, that strain against an easy reinforcement of the sensation of wading against the current. What he gives us in a few lines is a condensation of an episode in an epic historical novel, with all the dreariness as well as the awesomeness of mass suffering. The passage comes as close as

anything to exemplifying all the qualities that Hughes credits
Douglas with. What could be a better illustration of 'colloquial
prose readiness' combined with 'poetic breadth', than the line 'All
the funeral woe-drag from some overnight disaster'? The suggestion
of appalling jumble and dreariness, as well as appalling tragedy,
keeps the extraordinary hyperbole under control, stops it from
seeming a self-indulgent fantasy. At the same time the metaphor has
to break loose from the simple reinforcement of sensations: it has to
suggest an imagination invaded and unhinged by the river's fury. The
poetry does this while keeping itself whole and 'wakeful'.

The same fundamental quality is there in poems that seem much
more straightforward than this, in which the combination of receptiveness and control is expressed in shifts of tone rather than
metaphorical boldness. The following example is from one of the
best of Hughes's recent journal-poems, 'Coming down through
Somerset', which describes the finding and taking home of a dead
badger. The poem is collected in both *Moon-Bells* and *Moortown*.

I flash-glimpsed in the headlights—the high moment
Of driving through England—a killed badger
Sprawled with helpless legs. Yet again
Manoeuvred lane-ends, retracked, waited
Out of decency for headlights to die,
Lifted by one warm hindleg in the world-night
A slain badger. August dust-heat. Beautiful,
Beautiful, warm, secret beast. Bedded him
Passenger, bleeding from the nose. Brought him close
Into my life. Now he lies on the beam
Torn from a great building. Beam waiting two years
To be built into new building. Summer coat
Not worth skinning off him. His skeleton—for the future.
Fangs, handsome concealed. Flies, drumming,
Bejewel his transit. Heatwave ushers him hourly
Towards his underworlds. A grim day of flies
And sunbathing. Get rid of that badger.
A night of shrunk rivers, glowing pastures,
Sea-trout shouldering up through trickles. Then the sun again
Waking like a torn-out eye. How strangely
He stays on into the dawn—how quiet
The dark bear-claws, the long frost-tipped guard hairs!
Get rid of that badger today.
And already the flies.

More passionate, bringing their friends. I don't want
To bury and waste him. Or skin him (it is too late).
Or hack off his head and boil it
To liberate his masterpiece skull. I want him
To stay as he is. Sooty gloss-throated,
With his perfect face. Paws so tired,
Power-body relegated. I want him
To stop time. His strength staying, bulky,
Blocking time. His rankness, his bristling wildness,
His thrillingly painted face.
A badger on my moment of life.
Not years ago, like the others, but now.
I stand
Watching his stillness, like an iron nail
Driven, flush to the head,
Into a yew post. Something
Has to stay.

A disturbance runs through this poem, never stated explicitly as it is in 'Stealing Trout on a May Morning', but implicit in the brooding concentration on the badger's corpse, the hyper-consciousness of the tension between its actual beauty and its inevitable decay. The conflict is most apparent in the juxtaposition of the brisk, urgent, common-sense 'Get rid of that badger' with the lingering, loving, sensuous celebration of the body. It is also, however, detectable in more subtle shifts of tone throughout. Consider, for example, the sentence 'Flies, drumming,/Bejewel his transit.' When Hughes uses a literary-sounding phrase like 'Bejewel his transit' one rarely feels that he is using it with deliberate and fully-conscious irony, as when Eliot uses a phrase such as 'The nymphs are departed.' Hughes does not give the impression of slotting phrases neatly into place like that. But that phrase is not a naïve poeticism either. It has to co-exist with the horrible necrophilic implications of 'the flies./More passionate, bringing their friends.' The co-existence indicates the scope of the poet's response to the situation: the beauty of the flies is a fact, or a perception, that has to be assimilated together with their carrion nature. And beneath the visual image there is a striking paradox, which reflects the tension at the heart of the poem: the badger's flesh is 'transitory' but the poet is willing it to have the permanence of a jewel. The shift of tone from 'Bejewel his transit' to 'More passionate, bringing their friends' is not a simple irony but a manoeuvre of the poet's assimilating consciousness. Thus we are able to take 'masterpiece skull' at its face value, which would not be possible if 'Bejewel his transit' had been undermined in the intervening lines.

One inevitably comes back, however, to Hughes's astonishing metaphorical fertility and boldness. The range and density of metaphor is the most striking sign of the poet's receptiveness, and the high incidence of aptness and wholeness of effect, even in poems that at first seem like several radio stations transmitting on the same frequency, is the measure of his control. This last example, 'Cock-Crows', is from *Remains of Elmet*, one of his most recent volumes.

> I stood on a dark summit, among dark summits—
> Tidal dawn splitting heaven from earth,
> The oyster opening to taste gold.
>
> And I heard the cockcrows kindling in the valley
> Under the mist—
> They were sleepy,
> Bubbling deep in the valley cauldron.
>
> Then one or two tossed clear, like soft rockets
> And sank back again dimming.
>
> Then soaring harder, brighter, higher
> Tearing the mist,
> Bubble-glistenings flung up and bursting to light
> Brightening the undercloud,
> The fire-crests of the cocks—the sickle shouts,
> Challenge against challenge, answer to answer,
> Hooking higher,
> Clambering up the sky as they melted,
> Hanging smouldering from the night's fringes.
>
> Till the whole valley brimmed with cockcrows,
> A magical soft mixture boiling over,
> Spilling and sparkling into other valleys
>
> Lobbed-up horse-shoes of glow-swollen metal
> From sheds in back-gardens, hen-cotes, farms
> Sinking back mistily

Till the last spark died, and embers paled

And the sun climbed into its wet sack
For the day's work

While the dark rims hardened
Over the smoke of towns, from holes in earth.

The poem opens with two extraordinary metaphors for the appearance of dawn-light on the horizon, each one of which, 'unpacked', could furnish a neat little poem of its own. This throw-away generosity of imagination is one of the things that make one feel the poet is equal to the splendour and exuberance of his subject. As with all intense poetic activity, the word 'description' is hopelessly inadequate. The energy and complexity of the imagination constitute a thrilling engagement that transcends observation. A central conceit, running through 'kindling', 'bubbling', 'smouldering', 'boiling', develops the action of the sun on the cocks, but the imaginative engagement constantly bursts the limits of the conceit, in synaesthesia and in counterpointing metaphors. The rockets, for example, are another direction suggested by 'kindling', and convey the individually recognizable crows among the general 'magical soft mixture'; the 'sickle shouts' and 'Lobbed-up horse-shoes of glow-swollen metal' are another, suggesting the energy with which the bubbling mass of sound is shaped and articulated, and keeping the poem in touch with the domestic ordinariness of the scene, preparing for the return to 'sheds in back-gardens, hen-cotes, farms'. The diction, after the fanfare of the first three lines, is completely unassuming: much hinges on such phrases as 'tossed clear', 'flung up', 'clambering up', 'boiling over', 'lobbed-up'. This trust in simple, workaday phrases, eschewing any privileges of diction, is a prime characteristic of the 'utility general-purpose style': an ecstatic response to natural splendour is conveyed in a language that is, as Hughes puts it, 'in the end nothing but casual speech'. (This 'end', however, is reached through careful revision, and the effect of spontaneity is delusive—the line 'Lobbed-up horse-shoes of glow-swollen metal', for example, read 'Crestings and spurs of glow metal' in an earlier published version.[1])

The World Speaking

Introducing his reading of his own poetry on the record *The Poet Speaks*, no. 5, Ted Hughes said:

> I prefer poems to make an effect on being heard, and I don't think that's really a case of them being simple because for instance Eliot's poems make a tremendous effect when you hear them, and when I first heard them they did, and when I was too young to understand very much about them they had an enormous effect on me, and this was an effect quite apart from anything that I'd call, you know, understanding, or being able to explain them, or knowing what was going on. It's just some sort of charge and charm and series of operations that it works on you, and I think quite complicated poetry, such as Eliot's, can do this on you immediately.

Hughes's early career as a poet shows an increasingly sure grasp of the nature of this 'effect' and of its origins.

The familiar idea that good poetry makes a communication or 'charge' which precedes and perhaps outdistances conscious understanding is connected in Hughes's case with the relation of language to the physical world. There are two aspects of this relation: the ability of language to represent objects, and its roots in the physical nature of the speaker and the hearer. Hughes has spoken of 'capturing' the reality of things in words and illustrated the idea with his poem 'The Thought-Fox': 'every time anyone reads it the fox will get up somewhere out in the darkness and come walking towards them' (*Poetry in the Making*, p. 20). And the idea that the 'charge' of poetry and all 'effective' language is physiological is the basis of the project of Orghast, the language Hughes invented for a drama to be performed by Peter Brook's International Centre for Theatre Research at Persepolis. In notes for A. C. H. Smith, who accompanied Hughes and Brook to Persia, Hughes wrote:

> The deeper into language one goes, the less visual/conceptual its imagery, and the more audial/visceral/muscular its system of tensions. This accords with the biological fact that the visual nerves connect with the modern human brain, while the audial nerves connect with the cerebellum, the primal animal brain and nervous system, direct. In other words, the deeper into language one goes, the more dominated it becomes by purely

musical modes, and the more dramatic it becomes—the more unified with total states of being and with the expressiveness of physical action.

(A. C. H. Smith, *Orghast at Persepolis*, p. 45)[2]

Hughes evidently considers that language, particularly spoken language, has its roots in an inner life of which the speaker may not be conscious. This is consistent with what he has said about dialect: 'Whatever other speech you grow into, presumably your dialect stays alive in a sort of inner freedom, a separate little self' (*London Magazine* interview, January 1971, p. 11). The consequence of this for the poet is not necessarily a preoccupation with a private world. In *Poetry in the Making* Hughes called the inner life that the poet attempts to discover and make public 'the world of final reality' (p. 57). Bearing in mind this phrase and Hughes's remarks about neurology, a helpful parallel might be found in one of Jung's ideas. In Jung and Kerényi's joint book *Introduction to a Science of Mythology*, Kerényi writes: 'A "symbol" is not an "allegory", not just another way of speaking: it is an image presented, or rather represented, by the world itself' (p. 62). Jung provides a commentary on this sentence:

> The deeper 'layers' of the psyche lose their individual uniqueness as they retreat farther and farther into darkness. 'Lower down', that is to say as they approach the autonomous functional systems, they become increasingly collective until they are universalized and extinguished in the body's materiality, i.e. in the chemical bodies. The body's carbon is simply carbon. Hence 'at bottom' the psyche is simply 'world'. In this sense I hold Kerényi to be absolutely right when he says that in the symbol the *world itself* is speaking. The more archaic and 'deeper', that is the more *physiological*, the symbol is, the more collective and universal, the more 'material' it is.
>
> (p. 127)

Hughes appears to hold a similar view of language, and this theory can be used to provide a synthesis of the two aspects of language's relation to the physical world: the ability of language to represent the spirit or essence of things-as-they-are (as opposed to cataloguing attributes) derives from its origins in that 'layer of the psyche' which is 'things-as-they-are' itself.

Two caveats are in order here. First, the experimenter with a language of pure sound is also the author of several poems which express a distinct scepticism about the relation between language and the world. In 'Crow Goes Hunting', for example, the world's evasion of the hunting words is like the magical shape-changing of 'Tam Lin', and in 'A Disaster' (also from *Crow*) a word consumes humanity and then dies of starvation when it tries to digest 'the earth's bulge'. Secondly, we are not concerned with validating, scientifically or philosophically, Hughes's (or Jung's) speculations. The function of the poet's theories is to assist the production of good poetry, and for the critic they provide perhaps no more than a useful metaphor for describing the poetry's effect.

In his first volume Hughes most obviously attempts to create poetry with a material body by employing language which, when spoken, demands a conscious physical effort, dense with dental, plosive and gutteral consonants, and with alliteration and assonance. The opening lines of the title poem are an example of this technique:

I drown in the drumming ploughland, I drag up
Heel after heel from the swallowing of the earth's mouth,
From clay that clutches my each step to the ankle
With the habit of the dogged grave ...

The passage is melodramatically exaggerated, and it also illustrates the dangers of an extreme reliance on the obvious physical properties of words: the language is so physically dense that one is intensely conscious of the words *as* words, and of the activity of the poet in putting them together. In this particular case the result is felicitous—the clogged and desperate verbal devices are a striking analogue of the protagonist's floundering earthboundness. But we see by contrast real mastery and subtlety in the immediately following description of the hawk:

... but the hawk

Effortlessly at height hangs his still eye.

The effect of this is not ineffable—there is the assonance of 'height' and 'eye', the sprung rhythm with its fulcrum at the centre of the line—but the sense of the hawk's light and easy mastery precedes an awareness of the mechanics of the poetry: it has the 'charge and

35

charm' that we have heard Hughes talking about, the speed and directness of effect that he attributes to Shakespeare's language—'He goes direct from centre to centre but you never see him on the stairs or the corridors' (*London Magazine* interview, January 1971, p. 13).

The use of overtly physical language is not usually as felicitous as it is in the opening of this poem. Later in 'The Hawk in the Rain', for example, the poet describes himself as a

> Bloodily grabbed dazed last-moment-counting
> Morsel in the earth's mouth,

and at the end of 'Egg-Head', 'Braggart-browed complacency... Must stop the looming mouth of the earth with a pin-/Point cipher' and:

> Spurn it muck under
> His foot-clutch, and, opposing his eye's flea-red
> Fly-catching fervency to the whelm of the sun,
> Trumpet his own ear dead.

Examples could be multiplied. The bluster of the language numbs the reader and the words remain merely words. But this sort of writing does exemplify a determination not to allow language to fall into bland and inert patterns, which can also be detected in the frequent magniloquence and the use of adjectives as verbs—'crimsoning into the barbs' ('Macaw and Little Miss')—nouns as verbs—'something magnets and furnaces' ('Incompatibilities')—and so on.

In a perceptive and largely critical early essay (*Delta*, 25, Winter 1961) J. M. Newton remarked that Hughes, after having published his first two books, needed 'a greater inner stillness ... not to snatch at his inspiration, but to let its fruit come quietly, with all its *apparent* fragility and incompleteness, of its own accord'. Mr Newton had not noticed the considerable advance towards this greater inner stillness between the first two volumes, but it is interesting to note that the poet expresses a similar thought in *Poetry in the Making*, when he compares the imaginative process of such a poem as 'View of a Pig' ('Where did the poet learn to settle his mind like that on one thing?') to fishing with a float, which he calls 'a sort of mental exercise in concentration on a small point, while at the same time letting your imagination work freely to collect everything that might concern that still point'.

The best early poems often seem to centre on a moment of stillness, which in some cases gives meaning to the bluster that goes on around it. This is often a moment of *observed* stillness, as in 'The Hawk in the Rain':

> His wings hold all creation in a weightless quiet,
> Steady as a hallucination in the streaming air,

or the death of the pilot in 'The Casualty':

> suddenly the heart's beat shakes his body and the eye
>
> Widens childishly.

Such stillness as the *subject* of Hughes's poetry, in poems like 'Pike' and 'The Bull Moses', is not separable from the quality of mind that perceives and records it; but it is useful to isolate that quality of mind by looking at its exercise in a poem whose subject is the opposite of stillness, one of the handful of wholly successful poems in *The Hawk in the Rain*, 'Wind'.

> This house has been far out at sea all night,
> The woods crashing through darkness, the booming hills,
> Winds stampeding the fields under the window
> Floundering black astride and blinding wet
>
> Till day rose; then under an orange sky
> The hills had new places, and wind wielded
> Blade-light, luminous black and emerald,
> Flexing like the lens of a mad eye.
>
> At noon I scaled along the house-side as far as
> The coal-house door. I dared once to look up—
> Through the brunt wind that dented the balls of my eyes
> The tent of the hills drummed and strained its guyrope,
>
> The fields quivering, the skyline a grimace,
> At any second to bang and vanish with a flap:
> The wind flung a magpie away and a black-
> Back gull bent like an iron bar slowly. The house

Rang like some fine green goblet in the note
That any second would shatter it. Now deep
In chairs, in front of the great fire, we grip
Our hearts and cannot entertain book, thought,

Or each other. We watch the fire blazing,
And feel the roots of the house move, but sit on,
Seeing the window tremble to come in,
Hearing the stones cry out under the horizons.

There is hardly any attempt to mimic the violence of the wind in the language. Compare the line

the brunt wind that dented the balls of my eyes

with 'The Hawk in the Rain' where the wind

Thumbs my eyes, throws my breath, tackles my heart,
And rain hacks my head to the bone.

Having used 'brunt' (the only word in the poem obviously chosen for its physical properties), the single, precise verb 'dented' suffices to make the effect. By contrast the alliterative piling up of verbs in 'The Hawk in the Rain' suggests (like the opening of the poem) an agitation in the poet as well as the protagonist.

'Wind' differs from most of the *Hawk in the Rain* poems in the clarity of its language: one feels that the poet trusts the conceits to do their work, and they seem accordingly inevitable. The first line, in the simplest of words, gives us a metaphor that unifies the associations of the ensuing violent participles and summarizes the continuing sensations of the night. At a deeper level, it starts off the series of suggestions that undermine the reader's faith in the permanence and reliability of the landscape. Thus it intensifies 'The hills had new places' and brings out the underlying metaphor of a careening ship in the word 'scaled'. The final line of the third stanza is an excellent visual metaphor, reinforced by characteristically energetic verbs; yet it too derives its greatest power from this deeper level, by implying that the wind is *inside* the hills, the fabric of the land reduced to a bellying canvas.

The conceits are the result of 'concentration on a small point, while ... letting your imagination work freely to collect everything that might concern that still point'. The stillness-in-concentration can perhaps most clearly be seen in

> a black-
> Back gull bent like an iron bar slowly

which is not merely a precise visual image but a record and re-creation of a *slow* movement in the midst of violence and suddenness ('At any second to bang and vanish with a flap'). The line typifies the sustained steadiness of concentration which is awed but not deflected by the violence of the elements, and is also represented in the people at the end of the poem who are severed from each other and their own thoughts 'but sit on', the words suggesting a voluntary endurance of their subjection to a violence that threatens to engulf them.

'Wind' and 'The Thought-Fox' are perhaps the only poems in *The Hawk in the Rain* in which this steadiness is completely un-deflected, but in all the most impressive poems in the volume—'The Hawk in the Rain', 'The Jaguar', 'The Man Seeking Experience', 'Meeting', 'The Casualty', 'Bayonet Charge', 'Griefs for Dead Soldiers', 'Six Young Men'—Hughes's imagination can be seen operating in what is to become its most characteristic way. He describes this in *Poetry in the Making* when, after discussing 'the inner life, which is the world of final reality', he goes on to talk about

> the thinking process by which we break into that inner life and capture answers and evidence to support the answers out of it. That process of raid, or persuasion, or ambush, or dogged hunting, or surrender, is the kind of thinking we have to learn and if we do not somehow learn it, then our minds lie in us like the fish in the pond of a man who cannot fish.
> ... I am talking about whatever kind of trick or skill it is that enables us to catch those elusive or shadowy thoughts, and collect them together, and hold them still so we can get a really good look at them. (pp. 57–8)

His development is an increasing trust in that operation and a less frequent reliance on willed substitutes. In *Lupercal* there are more poems that are completely permeated by the steadiness of concentration and hardly any in which Hughes's characteristic strengths cannot be detected at all.

An important feature of most of these characteristically good early poems is the role of the protagonist as *perceiver*, registering some startling or frightening quality or energy in the world, but making no claim to embody it in his own personality. Outstanding examples are 'Wind', 'Six Young Men', 'The Bull Moses', 'View of a Pig', 'November', 'Bullfrog' and 'Pike'. This role is an advance upon and contrast to the persona of several poems in *The Hawk in the Rain*, in whom Hughes attempts to embody the same closeness to material reality that he strives for in his language. These poems can be powerful, as for example these lines from 'Billet-Doux':

> If, dispropertied as I am
> By the constellations staring me to less
> Than what cold, rain and wind neglect,
> I do not hold you closer and harder than love
> By a desperation, show me no home.

But this speaker is too self-conscious, and runs the danger of ending up in admiring self-contemplation. Hughes seems to have sensed this in 'Fallgrief's Girl-Friends', where he gives this figure a satirical name and asserts his failure to live up to his boast that he 'shall not seek more/Than a muck of a woman':

> The chance changed him:
> He has found a woman with such wit and looks
> He can brag of her in every company.

The level of unity with the material world that Hughes achieves in his best poetry is one at which there is no question of self-assertion.

The poem which Hughes chooses to illustrate what he means about learning to think takes a subject at the opposite extreme from 'Wind' and is almost, like its subject, 'too deadly factual'. But it illustrates exactly the process of holding shadowy thoughts still to look at them. Here are the first three stanzas of 'View of a Pig':

> The pig lay on a barrow dead.
> It weighed, they said, as much as three men.
> Its eyes closed, pink white eyelashes.
> Its trotters stuck straight out.

Such weight and thick pink bulk
Set in death seemed not just dead.
It was less than lifeless, further off.
It was like a sack of wheat.

I thumped it without feeling remorse.
One feels guilty insulting the dead,
Walking on graves. But this pig
Did not seem able to accuse.

The cleanly factual description takes on a strange dimension when
expressed as a thought by this particular man 'telling' the poem as
his own experience—'It was like a sack of wheat' is not just a simple
simile conveying bulk and weight; it expresses the way the pig now
seems unanimal, neither living nor dead, just material. The man is
breaking taboos in thinking this, and concentrates on the fact that he
is missing the normal response, the usual guilt that affirms a link
with death. This is some of the simplest poetry Hughes has written.
The diction has something of a Yorkshireman's glum factual sob-
riety, which is enhanced by the poet's own reading.[3] Though not in
any sense dialect it bears out Hughes's remarks about having grown
up with a dialect—it could not have been written by someone
brought up on received pronunciation. Much of its effect is made by
almost-casual phrases like 'Its trotters stuck straight out' and 'not
just dead'. The only simile might have been made by anyone. The
simplicity is of course that of art, of the poet who had to struggle out
of the language of such poems as 'Egg-Head'; but that is not inconsistent with saying that the language has been caught or found at the
same time and by the same process as the 'elusive or shadowy
thought' it expresses. The physical properties of the language, such
as the short, monosyllabic sentences, the even emphasis that is
almost no emphasis, the repeated 'k' and 't' sounds, undoubtedly
have an effect on the reader, but without drawing attention to the
words as words. The co-operation of sounds in 'thick pink bulk'
unobtrusively draws off any prettiness from 'pink', making it
emphatically the pink of dead flesh. 'Set', reinforced by the assonance of 'weight', subliminally suggests concrete, thus anticipating
'less than lifeless'. This language is more deeply interfused with the
material reality of its subject than 'clay that clutches my each step to
the ankle': we do not see the poet willing it to perform its function.

In its own way the poem has what Hughes has called 'animal music' (see *Shakespeare's Verse*, p. 12 and Smith, *Orghast at Persepolis*, p. 46).

'View of a Pig' goes on putting together various thoughts, anecdotes and pieces of information about pigs, and returns in the final stanza to the poet's concentrated stare at the dead pig with which it started. The imagination thus 'collects' while it 'concentrates'. The technique of 'Pike' is so similar that they must have been written close in time—both were first published in the summer of 1959, and must be among the poems Hughes was referring to when he said in an interview in the *Guardian*, 'A lot of my second book, "Lupercal", is one extended poem about one or two sensations. There are at least a dozen or fifteen poems in that book which belong organically to one another' (23 March 1965). The conclusion of 'Pike', however, takes us into a different dimension. The poem begins factually, 'Pike, three inches long', and reflects on the beauty and ferocity of the fish, and on its awesome 'stillness'. In the following lines from the fourth stanza we have the same thought as in Hughes's meditation on a jawbone, 'Relic':

> The jaws' hooked clamp and fangs
> Not to be changed at this date;
> A life subdued to its instrument;

but here as one note in a much more varied and resonant, less didactic poem. Anecdotes follow, about pike kept behind glass that ate each other, and two found high and dry, 'One jammed past its gills down the other's gullet'. And finally about the pond the poet fished, presumably as a boy:

> A pond I fished, fifty yards across,
> Whose lilies and muscular tench
> Had outlasted every visible stone
> Of the monastery that planted them—
>
> Stilled legendary depth:
> It was as deep as England. It held
> Pike too immense to stir, so immense and old
> That past nightfall I dared not cast

42

But silently cast and fished
With the hair frozen on my head
For what might move, for what eye might move.
The still splashes on the dark pond,

Owls hushing the floating woods
Frail on my ear against the dream
Darkness beneath night's darkness had freed,
That rose slowly towards me, watching.

Here we have something quite different from the blunt materiality
of the out-there, 'further-off' pig. Hughes's use of fishing as an
analogy for the workings of the poetic imagination could well have
originated in this poem. Just as in 'The Thought-Fox' the mimetic
language works two ways, evoking the movements of the fox which
in turn provide an image for the movement of the poem itself, so
here, on a deeper level, the quiet, echoing verse is the voice or
instrument of the memory the poet is 'collecting', and the memory
itself provides an image of the poetic activity: of quiet, attentive,
apprehensive waiting. The pike is also waiting and watching, and the
poem has something of its quality too. The boy is frightened of a real
pike but what 'rose slowly towards me, watching' is something
within him, unconscious and probably more-than-individual.

Rhythm, syntax, imagery and repetition work together to create
this effect. Repetition is the most obvious stylistic feature of the
passage, and the changes in its function chart the movement of the
poem towards its central vision: we move from the simply emphatic
'immense', through the paradoxical 'dared not cast/But silently
cast', to the darkness that has become something more terrifying
than a natural phenomenon. The repetition of 'move' works
together with the syntactical ambiguity of the two foregoing lines.
Should we read 'fished for what might move' or 'hair frozen (in
dreadful anticipation) for what might move'? Evidently both, since
the line in which 'move' is repeated shifts from a fisherman's alert-
ness to dread, the emphasis in the second half-line inevitably falling
on the new word 'eye', making the open vowel almost a cry.

More generally the repetition conveys an impression of deliber-
ated control, of the poet holding firmly on to language in the face of
his vision. This effect is also suggested, in the last three stanzas, by
the stressed monosyllabic endings of every line except the last (this
is peculiar to the mood of these stanzas—only half the lines in the

43

rest of the poem end like this), especially ('held/ Pike', 'woods/ Frail', 'dream/ Darkness') when the ensuing line opens with a stress. The sense one has of the poem's being menacingly open-ended derives in part from the interruption of this sequence by the isolated participle, 'watching'. That word completes the movement in which simultaneously the hunter becomes the hunted and the boy's concentration turns inward, towards the surfacing unknown self. In 'Owls hushing the floating woods' we hardly notice that the woods are a reflection. Such a literal-minded response to the line would, in fact, be irrelevant: that the woods, and the whole pheno-menal world, should float and become insubstantial seems natural as they are displaced by the dream. The poem anticipates and authenticates Hughes's later more explicit preoccupation with shamanism: the pike, like the thought-fox and most of his other animals, is akin to the 'helping spirits' of the shaman, which often take animal form, arousing feelings of terror, and act as inter-mediaries between the shaman and the mysterious pre-conscious animal world (see Eliade, *Shamanism*, pp. 88 ff.).

Narrative

When Sylvia Plath first met Ted Hughes in Cambridge in 1956 she wrote to her mother that he was a man 'with a voice like the thunder of God—a singer, story-teller, lion and world-wanderer, a vaga-bond who will never stop'. Ten days later she was writing:

> His humor is the salt of the earth; I've never laughed as hard and long in my life. He tells me fairy stories, and stories of kings and green knights, and has made up a marvelous fable of his own about a little wizard named Snatchcraftington, who looks like a stalk of rhubarb. He tells me dreams, marvelous colored dreams, about certain red foxes. . . .
>
> (*Letters Home*, pp. 233, 244)

This story-teller's gift has emerged most obviously in *Crow* (particu-larly the public readings) and subsequent work, but its presence in the earlier volumes, particularly *Wodwo*, is important to a discus-sion of Hughes's language. The success of such poems as 'Wind', 'View of a Pig' and 'Pike' clearly depends to some extent on the tone of personal narrative reminiscence. Between *Lupercal* in 1960 and *Wodwo* in 1967 Hughes reviewed a wide range of publications concerning folklore, from *The Loch Ness Monster* to *Shamanism*, and published four books for children. In the first version of 'Myth and Education' he refers to the use of stories by the Sufis.

> By stories alone, or almost alone, they claim to be able to bring a man to communion with his highest powers and abilities, to communion with God in fact. The hearer needn't necessarily understand the significance of the stories, as long as they work on his imagination. So, working on and altering his imagination, they alter his ideas about himself, about mankind, about the world and about all the strategies that operate in it. They use specific stories for specific purposes.
>
> (*Children's Literature in Education*, 1, p. 62)

He goes on to explain that he wrote his children's story *The Iron Man*, partly in reaction to the failure of children's literature he had read in America to reflect 'the collision with the American techno-logical world and, beyond that, the opening up, by physics and so on, of a universe which was completely uninhabited except by atoms and the energy of atoms' (p. 63). An Iron Man appears in the human world out of nowhere, and men try to destroy him. A little boy suggests that rather than fight him he should be provided with the means to live—a scrapyard, because he eats metal. Thus peace is made with the Iron Man and he later saves the world from a space-monster by outwitting it in a series of ordeals. The monster is tamed and turned into a spirit of harmony, who flies around the earth making the music of the spheres. Thus two threats are averted and turned to advantage by what Hughes calls 'negotiation' rather than by frontal assault—the threat of technology and of the cosmic chaos. The story has justly become a children's classic.

The influence that Hughes's reading in folklore and anthropo-logy, and his writing for children, seem to have had on his poetry is the introduction, or at least bringing to greater prominence, of mythical narrative in his work. Myth is a dangerous word to use about a work of literary art, and we must bear in mind the anthropological arguments that genuine myth is collectively pro-duced, and that it is inseparable from ritual. However, the word can be meaningfully used of Hughes's poetry, with the help of a passage from Malinowski:

> Myth as it exists in a savage community, that is, in its living primitive form, is not merely a story told but a reality lived. It

is not of the nature of fiction, such as we read today in a novel, but it is a living reality, believed to have once happened in primeval times, and continuing ever since to influence the world and human destinies. . . .

The stories live not by idle interest, not as fictitious or even as true narratives; but are to the natives a statement of a primeval, greater, and more relevant reality, by which the present life, fates, and activities of mankind are determined. . . .

(Myth in Primitive Psychology, pp. 21, 39)

The phrase 'a primeval, greater, and more relevant reality' has an obvious bearing on Hughes's concerns, and this passage provides a good guide to the status of the narratives in his work. We might also at this point recall Jung and Kerényi's remarks about 'the world speaking' through symbols and myths.

In suggesting that Hughes's writing for children was an important factor in the change in his poetry between *Lupercal* and *Wodwo* we are not merely pointing out that the sequence of publications for children was followed by the appearance of *Wodwo*. There are formal parallels between the children's stories and the poetry of *Wodwo*, as can be shown by a comparison between 'Still Life' and the story 'Why The Owl Behaves As It Does' from *How the Whale Became and other stories*. The anthropomorphism of 'Still Life' suggests a childlike starting point for the imagery: 'perhaps stone is only pretending to be dead and is really alive, but wants to live with as little effort as possible.' In the story about Owl, all the other birds are fooled into thinking that, in the farmer's stockyard to which Owl has led them, day is in fact night. They must keep their eyes closed during the night because the darkness in that country is so strong that it will kill them. After a year the birds decide that their existence is so worthless that they might as well commit suicide by opening their eyes to the darkness. They all begin to sing one last song together. They open their eyes and find that Owl has tricked them, since it is in fact dawn, and not dusk as they had been told. Owl is chased into his hole, to come out only at night for fear of being mobbed by the other birds.

And so it is still.
Every morning the birds sing, and the owl flies back into his dark hole.

46

So the beautiful dawn chorus originated as a 'swan-song'. In 'Still Life' the warted stone that thinks it will 'be in at the finish' forgets the harebell which actually contains 'the maker of the sea' from which the stone originated as sea-bed. In both the story and the poem the narrative structure and the final image indicate that the complacent Owl and stone are finally outdone in a beautiful ironic reversal. 'Still Life' needs to be heard in full as the momentum of the myth builds towards its simple and fragile conclusion.

> Outcrop stone is miserly
>
> With the wind. Hoarding its nothings,
> Letting wind run through its fingers,
> It pretends to be dead of lack.
> Even its grimace is empty,
> Warted with quartz pebbles from the sea's womb.
>
> It thinks it pays no rent,
> Expansive in the sun's summerly reckoning.
> Under rain, it gleams exultation blackly
> As if receiving interest.
> Similarly, it bears the snow well.
>
> Wakeful and missing little and landmarking
> The fly-like dance of the planets,
> The landscape moving in sleep,
> It expects to be in at the finish.
> Being ignorant of this other, this harebell,
>
> That trembles, as under threats of death,
> In the summer turf's heat-rise,
> And in which—filling veins
> Any known name of blue would bruise
> Out of existence—sleeps, recovering,
>
> The maker of the sea.

The final line is a simple outflanking stroke which indicates the profound skill of the teller of tales. In Hughes's recorded reading of this poem[4] his voice has an upward inflexion on the final word which seems to hint at not only the cyclic implications of the last line (visually emphasized by its separation on the printed page), but a shared knowledge of the phrase 'maker of the sea'. It is as though the poem is part of some larger continuing myth which Hughes implies we have heard before. In this way his reading re-creates the sense of authentic myth that underlies the tone of the whole poem.

This same voice of newly created but recognizable myth is also heard in 'Thistles', 'Sugar Loaf', 'The Bear', 'Gog', 'Wodwo' and 'Ghost Crabs'. In each case the myth represents 'a primeval, greater, and more relevant reality'. 'Ghost Crabs' begins:

At nightfall, as the sea darkens,
A depth darkness thickens, mustering from the gulfs and the
                                    submarine badlands,
To the sea's edge. To begin with
It looks like rocks uncovering, mangling their pallor.
Gradually the labouring of the tide
Falls back from its productions,
Its power slips back from glistening nacelles, and they are crabs.
Giant crabs, under flat skulls, staring inland
Like a packed trench of helmets.
Ghosts, they are ghost-crabs.

The crabs emerge from the gap between day and night, sea and land, known and unknown, conscious and unconscious. The poetry is narrative in that it dramatizes perception, as a novelist dramatizes the changing perceptions of a character—in *Pincher Martin*, for example, or the opening paragraph of *Edwin Drood*—or a film might place its drama in the audience's growing awareness of what it is looking at.[5] The poem's original title, 'Nightfall', was more helpful in this respect than the present one, which alerts the reader from the start. The narrative is a journey into the imagination, or the unconscious. It moves from a realistic sea at nightfall, through the dissolving, ambiguous processes of metaphor, to the assertion of a mythic other reality. The writing suggests that discoveries are being made line by line: 'and they are crabs./Giant crabs ... Ghosts, they are ghost-crabs.' A fearful intuition, aroused by nightfall and the depths of the sea, has found its representation, which then becomes an instrument for crystallizing half-conscious terrors, as the narrative sets the crabs in motion.

They emerge
An invisible disgorging of the sea's cold
Over the man who strolls along the sands.
They spill inland, into the smoking purple
Of our woods and towns—a bristling surge
Of tall and staggering spectres
Gliding like shocks through water.
Our walls, our bodies, are no problem to them.
Their hungers are homing elsewhere.
We cannot see them or turn our minds from them.
Their bubbling mouths, their eyes
In a slow mineral fury
Press through our nothingness where we sprawl on our beds,
Or sit in rooms. Our dreams are ruffled maybe.
Or we jerk awake to the world of possessions
With a gasp, in a sweat burst, brains jamming blind
Into the bulb-light. Sometimes, for minutes, a sliding
Staring
Thickness of silence
Presses between us.

(Selected Poems text)

So far the poem might be called an adult fairy-tale, with a fairy-tale's exaggerated grimness, designed to chasten the reader and to help him to cope imaginatively with the chastenings of unruly inward experience. Unfortunately the second half of the poem is more obviously deliberate and dogmatic.

As well as the poems we have named, in which a narrative-mythic tendency is dominant, there are many others in *Wodwo* that testify to Hughes's preoccupation with myth. 'Reveille' and 'Theology' very obviously anticipate the reinterpretations of biblical narrative in *Crow*. 'Ballad from a Fairy Tale' attempts to give mythical expression to personal experience: its anguished inexplicitness both intensifies and circumscribes its power. In 'Out' the horrors of his father's First World War experiences, which brooded over the poet's childhood, are called 'The Dream Time', an ironic reference to the paradisal early world of the ancestors in Australian mythology. The opening lines of 'The Rescue'—'That's what we live on: thinking of their rescue/And fitting our future to it'—seem intended to bestow on the ensuing narrative the archetypal and prophetic authenticity of myth.

The presence of the stories and the play in *Wodwo* are of course

further evidence of the narrative element in this development, but if
'Ghost Crabs' is (in this context) an advance on 'Pike', in which the
legendary fish only 'rose slowly towards me, watching', it remains
true that the poems in *Wodwo* give us only fragments of myth and
fragmentary narratives. As we have seen, a poem like 'Still Life'
brilliantly exploits this very fact, but Hughes's description of the
book, in the Author's Note, as a 'single adventure', tells us that he is
already aspiring to more than the small-scale mythical poem. The
progress of this aspiration—to achieve in his poetic work for adults
what he had achieved in a prose work for children by 1968 with *The
Iron Man*—seems to have been extraordinarily difficult. The relation between the poems of *Crow* and the 'epic folk-tale' or saga that
lies behind them is very uneasy and Hughes has admitted that the
story is not really relevant to the poems. A. C. H. Smith has testified
to the 'deep, personal power of myth-making' in *Orghast* (*Orghast
at Persepolis*, p. 98), but anyone who was not at Persepolis can
experience only the skeleton of the work. *Prometheus on his Crag* is
a series of meditations on a pre-existing myth. It is not until *Gaudete*
(1977), which we shall be discussing in a later chapter, that Hughes
achieves a large-scale poetic narrative.

Humour

Sylvia Plath's letter to her mother also stressed Hughes's
humour—'I've never laughed as hard and long in my life.' Few of his
best poems are entirely without humour, and in many of them it
belongs to the shock of registering something in the natural world
and establishing a relationship with it. It is there in 'a sag belly and
the grin it was born with' of 'Pike', and perhaps the first predominantly humorous poem of this kind is 'Bullfrog'.

> With their lithe long strong legs
> Some frogs are able
> To thump upon double-
> Bass strings though pond-water deadens and clogs.
>
> But you, bullfrog, you pump out
> Whole fogs full of horn—a threat
> As of a liner looming. True
> That, first hearing you

Disgorging your gouts of darkness like a wounded god,
Not utterly fantastical I expected
(As in some antique tale depicted)
A broken-down bull up to its belly in mud,
Sucking black swamp up, belching out black cloud

And a squall of gudgeon and lilies.
                                                    A surprise,
To see you, a boy's prize,
No bigger than a rat—all dumb silence
In your little old woman hands.

This is a witty and delicate poem spoilt only by the awkward couplet, 'Not utterly fantastical I expected/(As in some antique tale
depicted)'. The most obvious wit is at the expense of his own
fantasies but the heart of the poem is in the last three lines, in the
humour of the let-down that is not really a let-down but a glimpse of
the true wonder, the apparently belittling anthropomorphism that is
really an acknowledgement of the bullfrog's mysterious being. The
quietness of this conclusion is also important. Like that of 'Pike' and
'The Bull Moses' it is a sign of Hughes's increasing confidence in the
voice of his inspiration.

This mode emerges more strongly in the nature poems in *Wodwo*:
'Thistles', 'Still Life', 'Sugar Loaf', 'Fern', 'Skylarks', 'Gnat-Psalm'
and 'Full Moon and Little Frieda'. In each case anthropomorphism
is an important element in the humour.

Full Moon and Little Frieda

A cool small evening shrunk to a dog bark and the clank of a
                                                    bucket—

And you listening.
A spider's web, tense for the dew's touch.
A pail lifted, still and brimming—mirror
To tempt a first star to a tremor.

Cows are going home in the lane there, looping the hedges with
                                    their warm wreaths of breath—
A dark river of blood, many boulders,
Balancing unspilled milk.

'Moon!' you cry suddenly, 'Moon! Moon!'

The moon has stepped back like an artist gazing amazed at a
work

That points at him amazed.

This is rightly one of Hughes's most popular poems and he has called it a favourite of his own. The beauty and aptness of its movement could never have been predicted from most of the poems in *The Hawk in the Rain*—even 'The Thought-Fox' is mechanical in comparison. It is rare to find such freedom of line accompanied by such appropriateness and inevitability, so that it seems to have a form as tight as a sonnet—the whole evening in one long line, the listening child who is the focus of it in a balancing short one; the 'mirror' poised between the water of which it is composed and the star that it reflects; the herd of cows in a long, lazy line that nevertheless doesn't fall apart. The humour that belongs to the wonder is there throughout: in 'tempt'; in the cows being communally the river and individually the boulders that impede its progress; and above all in the final two lines, where something of the artist's wonder at the life of his work, the moon's ancient divinity, the child's suddenness and wholeness of attention, combine in a delicacy of suggestion that really does defy analysis.

In 'Thistles' the humour stems from the way the anthropomorphism takes an unexpected turn in the final stanza, and we find ourselves thinking of human tragedy as a metaphor for a natural process—not, as usually, the other way round.

Against the rubber tongues of cows and the hoeing hands of men
Thistles spike the summer air
Or crackle open under a blue-black pressure.

Every one a revengeful burst
Of resurrection, a grasped fistful
Of splintered weapons and Icelandic frost thrust up

From the underground stain of a decayed Viking.
They are like pale hair and the gutturals of dialects.
Every one manages a plume of blood.

Then they grow grey, like men.
Mown down, it is a feud. Their sons appear,
Stiff with weapons, fighting back over the same ground.

This humour becomes the dominant mode of *Season Songs*. It is
the delight it communicates that makes poems aimed at young
people completely satisfying to adult readers as well. Here, as
examples, are two sections from 'Spring Nature Notes':

> A spurt of daffodils, stiff and quivering—
> Plumes, blades, creases, Guardsmen
> At attention
>
> Like sentinels at the tomb of a great queen.
> (Not like what they are—the advance guard
> Of a drunken slovenly army
>
> Which will leave this whole place wrecked.)
>
> *   *   *
>
> With arms swinging, a tremendous skater
> On the flimsy ice of space,
> The earth leans into its curve—
>
> Thrilled to the core, some flies have waded out
> An inch onto my window, to stand on the sky
> And try their buzz.

There is, though, a more prominent and many would think more
characteristic vein of humour which does not give such simple
delight. Derwent May, in an essay published in 1970 (*The Survival
of Poetry*, ed. Martin Dodsworth), claims interestingly that some of
the poems which seem both menacing and argumentative, such as
'October Dawn' and 'Strawberry Hill', look better when regarded
as examples of 'extravagant but sardonic' and macabre humour. A
still better example, from *Wodwo*, is 'Sugar Loaf'.

> The trickle cutting from the hill-crown
> Whorls to a pure pool here, with a whisp trout like a spirit.
> The water is wild as alcohol—
> Distilling from the fibres of the blue wind.
> Reeds, nude and tufted, shiver as they wade.

I see the whole huge hill in the small pool's stomach.

This will be serious for the hill.
It suspects nothing.
Crammed with darkness, the dull, trusting giant
Leans, as over a crystal, over the water
Where his future is forming.

'Nude and tufted' is a brilliantly concise suggestion of comic human vulnerability, intruding into the emphatically material description of the first four lines. As in 'Still Life', 'Bullfrog', 'Full Moon and Little Frieda' and 'Thistles', anthropomorphism and wit go hand in hand. A bolder and, while still light, more menacing anthropomorphism comes in with the middle line, whose perfectly achieved combination of rhythm and assonance holds the comic potentialities of the conceit in suspension until they are crystallized in the mock solemnity of the ensuing two lines. The rare quality of this poem's poise lies in keeping its countenance in the face of nature's warnings, without any hubristic detachment or bravado.

A harsh, sardonic and macabre humour is a feature of many of Hughes's best poems discussed elsewhere in this book. Consider the way it both controls and intensifies the poignancy of the opening of 'The Green Wolf':

Your neighbour moves less and less, attempts less.
If his right hand still moves, it is a farewell
Already days posthumous.

And in the final section of 'Stations'—

Whether you say it, think it, know it
Or not, it happens, it happens as
Over rails over
The neck the wheels leave
The head with its vocabulary useless,
Among the flogged plantains.

the penultimate line is of the same order as Ralegh's 'want a head to dine next noon' in 'A Passionate Man's Pilgrimage', though it lacks the gallantry given by the supposed occasion of Ralegh's poem (the eve of his execution).

This kind of humour finds its fullest and by far its most overt expression in *Crow*. Here is 'A Childish Prank':

Man's and woman's bodies lay without souls,
Dully gaping, foolishly staring, inert
On the flowers of Eden.
God pondered.

The problem was so great, it dragged him asleep.

Crow laughed.
He bit the Worm, God's only son,
Into two writhing halves.

He stuffed into man the tail half
With the wounded end hanging out.

He stuffed the head half headfirst into woman
And it crept in deeper and up
To peer out through her eyes
Calling its tail-half to join up quickly, quickly
Because O it was painful.

Man awoke being dragged across the grass.
Woman awoke to see him coming.
Neither knew what had happened.

God went on sleeping.

Crow went on laughing.

Poems like this cause offence to many readers, partly perhaps because although the humour is sardonic and cruel there is also a lightness about it that is not very different from a quality of the humorous nature-poems we have just been examining, so that it can seem a blithe writing-off of human dignity and aspiration. The energy of this poem, too, derives from the likeness-in-unlikeness of a conceit, though any delight that this energy may give the reader does not (as it does in all those poems) spill over into delight in the world. It may seem perverse to talk about delight at all in this connection; or it may seem symptomatic of a nihilistic desire to 'do dirt on life', in Lawrence's phrase. What we have called a conceit

55

might seem better described as a childishly smutty joke. That reaction is, we think, the result of a kind of short-circuit in the operation of the poem, of the reader's mind failing to allow the conceit to open up and develop. It is true that even someone who liked the poem on first reading would suspect that it would rapidly lose its effectiveness on re-reading. Many readers would say that that is a correct prediction, but we attest that for ourselves, on frequent re-reading over nearly a decade, it is not.

Let us examine some of the qualities that get lost in the short-circuit. First, the poem is not reducible to its central joke or conceit, but is a development of it in which all the parts are important. The element of 'lightness' in the humour can tempt us to see the movement of the poem as a swift getting to the point and signing off. But in fact the movement is extremely slow and paradoxically weighty. This is emphasized in Hughes's own reading, but is fairly deducible from the words on the page. 'Scanning' free verse is a dangerous activity, but this seems reasonable:

> Crów laúghed.
> He bít the Wórm, Gód's ónly són,
> Into twó wríthing hálves.

In other words the movement invites the reader to pause over each word and ask such questions as: is the second of these lines a denial of redemption or a hint at its redefinition? This leads to the question whether Crow's intervention is a disastrous error, and whether we can feel comfortable in sharing his laughter.

Then consider the movement of these lines:

> He stuffed the head half headfirst into woman
> And it crept in deeper and up
> To peer out through her eyes
> Calling its tail-half to join up quickly, quickly
> Because O it was painful.

The way the movement enacts first the creeping up and then the urgency of the head's call to its tail is an important part of the development of the conceit, and of the tone of the poem, that can be lost in an unsympathetic reading. 'O it was painful' is only partly humorous.

In this case an 'interpretation' of the poem might help both to establish its fundamental seriousness and to show why it has to run the risk of appearing flippant or nihilistic. It is a little mythical narrative of the awakening of consciousness and consequent pains of separation. In our chapter on *Crow* we shall be arguing more fully that this is an important theme of the book. At the start of the poem man and woman may be 'dully gaping' and 'foolishly staring' but they are, for what it is worth, in Paradise, 'On the flowers of Eden'. This is one of several comic-serious reworkings of the Genesis story in *Crow*, and in this case the awakening of consciousness, sex, and the pain of human destiny are parts of a single action. The Worm, the principle of vitality, is incorporated into human life at the cost of its division and the consequent human sense of separation and isolation, and of being subjected to uncontrollable impulses, sex being the most intensely felt symptom of separation, as well as the most obvious hope of overcoming it.

This account shows how difficult it is to write about the subject without a solemnity and self-pity that invite a ribald response. Its effect is so different from that of the poem that it does not really merit the word 'interpretation'. But though it falsifies the poem we hope to have established that this is by doing it less, not more, than justice.

Later Developments

After the publication of *Crow* Hughes became involved in the *Orghast* project during which he wrote a sequence of twenty-one short poems, *Prometheus on His Crag,* based on the same myth as *Orghast*. These poems were published in a limited edition in 1973 and reprinted in *Moortown* (1979). They are curiously toneless and 'numb' (Hughes's own word, quoted by Keith Sagar, *The Art of Ted Hughes,* 2nd edition, p. 147). If they are free of the excesses of *Crow*, they also lack its energy, humour and variety. Here is an example:

Now I know I never shall

Be let stir.
The man I fashioned and the god I fashioned
Dare not let me stir.

57

This leakage of cry, these face-ripples
Calculated for me—for mountain water
Dammed to powerless stillness.

What secret stays
Stilled under my stillness?
Not even I know.

Only he knows—that bird, that
Filthy-gleeful emissary and
The hieroglyph he makes of my entrails

Is all he tells.

A phrase like 'leakage of cry' anticipates the diction of *Cave Birds* (compare 'The carapace/Of foreclosure/The cuticle/Of final arrest'), and we encounter a similar numbness again in the poems at the end of *Gaudete*. Nevertheless the volume underlines the impression of a hiatus in the development of Hughes's poetry following the completion or abandonment of *Crow*—certainly in comparison with what happened subsequently, for between 1973 and 1975 he substantially wrote *Season Songs, Gaudete* and *Cave Birds*. The significance of this unprecedented fertility of major work is not merely its volume but the variety and newness of its language.

Although, as we shall be arguing at length in Chapter 5, the language of *Crow* is far less limited and monotonous than is often claimed, the style of such a poem as 'A Childish Prank' (which is fairly characteristic) contains obvious dangers of self-parody. Hughes compared his stylistic decision in *Crow* to that of the fairy-tale hero who chooses a 'scabby little foal' for the 'next stage' of his adventure (*London Magazine* interview, January 1971, p. 20). How he could transfer to another horse for a further stage was not at all obvious to his readers after 1970. Having spent three years writing brief, harsh poems exorcizing illusions, speaking as it were through gritted teeth, there must be a danger of finding your jaw locked.

What Hughes seems to have discovered is the ability to engage more or less simultaneously in several different projects, demanding different voices, all more expansive and relaxed than the voice of *Crow*. It is tempting to speculate that the composition of *Season Songs* played an important part in stimulating this development and the accompanying productiveness. We must not oversimplify— five of the poems were written as 'Autumn Songs for Children's Voices' in 1968, in the middle of the composition of *Crow*—but the majority were written in 1973–4, and the book as a whole is the first strikingly new note sounded by Hughes after *Crow*. Introducing a reading of some of the poems on the radio he said that he wanted to keep 'within hearing of children', and that phrase is helpful in defining the peculiar tone of the poems. They are quite unlike the earlier children's poems such as *Meet My Folks!* and *Nessie the Mannerless Monster*, in that they are evidently the result of a far more concentrated attention and imaginative activity. In the American edition (beautifully illustrated by Leonard Baskin) there is no mention of its being a children's book. The subtle free verse of most of them is in stark contrast to the earlier jolly doggerel. At the same time there is an unmistakable feeling of relaxation, an expansiveness resulting, perhaps, from a relaxed sense of responsibility.

Spring Nature Notes

I
The sun lies mild and still on the yard stones.

The clue is a solitary daffodil—the first.

And the whole air struggling in soft excitements
Like a woman hurrying into her silks.
Birds everywhere zipping and unzipping
Changing their minds, in soft excitements,
Warming their wings and trying their voices.

The trees still spindle bare.

Beyond them, from the warmed blue hills
An exhilaration swirls upward, like a huge fish.

As under a waterfall, in the bustling pool.

Over the whole land
Spring thunders down in brilliant silence.

In his adult poetry Hughes would not, probably, permit himself the comparison with 'a woman hurrying into her silks'—not, at least, without more qualification than it has here. However, the comfortable anthropomorphism does not in this case pin down its subject in a static and sentimental picture. It is part of the sense of Spring's immanence, of everything being charged and active, that the poem is full of.

It is not hard to find parallels in the prose and verse of *Gaudete*:

> The wood creeps rustling back. The million whispering busyness of the fronds, which seemed to have hesitated, start up their stitchwork, with clicking of stems and all the tiny excitements of their materials....
> Clouds slide off the sun. The trees stretch, stirring their tops. A thrush hones and brandishes its echoes down the long aisles, in the emerald light, as if it sang in an empty cathedral. Shrews storm through the undergrowth. Hoverflies move to centre, angle their whines, dazzle across the sunshafts. The humus lifts and sweats. (pp. 29–30)

If the language of *Gaudete* also often seems loose and unedited, that is perhaps the price which had to be paid for the expansiveness necessary to a long poem.

The greater tenderness and overt humanity of *Cave Birds* in comparison to *Crow* can also be seen in relation to the language of *Season Songs*:

She had found her belly
In a clockwork pool, wound by the winding and unwinding sea.
First it was her toy, then she found its use
And curtained it with a flowered skirt.
It made her eyes shine.

She looked at the grass trembling among the worn stones

Having about as much comprehension as a lamb
Who stares around at everything simultaneously
With ant-like head and soldierly bearing

She had made it but only just, just—
('After there was nothing there was a woman')

Finally, the freedom and expansiveness of *Season Songs* can be seen in another large body of recent work, particularly *Moortown Elegies* and *Remains of Elmet*, which is directly personal and autobiographical. (The contents of *Moortown Elegies* and *Season Songs* in fact overlap—'Sheep', for example, appears in both.) The experience of writing 'within hearing of children' was perhaps influential on the following, wholly adult, poem about childhood, from *Remains of Elmet*.

Tick Tock Tick Tock
Peter Pan's days of pendulum
Cut at the valley groove.

Tick Tock Tick Tock
Everlasting play bled the whole unstoppable Calder
And incinerated itself happily
From a hundred mill chimneys.

Tick Tock Summer Summer
Summer Summer.
And the hills unalterable and the old women unalterable.
And the ageless boy
Among the pulsing wounds of Red Admirals.

Somebody else acted Peter Pan.
I swallowed an alarm clock
And over the school playground's macadam
Crawled from prehistory towards him
Tick Tock Tick Tock the crocodile.

3

Man and Nature

For Ted Hughes the vocation of being a poet is bound up with the subject-matter of his poetry in a way that can only be paralleled in a devotional poet. His subject is most simply described as the relation between man and nature, but that phrase conveys nothing of the intensity of the imaginative endeavour. This endeavour is to gain access to, and give expression to, a level of being at which the continuity between the processes of nature experienced within and observed without is unimpeded by consciousness. Here lies the source of all energy, creativity and delight. Individual consciousness, insisting all the time on its separateness, is the cause of painful and destructive alienation from this inner life—the obscure unhappiness of many of the human protagonists of Hughes's poems and stories. But consciousness is inescapable, and poems are ultimately acts of consciousness. The subterranean world that Hughes's poems explore can never be completely projected into language, nor can anyone permanently live in it. The poems are thus attempts at mediation, or reconciliation; none of them can be regarded as a final statement. Any didactic elements are therefore by their very nature suspect.

In the best of the earlier poems, on which we shall be concentrating in this chapter, the imaginative process is triggered by the observation of something in 'external' nature, usually an animal. Hughes's animal poems are very unlike Lawrence's. One never has the feeling that Hughes's animals are impenetrably alien, like Lawrence's fish and bat. It was Lawrence's achievement to honour the animal creation by asserting its independence of human ideas. The fact that Hughes frequently does not 'honour' his animal subjects in this way has offended some critics. His poems sometimes seem like an invasion of their subjects' being. The term 'otherness', which inevitably crops up in a discussion of this matter, is not very helpful. Hughes's animals are unmistakably 'other' in that they present a shock and a challenge to the poet. But Hughes would not say, with Lawrence, 'I did not know his God' ('Fish'). On the contrary, Hughes's poems are inspired by the conviction that he *does* know the God of the hawk, jaguar or pike. 'Know', that is, not in the sense of being able to define, but of being intimately acquainted with. For him the animal is not merely an analogue or emblem of the inner self but a part, with that self, of an indivisible whole.

This imaginative endeavour is the subject of the first part of this chapter. In the second part we discuss Hughes's treatment of the crucial characteristic of this indivisible reality on which all life is founded: the interdependence of creation and destruction, in which the relationship of consciousness to natural processes is again of paramount importance.

The first of Hughes's animal poems to be published was 'The Jaguar'.

> The apes yawn and adore their fleas in the sun.
> The parrots shriek as if they were on fire, or strut
> Like cheap tarts to attract the stroller with the nut.
> Fatigued with indolence, tiger and lion
>
> Lie still as the sun. The boa-constrictor's coil
> Is a fossil. Cage after cage seems empty, or
> Stinks of sleepers from the breathing straw.
> It might be painted on a nursery wall.
>
> But who runs like the rest past these arrives
> At a cage where the crowd stands, stares, mesmerized,
> As a child at a dream, at a jaguar hurrying enraged
> Through prison darkness after the drills of his eyes
>
> On a short fierce fuse. Not in boredom—
> The eye satisfied to be blind in fire,
> By the bang of blood in the brain deaf the ear—
> He spins from the bars, but there's no cage to him

More than to the visionary his cell:
His stride is wildernesses of freedom:
The world rolls under the long thrust of his heel.
Over the cage floor the horizons come.

This is a poem that has excited many readers and repelled others.
The reason for this is undoubtedly an awareness that the poet is in
some sense identifying himself with the jaguar. It is not a poem just
of observation but of longing and affirmation, particularly in its final
lines which broaden out to suggest a human possibility: an enticing
possibility but one that entails preserving intact the predatory ferocity, rage, blindness and deafness of our own nature. This is never
stated explicitly of course, but it is implicit in the way the poem's
own most intense life is concentrated in the undeviating thrust of the
jaguar's being. 'Drills' gives us the narrow intensity of the animal's
field of vision, but also suggests that he has bored holes in his prey
even before he reaches it, his predatory power concentrated into
his very eyesight. The penultimate line, with its superbly mimetic
juxtaposition of long stressed syllables, makes us imagine not only
that the jaguar's energy turns the world, but that with the same
action he spurns it, in his relentless pursuit of the 'horizons'. The
power of that final line derives from the sense that the vision of
horizons has, through his unquestioning absorption in the jaguar's
being, transferred itself to the poet.

The fact that it is caged makes the jaguar, of course, a natural
representation of a man's imprisoned animal energies. He is objectively caged but subjectively free, since he cannot formulate the
concept of imprisonment. He is an example to the man who longs to
live fully in those energies. Or is he? A man is not only conscious of
his prison, but his consciousness forms the very bars of his cell. Yet
in the last three lines it is the poet's conscious longing that attributes
freedom to the jaguar. In a sense, the jaguar only plays back the
wishfulness that the poet feeds into it; yet at the same time, in this
blind heroic commitment to the source of his own vitality, Hughes
creates a genuine embodiment of his animal subject. 'The Jaguar'
inaugurates the great quest of Hughes's poetry, but his per-
severance in the quest takes him beyond blind identification.

That the jaguar's freedom was the poet's illusion is implied in
'Second Glance at a Jaguar', collected in *Wodwo* a decade after the
first volume.

                    A gorged look,
Gangster, club-tail lumped along behind gracelessly,
He's wearing himself to heavy ovals,
Muttering some mantrah, some drum-song of murder
To keep his rage brightening, making his skin
Intolerable, spurred by the rosettes, the cain-brands,
Wearing the spots off from the inside,
Rounding some revenge.

This jaguar is also of course unconscious, but he does not transcend his cage: imprisonment has penetrated his body. The poem's powerful achievement is, over thirty-three lines, to maintain a relentless, threatening momentum that expresses the animal's unyielding ferocity yet carries a rhythmic embodiment of his tragic loss of grace in every line. As in Milton's devils, traces of his angelic nature remain, filling the reader with awe, but emphasizing the calamity of his fall. He is perhaps, in Hughes's own words, 'a symbol of man's baser nature shoved down into the id and growing cannibal murderous with deprivation' (*London Magazine* interview, January 1971, p. 8). Even so, this is no recantation of Hughes's earlier work. The initial response to the jaguar may have expressed a fantasy, but that is all the more reason for, somehow, giving him a real freedom.

The polarity of fierce energy and indolent inactivity expressed in 'The Jaguar' is also a dominant note of 'Thrushes'.

Terrifying are the attent sleek thrushes on the lawn,
More coiled steel than living—a poised
Dark deadly eye, those delicate legs
Triggered to stirrings beyond sense—with a start, a bounce, a stab

Overtake the instant and drag out some writhing thing.
No indolent procrastinations and no yawning stares,
No sighs or head-scratchings. Nothing but bounce and stab
And a ravening second.

If Hughes implicitly affirms a kinship with the jaguar, he shocks and enlightens the reader of this poem by undermining any sentimental sense one might have of kinship with the birds. Even so, the note of envious longing in the concluding lines of 'The Jaguar' is heard again in this opening stanza. The stanza is hinged on the double perception of the predatoriness of the thrushes and their delicacy, brilliantly fused in the word 'triggered'. To be so 'triggered' to the beyond-sense stirrings is to be in a state of bliss: in an interview in

65

the *Guardian* (23 March 1965) Hughes described the animals in his poems as 'living the redeemed life of joy'. On the practical level, this joy is perfect adaptation to the needs of life, and the total absorption of being in action.

The 'lawn' is slipped into the description as a customary setting for thrushes and as a concise suggestion of the limit of our relation to nature. However customary, the thrushes are made to seem start-lingly out of place on the lawn. But why the word 'terrifying' brood-ing over the whole stanza like a keynote? Simply as a realization that thrushes are expert killers it might well be melodramatic. But as a recognition that they represent the fulfilment of a longing, 'the redeemed life of joy', it is a breathtaking opening of chilled awe. The predatory freedom of the jaguar, romantically evoked in the earlier poem, the implied freedom of the human animal from the 'sighs or head-scratchings' of consciousness, is here observed in the field: 'Nothing but bounce and stab/And a ravening second.'

The poem does not sustain the taut energy with which this stanza so perfectly matches its subject (the genuine spring with which it jumps the line-endings of ll. 2–5 for example); nevertheless the rest of the poem gives us a further insight into this simultaneous terror and longing. In the second stanza Hughes asks what 'Gives their days this bullet and automatic/Purpose?' and comments:

> Mozart's brain had it, and the shark's mouth
> That hungers down the blood-smell even to a leak of its own
>
> Side and devouring of itself: efficiency which
> Strikes too streamlined for any doubt to pluck at it
> Or obstruction deflect.

He is perhaps trying to pack too much suggestion into 'Mozart's brain', but in the shark's mouth which absorbs the belly's hunger and the nose's smell and finally, literally, the shark's own flesh he has achieved a miracle of condensation. Yet again it is the language itself, performing its subject, that takes Hughes where he wants to go and to lead us; and the fulfilment brings a horrible recognition: that this 'efficiency' belongs not to the whole shark but to an eating mechanism with a separate existence.

This discovery would persuade most men to give up the quest of liberating the animal self. But Hughes reminds us of the necessity of pursuing it, with a summary of normal human existence.

With a man it is otherwise. Heroisms on horseback,
Outstripping his desk-diary at a broad desk,
Carving at a tiny ivory ornament
For years: his act worships itself—while for him,
Though he bends to be blent in the prayer, how loud and above
                                                         what
Furious spaces of fire do the distracting devils
Orgy and hosannah, under what wilderness
Of black silent waters weep.

This is the least satisfactory stanza: the paradoxes of human existence are reduced to epigram rather than captured in the energy of
language. Nevertheless the capacities hauntingly caught in 'orgy',
'hosannah' and 'weep', belonging not to the conscious man but to
the suppressed and ignored 'distracting devils', remind us explicitly
of the heart of Hughes's drama: the awakening of that tormenting
sense of not being in possession of one's own life and potentialities.
If there is a terrifying limitation in the thrushes' mechanically
instinctive being, it is placed beside this final human sense of loss,
and no simple relative valuation of the two modes of living is
possible.

   In one memorable *tour de force* in *Lupercal*, 'Hawk Roosting',
Hughes attempted to speak with the voice of his animal subject.

> I sit in the top of the wood, my eyes closed.
> Inaction, no falsifying dream
> Between my hooked head and hooked feet:
> Or in sleep rehearse perfect kills and eat.
>
> The convenience of the high trees!
> The air's buoyancy and the sun's ray
> Are of advantage to me;
> And the earth's face upward for my inspection.
>
> My feet are locked upon the rough bark.
> It took the whole of Creation
> To produce my foot, my each feather:
> Now I hold Creation in my foot
>
> Or fly up, and revolve it all slowly—
> I kill where I please because it is all mine.
> There is no sophistry in my body:
> My manners are tearing off heads—

The allotment of death.
For the one path of my flight is direct
Through the bones of the living.
No arguments assert my right:

The sun is behind me.
Nothing has changed since I began.
My eye has permitted no change.
I am going to keep things like this.

In the *London Magazine* interview the poet said, 'That bird is accused of being a fascist. . . . the symbol of some horrible genocidal dictator. Actually what I had in mind was that in this hawk Nature is thinking. Simply Nature' (January 1971, p. 8). For Nature thinking he finds a language quite different from the attempts, in his own voice, to perform an empathy with the animals. In place of the extravagant, energetic, fusing style of 'The Jaguar' and 'Thrushes', he writes in a cool, self-possessed, distanced language. Many of the words that establish the tone are surprisingly abstract, but wittily and elegantly so: 'rehearse', 'convenience', 'advantage', 'inspection', 'manners', 'allotment', 'permitted'. Coming as they tend to in brief, elliptical phrases they actually contribute to the poem's effect of brutal hardness, as if each use were a robbery from some humane, rational context. The elegance and confidence with which they are used serve in place of any direct description of the hawk's physical splendour.

The assurance of being at the centre of things, the focus of Creation, in the middle stanzas of the poem, is what most strongly supports the claim that this is 'Nature thinking'. The hawk's poise and serenity, its contemplative ease, mean that it is not terrifyingly limited like the thrushes: it is not concentrated into 'bounce and stab', though every line is tense with predatory ferocity.

Nevertheless, the poem's prime device, the use of the first person singular, carries with it an inevitable irony. A hawk may or may not have a self-conscious ego, but to be truly the medium of 'Nature thinking' is imaginable only as a consequence of losing the ability to say 'I': of being, like the skylarks in a later poem, 'shot through the crested head/With the command, Not die'. Hughes exploits this paradox of his chosen form in the last three lines, where Nature and the hawk think in the same words but to different effects. Introducing a reading of the poem (Lancaster, May 1978), Hughes described the bird as 'keeping up its hawkish morale', implying the effort to survive, the struggle *against* everything in Nature that opposes its survival. Thus while 'Nature' in the last three lines is speaking in the simple certainty that it services only itself, the hawk is rehearsing its own necessary blindness: what the hawk sees as a straight line with himself intact at each end of it is really, of course, a cycle that includes his own death.

But the irony is not at the hawk's expense, for this blindness *is* Nature, is Nature's way of dwelling in the individual creature, so that the whole magnificent structure of Creation is built upon ignorance of death. In short, the poem is essentially dramatic, enacting once again the writer's engagement with the threatening and enticing non-human reality. Hughes does not moralize upon the hawk, but there is no question of its being a model for imitation. For, as we shall be seeing in the next chapter, the determined and disciplined pursuit of knowledge of death is central to Hughes's achievement.

The poems we have been looking at are parts of a drama that incorporates the majority of Hughes's most interesting earlier poems. It is a drama of consciousness, not a didactic programme: a drama of the valuation of consciousness and unthinking activity, separation and oneness, human existence and animal existence as it is variously perceived by human consciousness itself. The animals are variously mesmerizing embodiments of energy, terrifying machines, points of creative unity—or, as Hughes himself has said:

> A jaguar after all can be received in several different aspects. . . . he is a beautiful, powerful nature spirit, he is a homicidal maniac, he is a supercharged piece of cosmic machinery, he is a symbol of man's baser nature shoved down into the id and growing cannibal murderous with deprivation, he is an ancient symbol of Dionysus since he is a leopard raised to the ninth power, he is a precise historical symbol to the bloody-minded Aztecs and so on. Or he is simply a demon. . . . a lump of ectoplasm. A lump of astral energy.
>
> (*London Magazine* interview, January 1971, p. 8)

What this conversational summary leaves out of course is the drama itself, which creates the tensions within and between the poems, and of which the weaknesses of the less successful poems are often a part. The most common weakness, which clearly belongs to the drama, is the indulgence of the desire to find an uncomplicated value in animal life, to see the animal as a 'beautiful, powerful nature spirit' that simply puts man in his place. 'Esther's Tomcat' is a pleasantly humorous poem about a tattered and battered old tom who 'Grallochs odd dogs on the quiet' and 'Walks upon sleep, his mind on the moon'. But didacticism creeps in when Hughes gives a version of the legend of the Barnburgh knight.

> A tomcat sprang at a mounted knight,
> Locked round his neck like a trap of hooks
> While the knight rode fighting its clawing and bite.
> After hundreds of years the stain's there
>
> On the stone where he fell, dead of the tom.

Actually in the legend the knight and the cat were both found dead, locked together. The suppression is important when Hughes goes on to say that the tomcat who is identical in spirit to the wildcat of the legend is 'unkillable'.[1]

More central to Hughes's achievement are the poems which insist on man's place in the material world, the perception of continuities and dependencies whose rejection by the conscious mind is death. An outstanding example is 'The Bull Moses', which makes its effect on the reader by what the poet has called 'some sort of charge and charm and series of operations' (*The Poet Speaks,* no 5) taking him from a simple external reality to the depth of his own mind. This movement, which is repeated at each stage of the poem, is the means by which the reader is drawn, like the boy (the perceiver), into the mystery of the bull's being:

> A hoist up and I could lean over
> The upper edge of the high half-door,
> My left foot ledged on the hinge, and look in at the byre's
> Blaze of darkness: a sudden shut-eyed look
> Backward into the head.

As Hughes himself has said, 'The bull represents what the observer sees when he looks into his own head' (*Guardian*, 23 March 1965). The second section's movement from sensuous, immediate reality leads deeper still:

Blackness is depth
Beyond star. But the warm weight of his breathing,
The ammoniac reek of his litter, the hotly-tongued
Mash of his cud, steamed against me.
Then, slowly, as onto the mind's eye—
The brow like masonry, the deep-keeled neck:
Something come up there onto the brink of the gulf,
Hadn't heard of the world, too deep in itself to be called to,
Stood in sleep. He would swing his muzzle at a fly
But the square of sky where I hung, shouting, waving,
Was nothing to him; nothing of our light
Found any reflection in him.

The poem moves towards its central mystery: why does the bull
accept a seemingly humiliating domination by our world?

Each dusk the farmer led him
Down to the pond to drink and smell the air,
And he took no pace but the farmer
Led him to take it, as if he knew nothing
Of the ages and continents of his fathers,
Shut, while he wombed, to a dark shed
And steps between his door and the duckpond.

The structure of the clause pivoting about the word 'led' suggests
the completeness of the farmer's domination and the bull's in-
difference. The images in the lines that follow—

The weight of the sun and the moon and the world hammered
To a ring of brass through his nostrils—

affirm a scale of power which seems to render the time and space of
'ages and continents' insignificant.
The poem concludes:

He would raise
His streaming muzzle and look out over the meadows,
But the grasses whispered nothing awake, the fetch
Of the distance drew nothing to momentum
In the locked black of his powers. He came strolling gently back,
Paused neither toward the pig-pens on his right,
Nor toward the cow-byres on his left: something

Deliberate in his leisure, some beheld future
Founding in his quiet.
                              I kept the door wide,
Closed it after him and pushed the bolt.

It would be arrogant to say that the mystery of the bull's meekness is solved: 'the locked black of his powers' remains inaccessible, locked and black. There is an anomaly at the heart of the perception—the bull is subject to the farmer, and yet so removed in being from the farmer's world as to be beyond the range of subjection—but the anomaly is fully developed and its psychological significance articulated. The ordinary common-sense reality in which it seems quite natural for the unconscious self to be subject to the mind's domination is occasionally breached by glimpses of that self so awesome as to make its subjection a mystery. The presence of the perceiver is of crucial importance in the poem, as the recognizer and self-recognizer. The quiet conclusion, the series of practical gestures expressing both awe in the face of the bull's mystery and relief at his disappearance into the byre, is beautifully managed, suggesting without emphasis or didacticism the relation of the protagonist's conscious self to the internal elements figured in the bull—a recognition accompanied by fear and holding in check of what is recognized. The poem's effect, the stillness that is not apathy, which the poem both describes and exemplifies, is similar to that of the equally fine poem, 'Pike', where the awesome stillness is once again both within and without.

If consciousness separates man from the so-called 'automatic purpose' of other creatures, it does enable him to observe his own response to the depths from which their vitality springs. Thus he is able to perceive that any connection he might eventually feel with the natural world will be determined by his definition of material reality. There are several early poems in which Hughes confronts directly the problem of defining on a larger scale the relationship between the forces that sustain the survival of life and the processes of dissolution and death.

The interest of the otter for Hughes is precisely in the difficulty of its definition. Living between water and land the otter must be defined in comparison with eel and tomcat. Ultimately only legends can pin down the qualities of his rootless yet surviving spirit. Here are the opening stanzas of 'An Otter':

Underwater eyes, an eel's
Oil of water body, neither fish nor beast is the otter:
  Four-legged yet water-gifted, to outfish fish;
    With webbed feet and long ruddering tail
    And a round head like an old tomcat.

    Brings the legend of himself
From before wars or burials, in spite of hounds and vermin-poles;
  Does not take root like the badger. Wanders, cries;
    Gallops along land he no longer belongs to;
    Re-enters the water by melting.

The two words 'wanders, cries' placed in the midst of the exposition contribute to the sense of a lost ghost in the anguish of its unease that is developed in the first part of the poem. The magical quality of his 'melting' into water suggests that he has been displaced from the material world to survive by some mysterious, supernatural force. The second part of the poem evokes the spirit by which the otter survives the hunt and places that spirit firmly in a series of larger natural processes.

    The hunt's lost him. Pads on mud,
    Among sedges, nostrils a surface bead,
    The otter remains, hours. The air,
    Circling the globe, tainted and necessary,

    Mingling tobacco-smoke, hounds and parsley,
    Comes carefully to the sunk lungs.
    So the self under the eye lies,
    Attendant and withdrawn. The otter belongs

    In double robbery and concealment—
    From water that nourishes and drowns, and from land
    That gave him his length and the mouth of the hound.

Once again Hughes employs the method exemplified in 'Bull Moses' by which he characteristically moves from physical detail to general idea, from a specific moment to universal processes. The dualities of 'tainted and necessary', 'attendant and withdrawn', 'robbery and concealment' and 'nourishes and drowns' place the otter's mysterious spirit at the centre of the tensions in the elements themselves. The poem, like 'The Jaguar' and 'Thrushes', is full of mimetic energy (for example, 'The heart beats thick,/Big trout muscle out of the dead cold'), but the emphasis on dualities indicates the development of a more clearly metaphysical preoccupation and language.

In 'Relic', Hughes attempts to explore further the implications of 'water that nourishes and drowns'. But although such a balanced concept seems to be assumed in such expressions as 'continue the beginning', the dominant emphasis is on a universe of destructive forces to which all living is finally subdued, hence the casual pose given to the sea in the opening lines and the deliberate omission of any evidence of the vitality derived from the function of jaws.

> I found this jawbone at the sea's edge:
> There, crabs, dogfish, broken by the breakers or tossed
> To flap for half an hour and turn to a crust
> Continue the beginning. The deeps are cold:
> In that darkness camaraderie does not hold;
> Nothing touches but, clutching, devours. And the jaws,
> Before they are satisfied or their stretched purpose
> Slacken, go down jaws; go gnawn bare. Jaws
> Eat and are finished and the jawbone comes to the beach:
> This is the sea's achievement; with shells,
> Vertebrae, claws, carapaces, skulls.
>
> Time in the sea eats its tail, thrives, casts these
> Indigestibles, the spars of purposes
> That failed far from the surface. None grow rich
> In the sea. This curved jawbone did not laugh
> But gripped, gripped and is now a cenotaph.

The matter-of-fact tone of the poem is consistent with the vision that is expressed in these statements: that all life in the sea eats and is eaten, and that this must be accepted without sentimentality or imposing values such as 'camaraderie'. Again the essential meaning is acted out by the language. According to the dictionary 'touch' and 'clutch' are a perfect rhyme, but the associations of the meaning make one intuitively credit 'touch' with the softness of its origin in the French *toucher*. In the progression 'touches but, clutching' Hughes brings out the latent contrast hidden beneath similarity in the sounds of the words, irresistibly conveying the corresponding progression in action.

'Relic' achieves a powerful grim singleness of vision, but in 'Crow Hill' Hughes finds a contrasting steady duality in contemplating universal processes directly. Perhaps because it is a poem directly expressing universals, and therefore tending to abstraction, it lacks the exploring energy of 'Bull Moses' and 'Pike'. But it catches, in a summary of images, the central concepts at the heart of Hughes's metaphysical drama. It seems to have been overlooked in previous studies, perhaps because its visualized description seems to be simply evoking the atmosphere of a specific place (there is a Crow Hill above Haworth). But four lines stand out as particularly finely balanced expressions of what interests Hughes. Firstly human life is humbled between elemental forces that are threatening and permanent, but achieves a modest vitality:

> Between the weather and the rock
> Farmers make a little heat.

The spirit represented by 'a little heat' is later to be quietly asserted in a number of Hughes's best poems such as 'Still Life', 'Full Moon and Little Frieda' and 'Littleblood'. Having placed man in relation to the elements that threaten him, Hughes goes on to relate animal vitality to the processes that shape the landscape:

> What humbles these hills has raised
> The arrogance of blood and bone.

The importance of this is that animal vitality is seen to be part of the same cycle of conflicting forces at work in the landscape. The creative-destructive tension in animals is a natural part of the larger cycle of forces in the universe.

In poems such as 'An Otter', 'Relic' and 'Crow Hill', Hughes is feeling towards an understanding of the necessity of 'the war between vitality and death' by placing the animal evidence of vitality sustained by death in the wider context of a creative-destructive universe. As the fully conscious but humble perceiver, the writer defines the tensions in the natural world that are parallel to those which appear to separate him from nature. The implication is that conscious awareness and acceptance of the tensions at the heart of 'Pike', 'An Otter' and 'Crow Hill' are necessary if man is to achieve the sort of completeness that comes from the commitment to those tensions exemplified by 'Skylarks'.

'Skylarks' is one of a number of poems in *Wodwo* that explore the personal paradoxes of living with intensity 'at the limit'. But more than 'Gnat-Psalm', for example, 'Skylarks' captures most completely the costs of intensity. It is also interesting as the beginning of a tendency towards the use of sequence in Hughes's poetry. The movement of the sections of this poem is not only a narrative one from the rise to the descent of the lark, but of widening perspectives to include the observer and his response.

The poem begins by suggesting that the lark is a responsive representative of an unease at the heart of its natural environment:

> The lark begins to go up
> Like a warning
> As if the globe were uneasy—

That vague unease is made tangible in the physical paradox of the lark's being 'leaden' with muscle for flight. The physical effort and its dangers of self-destruction are economically caught in:

> Leaden
> Like a bullet
> To supplant
> Life from its centre.

In the burst of that last line the force for life is identified with that of death.

In the second section the lark's fate to re-enact a life that narrowly escapes death is expressed in a metaphor that is more precise than it might first appear.

> Crueller than owl or eagle
>
> A towered bird, shot through the crested head
> With the command, Not die
>
> But climb
>
> Climb
>
> Sing
>
> Obedient as to death a dead thing.

76

'Towered', in the sense in which it is used here, refers to the upward flight of a wounded bird before it drops. But the 'shot' is the command to live. The skylark's nature almost makes it a predator of itself. We are reminded of the shark in 'Thrushes' and the pike that killed itself by eating another, but the effect here is not as exclusively grim. The lark is crueller than owl or eagle because it must act out its 'wounding' with an obedience paralleled only by the obedience of dead things to death. But at the same time it must sing as though dead to death. Thus the lark's song is

> incomprehensibly both ways—
> Joy! Help! Joy! Help!

The third part takes the question of obedience further. The lark appears to be as much acted upon as acting:

> I suppose you just gape and let your gaspings
> Rip in and out through your voicebox
> > O lark

> And sing inwards as well as outwards
> Like a breaker of ocean milling the shingle
> > O lark

The lark's condition is reminiscent of two sentences from Alan Watts: 'I am the whole process waving a flag named me' (*Beyond Theology*),[2] and (quoting Lieh-Tzu) 'I knew not whether the wind was riding on me or I on the wind' (*The Way of Zen*, p. 42).

The fifth section (fourth in *Wodwo*) is typical of the rhythmical and metaphorical boldness of the sequence. The frenzy of the lark and the sudden calm of the poet's perceptions when it disappears are both caught in unusually long lines, the first of abrupt, separated, short stresses—'Its feathers thrash, its heart must be drumming like a motor'—the second much more evenly accented on predominantly long syllables: 'Till my eye's gossamer snaps/and my hearing floats back widely to earth'. In this section the lark 'evaporates' towards the destructive fierceness of the 'whirling' sun, and this anticipates the sixth section (fifth in *Wodwo*), in which the demented cries of the larks are presented as those of tortured sacrifices:

77

Heads flung back, as I see them,
Wings almost torn off backwards—far up

Like sacrifices set floating
The cruel earth's offerings

The mad earth's missionaries.

In Hughes's poetry apparent restatements like the last three lines
are seldom repetitions of quite the same idea. The intelligence at
work in the poem controls the shift from 'sacrifices' to 'missionaries': the larks are not merely acted upon, but actively fulfil a
mission through their suffering.

The following section was the final one in the version printed in
Wodwo and we still think it makes the most appropriate conclusion
to the poem.

Like those flailing flames
That lift from the fling of a bonfire
Claws dangling full of what they feed on

The larks carry their tongues to the last atom
Battering and battering their last sparks out at the limit—
So it's a relief, a cool breeze
When they've had enough, when they're burned out
And the sun's sucked them empty
And the earth gives them the O.K.

And they relax, drifting with changed notes

Dip and float, not quite sure if they may
Then they are sure and they stoop

And maybe the whole agony was for this

The plummeting dead drop

With long cutting screams buckling like razors

But just before they plunge into the earth

They flare and glide off low over grass, then up
To land on a wall-top, crest up,

Weightless,
Paid-up,
Alert,

Conscience perfect.

This section exemplifies the way the whole sequence is balanced on the edge of human ability to register non-human life. It opens with a seemingly relentless insistence on the non-human, a determination to crystallize that part of Hughes's perception of the larks in which they are almost abstract embodiments of forces and laws: 'flames', 'atom', 'spark'. But this can only be kept up for five lines, or as long as the larks are 'at the limit'. As soon as the descent begins, words like 'relief' and 'relax' come in, and although 'burned out' and 'sucked them empty' prolong the language of the first five lines, 'the earth gives them the O.K.' reminds one irresistibly of a pilot receiving instructions. Anthropomorphic empathy reaches a peak in 'not quite sure if they may/Then they are sure and they stoop', only for the reader's corresponding relaxation (and perhaps complacency) to be jolted by 'The plummeting dead drop/With long cutting screams buckling like razors'. The larks have re-entered a phase of their being for which only material metaphors are available. Thus the return to anthropomorphism in the last line is bewildering: it is as if, beneath the comforting finality, the larks are mocking poet and reader, by their perfect imitation of a familiar human feeling, but as the outcome of a terrifying departure from the normal human range. This is not an attack on anthropomorphism (we have seen how frequently Hughes uses it) but a remarkable investigation of both its inevitability and its limits.

For the *Selected Poems* of 1972 Hughes added the following section:

Manacled with blood,
Cuchulain listened bowed,
Strapped to his pillar (not to die prone)
Hearing the far crow
Guiding the near lark nearer
With its blind song

> '*That some sorry little wight more feeble and misguided*
> *than thyself*
>
> *Take thy head*
> *Thine ear*
> *And thy life's career from thee.*'

It is not clear whether the crow is addressing Cuchulain or the lark, but he certainly represents the spirit of Hughes's own Crow, and mocks Cuchulain's heroic gesture. We are reminded of the 'heroisms on horseback' of 'Thrushes'. The crow's words undermine the possibility of assimilating the larks to the human ideal of heroism, and are perhaps intended to prevent any expansive response to the poem by dismissing the larks themselves as 'feeble and misguided'. Keith Sagar is probably right in suggesting that Hughes 'wanted to guard against the possibility of a sentimental reading of "Skylarks" or a reading which takes it to be no more than a very fine descriptive poem', and he is surely also right in saying that the poet has 'violated the unity of the poem' with this new ending (*The Art of Ted Hughes*, 2nd edition, pp. 93–4). The strength of the original poem is that the metaphysical and psychological perceptions operate within the drama of the lark's flight and the poet's response to it. By stepping outside the drama and introducing a didactic note, Hughes muffles the effect of a poem which epitomizes the integrity and clairvoyance of his engagement with the natural world.

In this chapter we have attempted to trace, in the early animal poems, two separate but interdependent themes: the sustained attempt of the conscious mind to articulate the continuities between the human self and the animal world; and an exploration of the creative-destructive nature of the material reality on which all life is founded. These concerns continue to predominate in Hughes's work after *Wodwo*, and the changes of artistic strategy in the later work perhaps reflect a sense that the poet has reached the limit of what he can do with the short lyric poem focused on a particular animal. The themes that we have discussed are at the centre, respectively, of *Gaudete* and *Crow*. In *Crow* Hughes uses the poem-sequence (which we have seen him beginning to exploit in 'Skylarks') and some of the imaginative strategies of primitive myth to develop his metaphysical inquiry. In *Gaudete*, through the experience of a somewhat paranormal human being, he extends his investigation into the relations between the animal self and the rest of the natural world. In both works the mother-goddess who has always been a part of his imaginative world becomes part of the expression. In the third and greatest of his 'mythical' works, *Cave Birds*, he finds a form to embody the 'drama of consciousness' that we have discussed in this chapter.

❧ 4 ❧

Knowledge of Death

'From now on, and for a period of eight days, I want you to lie
to yourself. Instead of telling yourself the truth, that you are
ugly and rotten and inadequate, you will tell yourself that you
are the complete opposite, knowing that you are lying and that
you are absolutely beyond hope.'
'But what would be the point of lying like that, don Juan?'
'It may hook you into another *doing* and then you may
realize that both *doings* are lies, unreal, and that to hinge
yourself to either one is a waste of time, because the only thing
that is real is the being in you that is going to die. To arrive at
that being is the *not-doing* of the self.'
(Carlos Castaneda, *Journey to Ixtlan*, pp. 213–14)

Don Juan's words to Carlos Castaneda make a suitable epigraph for
this chapter because they exemplify a preoccupation with death that
is not at all morbid or life-refusing. They are part of an argument
about, or revelation of, the reality of the self, and the unimportant
and ephemeral nature of self-images.[1] This is not to assert that there
is nothing morbid in Hughes, but that in much of his best poetry
(which may well have originated in a struggle with morbid impulses)
the preoccupation with death is similarly a preoccupation with the
real. Such a poem is 'Six Young Men':

The celluloid of a photograph holds them well,—
Six young men, familiar to their friends.
Four decades that have faded and ochre-tinged
This photograph have not wrinkled the faces or the hands.

Though their cocked hats are not now fashionable,
Their shoes shine. One imparts an intimate smile,
One chews a grass, one lowers his eyes, bashful,
One is ridiculous with cocky pride—
Six months after this picture they were all dead.

All are trimmed for a Sunday jaunt. I know
That bilberried bank, that thick tree, that black wall,
Which are there yet and not changed. From where these sit
You hear the water of seven streams fall
To the roarer in the bottom, and through all
The leafy valley a rumouring of air go.
Pictured here, their expressions listen yet,
And still that valley has not changed its sound
Though their faces are four decades under the ground.

This one was shot in an attack and lay
Calling in the wire, then this one, his best friend,
Went out to bring him in and was shot too;
And this one, the very moment he was warned
From potting at tin-cans in no-man's land,
Fell back dead with his rifle-sights shot away.
The rest, nobody knows what they came to,
But come to the worst they must have done, and held it
Closer than their hope; all were killed.

Here see a man's photograph,
The locket of a smile, turned overnight
Into the hospital of his mangled last
Agony and hours; see bundled in it
His mightier-than-a-man dead bulk and weight:
And on this one place which keeps him alive
(In his Sunday best) see fall war's worst
Thinkable flash and rending, onto his smile
Forty years rotting into soil.

That man's not more alive whom you confront
And shake by the hand, see hale, hear speak loud,
Than any of these six celluloid smiles are,
Nor prehistoric or fabulous beast more dead;
No thought so vivid as their smoking blood:
To regard this photograph might well dement,

Such contradictory permanent horrors here
Smile from the single exposure and shoulder out
One's own body from its instant and heat.

The relaxed tone of the first three stanzas is expressing an affection for ordinary life, a recognition of bright vitality where Hughes more characteristically detects complacency and inertia. But the response which raises this poem above an elegy in a Georgian or even 'Movement' manner first appears in the paradoxical but grimly accurate formulation of the sudden intimacy with death at the end of the third stanza. In the final stanza the idea of holding death closer than the hope of avoiding it is imaginatively experienced by the person holding the photograph. The intensity of vitality caught in a photograph brings the permanent reality of death so brutally into the life of the perceiver that his vulnerability is brilliantly reflected in the verb of 'shoulder out/One's own body from its instant and heat'. If there are signs in the wordiness of the fourth stanza that this is an early poem its central intuition anticipates one of Hughes's finest poems, 'Stations'.

'Six Young Men' owes some of its strength to the details of trench warfare in the third stanza, but war itself is the occasion rather than the subject of the best 'war poems' in *The Hawk in the Rain*. Their subject is death and grief. The opening section of 'Griefs for Dead Soldiers' is an ironically grandiloquent account of the unveiling of a cenotaph. This is the 'mightiest' grief, but the poem's strength is in its second section.

Secretest, tiniest, there, where the widow watches on the table
The telegram opening of its own accord
Inescapably and more terribly than any bomb
That dives to the cellar and lifts the house. The bared
Words shear the hawsers of love that now lash
Back in darkness, blinding and severing. To a world
Lonely as her skull and little as her heart

The doors and windows open like great gates to a hell.
Still she will carry cups from table to sink.
She cannot build her sorrow into a monument
And walk away from it. Closer than thinking
The dead man hangs around her neck, but never
Close enough to be touched, or thanked even,
For being all that remains in a world smashed.

Again the word 'closer' conveys the invasion of life by death, but in this case with a paradox. The widow's grief is real and inescapable, but the poignancy of the poem is generated mostly by the sense of the vacancy of grief, its power to make life unreal by abolishing everything except what has been lost. The sensitivity and psychological subtlety of this should be acknowledged. *The Hawk in the Rain* has not often been praised for these qualities.

Perhaps it was the sense that what we ordinarily think of as true grief makes for detachment from reality that prompted the brutally didactic final section of this poem. The 'Truest, and only just' grief is that of the burial party at the 'mass grave/Where spades hack, and the diggers grunt and sweat/... thud of another body flung/Down, the jolted shape of a face, earth into the mouth—/Moment that could annihilate a watcher!' Despite the obvious limitations of the language in comparison with the subtlety of Part 2, and despite also the deceptive shift of emphasis from grief to horror, this section exemplifies the strength of Hughes's vision, by its determination to acknowledge the reality and fate of the destroyed material body.

This explicit concern with the direct or imagined experience of human death goes underground in *Lupercal*. 'View of a Pig', which we have discussed in Chapter 2, more successfully develops the subject of Part 3 of 'Griefs for Dead Soldiers', and 'A Woman Unconscious' incorporates a moving description of a hospital death into a trite refusal to be frightened of a nuclear holocaust; but generally (as we have argued in Chapter 3) death in *Lupercal* is contemplated as a process operating in the material world, rather than as the inevitable end of individual human life.

It is in *Wodwo* and subsequent volumes that a poetry of death emerges which justifies the highest claims. According to Mircea Eliade one of the functions of the shaman is to 'contribute decisively to the *knowledge of death*' (*Shamanism*, p. 509), and Hughes's identification of the poet's role with that of the shaman may have been partly prompted by the aspiration that we have already seen in *The Hawk in the Rain*. The relevance of his interest in the *Tibetan Book of the Dead*, which he has called 'basically a shamanistic flight and return' (*London Magazine* interview, January 1971, p. 17), hardly needs to be stated. The 'knowledge' in question is not a matter of 'meanings', but rather of experience offered in the poetry. We might use the word 'understanding' if we accept that there is a kind of understanding inseparable from the experience through which it comes. In the case of a poet the beginning and end of the endeavour is to find a language in which to write about death. That endeavour is at best fragmentarily successful in the *Hawk in the Rain* poems, and its achievement is a main condition of the success of such a poem as 'Stations'.

'Stations' is a sequence, originally of four parts, increased to five in *Selected Poems*. The word is familiar to Catholic Christianity through the Stations of the Cross and the devotional exercises associated with them, but more directly relevant is its use to translate the Sufi *maqamat*, or stages on the road to the annihilation of individual consciousness (Hughes reviewed Idries Shah's *The Sufis* in 1964) Hughes's 'Stations' do not seem to correspond directly to these stages, but their tendency is the same. The reader is guided towards a contemplation of his own death, a process exemplified by the changes, in the course of the sequence, from third to second person, and past to present tense. Here is the first part:

Suddenly his poor body
Had its drowsy mind no longer
For insulation.

Before the funeral service foundered
The lifeboat coffin had shaken to pieces
And the great stars were swimming through where he had been.

For a while

The stalk of the tulip at the door that had outlived him,
And his jacket, and his wife, and his last pillow
Clung to each other.

The first line introduces a pathos which, despite the grim humour that subsequently accompanies it, is never entirely lost from the poem. But the object of the pathos is the body: the material object whose very qualification for pathetic treatment is its detachment from the 'he' to whom it once belonged. 'He', in fact, slips out through the syntax of the first three lines. The 'drowsy mind' is 'its', i.e. the body's, and served, it seems, as no more than 'insulation' against the process of decomposition that has just started. The word 'insulation' has another meaning: the mind's 'drowsiness' was presumably also an insulation against 'his' knowing the reality that has 'suddenly', just at the moment of 'his' slipping out of existence, started for the body. The revelation of this reality is guided by the careful, precise versification, which draws the maximum attention to the word 'insulation', while establishing a slow, thoughtful rhythm that is sustained for most of the sequence.

We have already seen indications of Hughes's characteristic wit in 'Stations', and the wit emerges more strongly in the conceit of the three lines that follow.

Before the funeral service foundered
The lifeboat coffin had shaken to pieces
And the great stars were swimming through where he had been.

The ironic oxymoron 'lifeboat coffin' concentrates in its harsh paradox the astringency that both delights and unnerves us in this poem, and which in the section's last lines is brilliantly fused with the re-emerging pathos.

For a while

The stalk of the tulip at the door that had outlived him,
And his jacket, and his wife, and his last pillow
Clung to each other.

The fusion is centred on the word 'clung', which poignantly conveys the wife's grief, while being grammatically governed by an impersonal and arbitrarily ordered list of nouns.

We'll quote the second and third sections together.

II
I can understand the haggard eyes
Of the old

Dry wrecks

Broken by seas of which they could drink nothing.

III
They have sunk into deeper service. They have gone down
To labour with God on the beaches. They fatten
Under the haddock's thumb. They rejoice

87

Through the warped mouth of the flounder
And are nowhere they are not here I know nothing
Cries the poulterer's hare hanging
Upside down above the pavement
Staring into a bloody bag Not here

Cry the eyes from the depths

Of the mirror's seamless sand.

The third section is not in the sequence as printed in *Wodwo*: there it formed part (much the best part) of a separate poem entitled 'Karma'. In addition to a few verbal improvements, the poem gains from its new context (and makes Part 2 more substantial—we can't help reading straight on). But the original title is helpful. The Western mind naturally has difficulty in understanding that reincarnation is something to be escaped from. That is the object of the splendid wit of this poem: the arrogant, but also pathetically desperate, attempt to turn the rest of the material world into a haven from one's own 'absence'.

The 'seas' which break the old people in Part 2 are, one guesses, those in which the funeral service foundered, and also perhaps wash the beaches on which the dead 'labour with God'. The continuity, at least, is hard to ignore. The associated uses of the image suggest the impersonal material reality that works through our lives, 'breaks' us and takes over after our deaths. The sea is also, both traditionally and in evolutionary theory, the source of life, and this gives us the chance to catch materialism by the tail: going back into the sea, we may hope to emerge from it again in some form.

The solemnity of 'They have sunk into deeper service' is a trap, which begins to close with the next sentence. The irony is clearly there in the hint of Churchillian rhetoric—'we shall fight them on the beaches'. This may be far-fetched, but one of the poem's earlier titles was 'Public Speech'. In any case, the poem as a whole demands to be read ironically. The labour in question is the labour of creation and evolution, and the reward is a degrading survival of the identity at any cost, in which the labourers grotesquely 'fatten' and 'rejoice'. (The haddock has a large blackish spot over each pectoral fin, traditionally supposed to be the marks made by the thumb and finger of St Peter when he picked the fish out of the water to provide the tribute money. The flounder's mouth is warped because, being a flat-fish, it is asymmetrical. Hughes's own regard for these lines can be deduced from the fact that, before 'Stations' and 'Karma', they appeared in an uncollected poem 'On Westminster Bridge', published in *Poetry*, December 1963.)

The pace and rhythm of the poem suddenly change as, dropping punctuation, it moves into the vivid material reality of the hare which belongs to itself, and will admit no identity but its own. The wit is maintained, becoming almost savage in its admonition against the arrogance we referred to earlier. The image of the mirror, with all its folklore resonances, completes the rejection of the illusion satirized in the first four lines. You cannot escape into the looking-glass world: it is 'seamless'. Indeed, it is not there to provide an escape: the eyes in its depths are merely reflections of the eyes looking in and asking.

The fourth poem is addressed to a bird. The word 'absence', which we have used already in our commentary, is at the centre of this poem.

> You are a wild look—out of an egg
> Laid by your absence.
>
> In the great Emptiness you sit complacent,
> Blackbird in wet snow.
>
> If you could make only one comparison—
> Your condition is miserable, you would give up.
>
> But you, from the start, surrender to total Emptiness,
> Then leave everything to it.
>
> Absence. It is your own
> Absence
>
> Weeps its respite through your accomplished music,
> Wraps its cloak dark about your feeding.

The tone has become epigrammatic, and in the first couplet the epigram is shaped by the energy of Hughes's wit at its strongest, combining a conceptual paradox with a startlingly vivid image. In

89

the second couplet the idea is reduced to its simplest visual terms. The conception of existence as a respite between two absences is powerful, though we should have carried from the previous poem the awareness that the 'Emptiness' is in fact peopled with other presences. The third and fourth couplets emphasize the blackbird's unreflective existence, absolved from metaphysics, all that distinguishes him from the human beings who often do 'give up'. But in the final four lines a modulation occurs: it is impossible to keep separate the blackbird's song and our own 'distinguished music', including that of the poem itself. 'Absence weeps its respite' through both. The poem's fullest power comes from this paradox, which touches the nerve of common but obscure experience, of one's own absence as a presence in one's life, expressing itself in art, and brooding over the means taken to preserve life. The odd power of the abstract word, given both witty and poignant intensity here, reaches back into the earlier parts of the sequence—so that its use in inverted commas seemed the best way of closing our commentary on the first poem.

The final poem is truly a conclusion: in its sudden increase of pace, reminiscent of the abrupt signing-off of a piece of music; in its harsh exclusion of the pathos that has been an important element in the sequence; and in its reflection on the saying, thinking and knowing which have been so much the point of the sequence, but make no difference to the reality. The polysyllabic abstract word 'vocabulary' is uncomfortably out of place here.

> Whether you say it, think it, know it
> Or not, it happens, it happens as
> Over rails over
> The neck the wheels leave
> The head with its vocabulary useless,
> Among the flogged plantains.

'Stations' is immediately followed in *Wodwo* by 'The Green Wolf', which we'll look at more briefly. It begins with a realistic description of a man dying from a stroke.

> Your neighbour moves less and less, attempts less.
> If his right hand still moves, it is a farewell
> Already days posthumous.

But the left hand seems to freeze,
And the left leg with its crude plumbing,
And the left half jaw and the left eyelid and the words, all the
                                                        huge cries

Frozen in his brain his tongue cannot unfreeze—
While somewhere through a dark heaven
The dark bloodclot moves in.

With greater realism, more detailed concentration on the dying man himself, Hughes again achieves, as in the first part of 'Stations', a modern elegiac language, which combines poignancy and wit, expressing sympathetic involvement with the dying individual, and a firm objectivity about the fact of death. The wit is subtly and impressively there in the paradoxical word 'attempts'—paradoxical because we usually associate the word with choice (we choose to attempt less rather than more) whereas here choice, or even the illusion of choice, has been removed. The poignancy is there above all in 'a farewell/Already days posthumous'. The gesture, in itself full of meaning, into which the survivors would want to put so much meaning, is from the dying man's point of view a random nervous convulsion. And note that it is not merely too late but 'posthumous'—the single word raises the question, highly relevant to the given case, of where life ends and death begins.

The phrase 'a dark heaven' has introduced a metaphysical dimension, and this dimension takes over in the second half of the poem.

You watch it approaching but you cannot fear it.
The punctual evening star,
Worse, the warm hawthorn blossoms, their foam,

Their palls of deathly perfume,
Worst of all the beanflower
Badged with jet like the ear of the tiger

Unmake and remake you. That star
And that flower and that flower
And living mouth and living mouth all

One smouldering annihilation
Of old brains, old bowels, old bodies
In the scarves of dew, the wet hair of nightfall.

As in 'Stations', the reader's attention is shifted from the described death to his own, as it opens out from the deathbed to the signs in the world that portend death, and finally to a vision of the world as a continuous breaking down of one thing into another.

This poem is slightly weakened by a forced note of menace. The hawthorn and the beanflower have folklore associations with death (and are used, in conjunction, to similarly menacing effect in Sylvia Plath's 'The Bee Meeting') but there is nothing in the progression of images to justify the cumulative 'Worse . . . Worst of all', which gives the poem a worked-up quality. But Hughes recovers in his powerfully equivocal conclusion, combining the eerie, the predatory and the erotic, which leaves the reader grasping at a beautiful but menacing transformation. This conclusion is Hughes's answer to the aspirations satirized in the 'Karma' section of 'Stations': this is not 'rejoicing through the warped mouth of the flounder' but a metamorphosis that demands the total extinction of the self.

In 1966, a year before the appearance of *Wodwo*, Hughes published a limited edition of poems entitled *Recklings*. The poems in this book were written over the same period as the *Wodwo* poems and are presumably those that the author decided to exclude from his major collection but not to suppress altogether. One poem, 'Logos', appears in both *Recklings* and *Wodwo*, and three of the *Recklings* poems form the sequence 'Root, Stem, Leaf', included in the American edition of *Wodwo* and the *Selected Poems*. Here is the second section, originally called 'On the Slope'.

> Having taken her slowly by surprise
> For eighty years
> The hills have won, their ring is closed.
>
> The field-walls float their pattern
> Over her eye
> Whether she looks outward or inward.
>
> Nothing added, nothing taken away.
> Year after year the trout in the pools
> Grow heavy and vanish, without ever emerging.
>
> Foxglove, harebell neither protest nor hope
> On the steep slope where she climbs.
> Out of nothing she grew here simply

Also suffering to be merely flowerlike

But with the stone agony growing in her joints
And eyes, dimming with losses, widening for losses.

The poem is a reminder of how Wordsworthian Hughes can be (cf., from the earlier volumes, 'The Horses': 'In the din of the crowded streets, going among the years, the faces,/ May I still meet my memory in so lonely a place' and 'November': 'I thought what strong trust/Slept in him'). One thinks of 'Michael' and the Lucy poems, though all the details are suffused with Hughes's distinctive tone and vision—'the hills have won', 'grow heavy and vanish', the pun on 'suffering' and the symbolic significance given to arthritis with the phrase 'stone agony'. The poem exemplifies its ideal of 'neither protest nor hope' and such an achievement entitles it to be better known, although it does not confront the harshness of annihilation as boldly as 'Stations' and 'The Green Wolf'.

There is, of course, a danger of seeing death as the only reality, and 'Heptonstall' might seem to provide an example were it not for the reality of its detail and the spirit of 'trying' which it celebrates. The version quoted here is from *Selected Poems*.

> Black village of gravestones.
> Skull of an idiot
> Whose dreams die back
> Where they were born.
>
> Skull of a sheep
> Whose meat melts
> Under its own rafters.
> Only the flies leave it.
>
> Skull of a bird,
> The great geographies
> Drained to sutures
> Of cracked windowsills.
>
> Life tries.
>
> Death tries.
>
> The stone tries.
>
> Only the rain never tires.

Heptonstall is, in fact, a 'village of gravestones' in that its extended cemetery seems to dominate it. Many people who have visited this windswept hilltop village of black stone houses and gravestones testify to this poem's representing the spirit of the place and the necessity for life, and indeed death and stone, equally to 'try' against the elements there. The poetic achievement is strongest in the third stanza: the piercing rapidity of the movement from the lines of a vast landscape to the joints of a skull and the vulnerability of human habitation.

The development from the achievement of 'Stations' and 'The Green Wolf', synthesizing Hughes's preoccupation with death as a measure of reality with a poignancy that acknowledges grief and loss, is to be found in 'That Moment' from *Crow*:

> When the pistol muzzle oozing blue vapour
> Was lifted away
> Like a cigarette lifted from an ashtray
>
> And the only face left in the world
> Lay broken
> Between hands that relaxed, being too late
>
> And the trees closed forever
> And the streets closed forever
>
> And the body lay on the gravel
> Of the abandoned world
> Among abandoned utilities
> Exposed to infinity forever
>
> Crow had to start searching for something to eat.

This is unlike many of the poems in *Crow*, which are much more crudely shocking, their language less obviously considered and certainly less restrained; many respond with a quite raucous humour to experiences even more painful than this. For this reason it is not surprising that the poem has met with some favour even from critics who are repelled by the book as a whole. For another reason, though, it is surprising, for the poem does something usually depre-cated by modern critics: it develops a powerful feeling from a deliberately unspecific occasion. It is not even certain whether the death is a suicide or a murder: the casualness of the lifting away of the gun makes murder seem more likely, but perhaps the shock that the poem communicates owes something to the sense that even the distinction between murder and suicide is unimportant at the moment of loss. We don't know for whom the dead face is 'the only face left in the world', whose hands 'relaxed, being too late', what relation the observer has to the victim and the murderer, or what relation Crow has to any of it.

Against this vagueness of occasion, however, there is a striking precision of language and image: the subtle and concise notation, for example, of the manner in which the gun is lifted away; the face broken between relaxed hands; the body lying on the *gravel* of the abandoned world. Furthermore, there is an almost positive anti-indulgence of emotional language: if the poem derives a strong feeling from an imprecise occasion, it is not in order to luxuriate in the feeling.

In 'The Green Wolf' the portents of death in the hawthorn blossom and the beanflower were menacing, but they were themselves alive. The 'old brains, old bowels, old bodies' were annihilated but reabsorbed: there was something beyond them, which they served. Here, the sense of loss is total—Hughes develops, through 'the only face left in the world', 'the trees closed forever', and the emphasis on the sterile 'gravel', the feeling that this individual death is or portends the end of all things—and the body, instead of being wrapped in 'the scarves of dew, the wet hair of nightfall', is 'Exposed to infinity forever'.

If in the *Wodwo* poems, then, Hughes created a modern elegiac language, in this poem he is striving to express the experience of loss within a perception of the world that nearly resembles a vacuum. The vacuum is perhaps created by the loss—the utilities are abandoned and therefore absurd because of the death—but a large part of the poem's power comes from the condition that the world is left in by the death. The removal of 'the only face left in the world' (whether literally or in the mind of an observer is unimportant) removes also the possibilities of meaning which make the world something other than a Beckettian wilderness.

We have come so far without mentioning the real point of the poem, which is contained in its last line. This is deliberate. Unless we are aware of how much has already been done, how complete the sense of loss is, this final line might seem a facile ironic twist. The power, restraint and integrity of the first twelve lines guarantee the seriousness of the thirteenth; conversely, a retrospective glance at the grammatical structure of the poem shows us that all that sense of loss was contained in a series of subordinate clauses, and the main clause is Crow's physical hunger: this blunt reality has all the time been putting a structural and rhythmic restraint on the poem and helping to ensure against sentimentality.

It is interesting to place beside 'That Moment' a more recent poem, in which the experience of loss is again central, and which anticipates a large body of later work in its directly personal tone.

The stone

Has not yet been cut.
It is too heavy already
For consideration. Its edges
Are so super-real, already,
And at this distance,
They cut real cuts in the unreal
Stuff of just thinking. So I leave it.
Somewhere it is.
Soon it will come.
I shall not carry it. With horrible life
It will transport its face, with sure strength,
To sit over mine, wherever I look,
Instead of hers.
It will even have across its brow
Her name.

Somewhere it is coming to the end
Of its million million years—
Which have worn her out.
It is coming to the beginning
Of her million million million years
Which will wear out it.

Because she will never move now
Till it is worn out.
She will not move now
Till everything is worn out.

We quote this poem here to show that a moving simplicity of seemingly spontaneous personal statement has been earned by the resolution and integrity of the encounters with death in the earlier poems, the repeated attempts to find a language in which to make death known. By the simplest and most natural means Hughes conveys the invasion of the personal realm of being by an irresistible material reality. The stone is of course the headstone of the grave but it also represents, in the most emotionally charged form, the portents of non-being that we have seen in other poems. Stone, or a stone, has frequently featured in this way in Hughes's work. In *Crow*, for example, there is a Manichaean battle between Crow and Stone:

> Crow was nimble but had to be careful
> Of his eyes, the two dewdrops.
> Stone, champion of the globe, lumbered towards him.

And in 'Still Life' the massive, inert, 'miserly' outcrop stone of the moorland is contrasted with the frail, trembling life of a harebell. In 'The stone' the mind, numbed with grief, enacts, with its short, heavy, two-stressed phrases, the lumbering progress of the portent. In some respects the poem recalls Wordsworth's great elegy, 'A slumber did my spirit seal':

> No motion has she now, no force.
> She neither hears nor sees.

But, while there seems to be a striving towards the acceptance achieved in Wordsworth's poem, it is thwarted by a horror incongruously and disturbingly reminiscent of Yeats's rough beast, dragging its slow thighs, as it slouches towards Bethlehem to be born.

'The stone', collected in *Moortown*, was first published in 1974. It brings us to the brink of *Gaudete* and *Cave Birds*. It would not be helpful to extract the preoccupation with death in *Gaudete* from the total effect of that work, but a brief discussion of two of the best *Cave Birds* poems will make a fitting conclusion to this chapter.

The executioner

Fills up
Sun, moon, stars, he fills them up

With his hemlock—
They darken

He fills up the evening and the morning, they darken
He fills up the sea

He comes in under the blind filled-up heaven
Across the lightless filled-up face of water

He fills up the rivers he fills up the roads, like tentacles
He fills up the streams and the paths, like veins

The tap drips darkness darkness
Sticks to the soles of your feet

He fills up the mirror, he fills up the cup
He fills up your thoughts to the brims of your eyes

You just see he is filling the eyes of your friends
And now lifting your hand you touch at your eyes

Which he has completely filled up
You touch him

You have no idea what has happened
To what is no longer yours

It feels like the world
Before your eyes ever opened

Earlier, when talking about the title of 'Stations', we said that the poem is akin to a devotional exercise. This is more strikingly true of 'The executioner', in which the reader is invited and encouraged, step by step, to contemplate his own non-being. The poem has a rhetorical structure directed to this end, of which the incantatory effect produced by the repetitions is only the most obvious feature. In the context of the *Cave Birds* sequence the 'you' being addressed is a persona, who goes through a series of spiritual adventures. But, whether we read the poem in or out of context, we can't help knowing that the protagonist is essentially ourself, just as the protagonist becomes the reader in the latter stages of 'Stations'.

'The executioner' begins by unravelling, or cancelling, the Biblical account of the first three days of Creation. All the images in the first eight lines, apart from the hemlock, refer directly to Genesis 1: 1–18 and draw from the force of its rhythm and imagery in reversing the process. But suddenly in a terrifying implacable dream-world vision the poem moves closer to the reader's intuitive awareness of the death that is part of him:

> The tap drips darkness darkness
> Sticks to the soles of your feet.

The final stage draws simultaneously on several levels of suggestion. The mirror and the cup are domestic details with strong folklore resonances: the shock (as in 'Crow's Vanity') of no longer seeing one's own face in the mirror; the poisoned chalice. What is movingly created from these lines onwards is the *feeling* of the helpless drift into non-being: 'You touch him.'

In discussing this poem we have substituted the word 'non-being' for 'death', partly because it seems called for by the final couplet:

> It feels like the world
> Before your eyes ever opened

and also because 'The executioner' comes quite early in the *Cave Birds* sequence: it is the conclusion of one stage in the protagonist's adventures. The experience in which we are invited to participate, then, is not necessarily final, though presumably it must prepare us for something final. There is an obvious influence of Oriental religious traditions here, and in particular the Sufi pursuit of *fana* or annihilation. Hughes said of the Sufis:

> they undergo many years of rigorous mental and spiritual training in the Sufi schools, a highly refined course of moral self-development, annihilating themselves without heaven or hell or religious paraphernalia of any kind, and without leaving life in the world, into the living substance of Allah, the power of Creation.
>
> (*Listener*, 29 October 1964, p. 678)

99

The Oriental influence, important though it undoubtedly is, may be put in perspective by noting a similar idea in a writer as Western as D. H. Lawrence. Here he is speaking through the character of Birkin in *Women in Love*.

> 'Only there needs the pledge between us, that we will both cast off everything, cast off ourselves even, and cease to be, so that that which is perfectly ourselves can take place in us.'
> (Chapter 13)

Death, as we have said in a previous chapter, is for Hughes the type of the inescapable. If his imagination is to a considerable extent death-oriented it is because the fact of death, resolutely contemplated, is the ultimate type of that unity of the inner self and 'external' nature which he attempts to express in his poems celebrating intense life. Perhaps the finest expression of this unity, combining an uncompromising statement of the material body's fate with a religious honouring of the earth to which it returns, is in these lines from 'The knight' (quoted in full on page 15):

> He has conquered in earth's name.
> Committing these trophies
>
> To the small madness of roots, to the mineral stasis
> And to rain.
>
> An unearthly cry goes up.
> The Universes squabble over him—
>
> Here a bone, there a rag.
> His sacrifice is perfect. He reserves nothing.
>
> Skylines tug him apart, winds drink him,
> Earth itself unravels him from beneath—
>
> His submission is flawless.
>
> Blueflies lift off his beauty.
> Beetles and ants officiate
>
> Pestering him with instructions.
> His patience grows only more vast.

Hughes has said, in his introduction to Popa,

I think it was Milosz, the Polish poet, who when he lay in a doorway and watched the bullets lifting the cobbles out of the street beside him realized that most poetry is not equipped for life in a world where people actually do die. But some is.

(Vasko Popa, *Selected Poems*, pp. 9–10)

We have tried to show in the most direct way possible that Hughes's own work is so equipped. 'The knight' not only gives us a world in which people die but, in its subtle imaginative fusion of human hero and dead bird, places human death solidly in the context of larger natural processes.

5

Crow

The Language of *Crow*

The first idea of *Crow* was really an idea of a style. In folktales
the prince going on the adventure comes to the stable full of
beautiful horses and he needs a horse for the next stage and
the king's daughter advises him to take none of the beautiful
horses that he'll be offered but to choose the dirty, scabby little
foal. You see, I throw out the eagles and choose the Crow. The
idea was originally just to write his songs, the songs that a
Crow would sing. In other words, songs with no music whatsoever, in a super-simple and super-ugly language which
would in a way shed everything except just what he wanted to
say without any other consideration and that's the basis of the
style of the whole thing.

(*London Magazine* interview, January 1971, p. 20)

Hughes's statement about the origin of *Crow* tells us several
important things: that it is a stylistic experiment, that it is not an
absolute apocalypse but a 'stage' of the poet's 'adventure', that in at
least one sense the experiment is reductive.[1] On the other hand it
dangerously over-simplifies the range of technique to be found in
the poems. A study of the style of *Crow* will certainly not find
unrelieved ugliness or a complete absence of 'music'. Hughes is in
fact describing a prominent but not predominant *part* of the style:
the deliberate use of crude colloquial and journalistic language
in unexpected contexts. This part of the style is easy to illustrate by passages from a large number of the poems. Here are
just a few.

When God said: 'You win, Crow,'
He made the Redeemer.

When God went off in despair
Crow stropped his beak and started in on the two thieves.
('Crow's Song of Himself')

So he just went and ate what he could
And did what he could
And grabbed what he could
And saw what he could

Then sat down to write his autobiography

But somehow his arms were just bits of stick
Somehow his guts were an old watch-cháin
Somehow his feet were two old postcards
Somehow his head was a broken windowpane
('A Bedtime Story')

Words came with Life Insurance policies—
Crow feigned dead.
Words came with warrants to conscript him—
Crow feigned mad.
Words came with blank cheques—
He drew Minnie Mice on them.
('The Battle of Osfrontalis')

It is, however, more difficult to find poems that are written entirely
in this kind of rock-bottom language, and the ones that are written
like this are among the worst. 'A Grin', for example, doesn't achieve
more than a facile journalistic grimness; 'Conjuring in Heaven' is
cheaply facetious; 'Song for a Phallus', the most extreme example, is
an exception, having originally been written as 'a satyr-song to
accompany a mime profane burlesque satyr-play' at the end of Peter
Brook's production of Seneca's *Oedipus*: 'it can only ever exist as an
addendum, a commentary, a goblin appendix to the human tragedy'
(letter to ourselves, October 1979). It would perhaps be more
effectively printed at the end of Hughes's translation of *Oedipus*.
What we more commonly find, and invariably so in the best

poems, is that this language has a specific function in a context of more complex and often quite literary effects. Even the simple humour of 'The Battle of Osfrontalis' becomes more interesting and sharper when Hughes juxtaposes, with the minimal statements of Crow's reactions, a fanciful and satirical yoking of the languages of warfare and phonology:

> Words attacked him with the glottal bomb—
> He wasn't listening.
> Words surrounded and over-ran him with light aspirates—
> He was dozing.
> Words infiltrated guerrilla labials—
> Crow clapped his beak, scratched it.
> Words swamped him with consonantal masses—
> Crow took a sip of water and thanked heaven.

In the best poems the 'super-simple and super-ugly' language sometimes has the most immediately striking effect, because it is the most obvious and usually comes at the end; but if we try to account for the full, pondered effect we find that it comes from a large and varied range of poetic resource, though handled with a brevity and directness that perhaps illustrates the true spirit of Hughes's 'idea of a style'.

A Horrible Religious Error

When the serpent emerged, earth-bowel brown,
From the hatched atom
With its alibi self twisted around it

Lifting a long neck
And balancing that deaf and mineral stare
The sphynx of the final fact

And flexing on that double flameflicker tongue
A syllable like the rustling of the spheres

God's grimace writhed, a leaf in the furnace

And man's and woman's knees melted, they collapsed
Their neck-muscles melted, their brows bumped the ground
Their tears evacuated visibly
They whispered 'Your will is our peace.'

104

But Crow only peered.
                    Then took a step or two forward,
Grabbed this creature by the slackskin nape,

Beat the hell out of it, and ate it.

There is first of all the clarity, control and expressiveness of the long sentence: the typographic isolation and accentual prominence of the main clause, the elegance of the description of the snake against the jumble of clauses describing man's and woman's reaction. There are the striking and pregnant juxtapositions such as 'deaf and mineral stare' and 'alibi self' (the snake's disappearing-trick, given this abstract expression, suggests that it is the nature of whatever the snake represents to be somewhere other than where you are looking, and also that—as in Genesis—it is not there when the crime for which it is responsible is being investigated). As for 'music', there is verbal music of the most obvious and traditional kind in:

> And flexing on that double flameflicker tongue
> A syllable like the rustling of the spheres

and a more subtle and complex kind in the way those lines combine with the rhythmic effect of the long sentence already mentioned. The super-simple and super-ugly language of the last few lines is actually a part of that music, as a few simple abrupt chords are musical when they occur at the end of a symphony. These concluding lines, of course, make more of a difference to the poem than that particular musical analogy would suggest. But the poem is not reductive in the sense that the 'practical', unreflective, no-nonsense attitude conveyed by those lines (and implied in their diction) is being offered for admiration. On the contrary, the poem's title (and the commentary with which Hughes prefaces readings of the poem[2]) reinforces the conclusion prompted by the language itself, that some more subtle action than Crow's, and certainly a more subtle consciousness than can be encompassed in the language of the poem's last lines, is necessary to meet the challenge of 'the world of final reality' that the serpent represents.

  'Crow on the Beach' is another fine poem—one of the poems that our high valuation of *Crow* is based on—that owes its effect to a range of poetic resource and in which the super-simple language, though again coming at the end, is even more obviously not the whole point.

Hearing shingle explode, seeing it skip,
Crow sucked his tongue.
Seeing sea-grey mash a mountain of itself
Crow tightened his goose-pimples.
Feeling spray from the sea's root nothinged on his crest
Crow's toes gripped the wet pebbles.
When the smell of the whale's den, the gulfing of the crab's last
                                                      prayer,
Gimletted in his nostril
He grasped he was on earth.
                                    He knew he grasped
Something fleeting
Of the sea's ogreish outcry and convulsion.
He knew he was the wrong listener unwanted
To understand or help—

His utmost gaping of brain in his tiny skull
Was just enough to wonder, about the sea,

What could be hurting so much?

In the first half of the poem rhythm, metaphor, assonance, and so on, combine to create a sensuous effect that is musical but not merely musical, that is not merely sound echoing the sense or the successful embodiment of ideas in language with suitable physical properties; the language here actually provokes in the reader the same physical reactions that it is attributing to Crow. This is not an unusual effect but it is done particularly well and is particularly important in the opening of this poem where Crow's experience of the physical world produces a heightened sense of being physically himself—tongue, skin, crest, toes—and of being where he is. 'He grasped he was on earth', though by the time this is said in so many words the sense of undeniable reality in the opening lines has already begun to slip away. Crow's final, uncomprehending question is already anticipated in 'the gulfing of the crab's last prayer', and the literal 'gripped' has become a metaphorical 'grasped', to develop into the more tenuous 'knew he grasped'. What he 'knew he grasped' is actually something much more doubtful than the initial experience of which it seems to be a natural development, and there is something ironic in the humility of 'knew he was the wrong listener unwanted' since the idea of the sea's pain has been created by his listening. Crow's brain is incapable of generating a conceptual equivalent for the 'just being in the same world as the sea' of the beginning (which he tries and fails to do in 'Crow and the Sea'). It is true that there is an element of apprehension in the heightened awareness of the opening lines, but the apprehension becomes detached and elaborated until, in the final line, Crow is unwittingly asking a question about himself. The simplicity of the final question is clearly an expression of Crow's limited consciousness, contrasting strongly with the language of the opening. This is not to say that Hughes is simply mocking Crow. The poem is sympathetic about the inevitability of conceptualization, and the difficulty and even suffering that it entails. Maintaining this sympathy in a poem that celebrates the awesome unapproachableness of the natural world is a remarkable achievement.

The same theme is explored in 'Owl's Song', which comes as close as any poem in the volume to 'shedding everything except what he wanted to say', yet which cannot be said to have 'no music whatsoever'.

> He sang
> How the swan blanched forever
> How the wolf threw away its telltale heart
> And the stars dropped their pretence
> The air gave up appearances
> Water went deliberately numb
> The rock surrendered its last hope
> And cold died beyond knowledge
>
> He sang
> How everything had nothing more to lose
>
> Then sat still with fear
>
> Seeing the clawtrack of star
> Hearing the wingbeat of rock
>
> And his own singing

The poem opens with a series of statements which, while difficult to pin down individually, cumulatively suggest the rejection of animism, folktale, astrology and similar accommodating constructions. The repetitive structure itself creates the simplest kind of music, and the haunting echoes of what is being rejected contribute to a distinctive bleak lyricism that runs throughout the poem. The pattern of melancholy cadences culminating in 'He sang/How everything had nothing more to lose', the pivot of 'Then sat still with fear' and the awesome resurgence of the final three lines clearly reflect the movement of Owl's consciousness, singing himself into a state of non-illusion and then frightened by his experience of a world that he has defensively filled with himself.

There is one poem, 'Crow and the Birds', in which we see Hughes throwing out the eagles and choosing the crow, both literally and linguistically.

When the eagle soared clear through a dawn distilling of emerald
When the curlew trawled in seadusk through a chime of
                                                        wineglasses
When the swallow swooped through a woman's song in a cavern
And the swift flicked through the breath of a violet

When the owl sailed clear of tomorrow's conscience
And the sparrow preened himself of yesterday's promise
And the heron laboured clear of the Bessemer upglare
And the bluetit zipped clear of lace panties
And the woodpecker drummed clear of the rotovator and the
                                                        rose-farm
And the peewit tumbled clear of the laundromat

While the bullfinch plumped in the apple bud
And the goldfinch bulbed in the sun
And the wryneck crooked in the moon
And the dipper peered from the dewball

Crow spraddled head-down in the beach-garbage, guzzling a
                                                dropped ice-cream.

Keith Sagar compares this with Eliot's 'Cape Ann' in which, after evoking the 'delectable' birds of the place, the poet tells us we must 'resign' it to 'its true owner, the tough one, the sea-gull'. Hughes's poem however has a more complex structure than Eliot's: not a simple contrast between Crow and the other birds but a dialectical structure which answers the questions of Ian Robinson and David Sims, 'Why is [the last line] truer, more serious than the lines before? Is Crow more interesting than the goldfinch?' (*Human World*, 9, p. 32). This answer is not simply the reductive ugliness of the language of the last line and the picture of Crow that it gives. The language of that line stands, like Crow's posture, in a complex relation to the language of the preceding lines. Each line of the poem is built around a perceptibly chosen verb which presents the bird in a characteristic attitude: 'soared, trawled, swooped, flicked, sailed, preened, laboured, zipped, drummed, tumbled, plumped, bulbed, crooked, peered, spraddled'. Crow's verb stands out as a neologism[3] and as the ungainliest of the attitudes, but it is one end of a spectrum that includes 'laboured' and 'tumbled' as well as 'soared' and 'sailed'. The attitude of Crow as conveyed by the striking verb itself is not set over in a simple and obvious way against the attitudes of the other birds. The verbs of course are affected by the other words in their respective lines so that we see the birds, embodied as it were in their verbs, affected by the verbal embodiments of various actual environments or imaginative contexts.

The mode of the first stanza is parodic: each bird is engulfed in a gratuitous romantic idea. This is most obvious in the line about the swallow, less so in the case of the swift, where 'the breath of a violet' *could* be interpreted as a botanical observation; coming at the end of the stanza, however, and prepared for by the preceding lines, a more 'precious' reading of that phrase is almost inevitable. These birds are trapped in an oppressive poetic sensibility, their verbs, in themselves finely evocative, enfeebled by their imaginative contexts.

If the line about Crow were to follow straight upon this stanza, it would indeed be a simple and obvious poem. But in the second stanza we see the birds in a different set of attitudes, and the verbs affected in a different way by their contexts. These birds are all trying to escape from the human world, either moral or physical, and in several, at least, of the lines the verbs take on a comic effect because of their appropriateness not only to the birds but also to what the birds are evading. Behind the observation of a peewit's actual flight in 'tumbled', for example, there is the absurd image of the bird in a tumble-drier.

After this series of comic pictures of the war between the natural

109

and human worlds we come to a group of simple observations of birds in their natural settings. Here for the first time the birds are all at rest and, also for the first time, there is no conflict within the lines. The simplicity allows the verbs, with the observations they contain, to dominate the lines, and we have the impression that the birds are just being themselves. But there is, in the end, something too easy, perhaps even complacent, certainly limiting about that style of observation. The birds are just too neatly placed in their appropriate circumstances, almost like specimens.

And, after the birds who try to escape from human interference in the landscape, and those who are protectively enshrined in their 'natural' contexts, there *is* something uniquely interesting in the bird which adapts to and thrives on the detritus of a seaside resort, and in the simply ugly language which, in this case, has an attractive energy and bravado. Hughes's celebration of Crow here is hearty and genuinely admiring, not at all sneering, grim or, really, reductive.

About a third of the poems in *Crow* have a repetitive, formulaic pattern similar to the most obvious pattern in 'Crow and the Birds', but not in all of them is the repetition so subtly handled. The easily achieved sense of rhythm and pattern and, occasionally, the vatic tone that the repetitive formula offers, are temptations to which Hughes succumbs in this book.

Crow's Song of Himself

When God hammered Crow
He made gold
When God roasted Crow in the sun
He made diamond
When God crushed Crow under weights
He made alcohol
When God tore Crow to pieces
He made money
When God blew Crow up
He made day
When God hung Crow on a tree
He made fruit
When God buried Crow in the earth
He made man
When God tried to chop Crow in two

He made woman
When God said: 'You win, Crow,'
He made the Redeemer.

When God went off in despair
Crow stropped his beak and started in on the two thieves.

Something is clearly happening in the last four lines which gives the
poem some point and seriousness, but on reflection the rest of it
seems just a build-up: the poet could go on like that indefinitely, or
remove several of the couplets, with neither greater nor lesser
effect. The same habit can be seen at greater length and with more
obvious self-indulgence in 'Crow Improvises'. The poems that make
successful use of the repetitive formula are usually powered by a
progression which gives each line some particular weight. We have
seen a dialectical progression in 'Crow and the Birds' but even a
simple linear progression can be enough to sustain one of these
poems, as in 'The Black Beast':

Where is the Black Beast?
Crow, like an owl, swivelled his head.
Where is the Black Beast?
Crow hid in its bed, to ambush it.
Where is the Black Beast?
Crow sat in its chair, telling loud lies against the Black Beast.
Where is it?
Crow shouted after midnight, pounding the wall with a last.
Where is the Black Beast?
Crow split his enemy's skull to the pineal gland.
Where is the Black Beast?
Crow crucified a frog under a microscope, he peered into the
                                        brain of a dogfish.
Where is the Black Beast?
Crow killed his brother and turned him inside out to stare at his
                                        colour.
Where is the Black Beast?
Crow roasted the earth to a clinker, he charged into space—
Where is the Black Beast?
The silences of space decamped, space flitted in every direction—
Where is the Black Beast?
Crow flailed immensely through the vacuum, he screeched after
                                        the disappearing stars—
Where is it? Where is the Black Beast?

A list of the poems in *Crow* that we most admire would be revealing: 'A Childish Prank', 'That Moment', 'Crow Tyrannosaurus', 'Crow's Account of the Battle', 'A Disaster', 'Crow and the Birds', 'Crow on the Beach', 'A Horrible Religious Error', 'Crow's Nerve Fails', 'Owl's Song', 'Crow's Undersong', 'Crow Blacker than Ever', 'Apple Tragedy', 'Crow and the Sea', 'Glimpse', 'How Water Began to Play', 'Littleblood'. Many of these poems are concerned with problems of consciousness; they are linguistically varied and interesting; only a few of them are among the most immediately 'shocking' in the book; although there is no lack of violence in them, only one of them ('Crow's Account of the Battle') is an example of the apocalyptic violence that some readers would consider the most obvious characteristic of the book.

Now let us confront ourselves with another list: 'A Kill', 'Crow and Mama', 'Crow's Account of the Battle', 'A Grin', 'Crow's Account of St George', 'Oedipus Crow', 'In Laughter', 'Magical Dangers', 'Crow Improvises', 'Crow's Battle Fury', 'Crow's Song of Himself', 'Song for a Phallus', 'Truth Kills Everybody', 'Notes for a Little Play'. These poems are all more or less violent and apocalyptic. Crow suffers violence at the hands of some metaphysical entity, or is the more or less helpless agent of violence, or tells some apocalyptic story. They tend to be repetitive in form and their language varies between gangster-movie crudity and surrealism. They include a high proportion of the most obviously 'cartoon-like' poems. The view that these poems represent the central achievement of *Crow* (and that our own list is a symptom of, shall we say, evasiveness) clearly stands or falls by whether their visions are actually more disquieting, real or relevant than the more intimate, inward alarms of 'Crow's Nerve Fails' or 'That Moment'.

Truth Kills Everybody

So Crow found Proteus—steaming in the sun.
Stinking with sea-bottom growths
Like the plug of the earth's sump-outlet.
There he lay—belching quakily.

Crow pounced and buried his talons—

And it was the famous bulging Achilles—but he held him
The oesophagus of a staring shark—but he held it
A wreath of lashing mambas—but he held it

It was a naked powerline, 2000 volts—
He stood aside, watching his body go blue
As he held it and held it

It was a screeching woman and he had her by the throat—
He held it

A gone steering wheel bouncing towards a cliff edge—
He held it

A trunk of jewels dragging into a black depth—he held it

The ankle of a rising, fiery angel—he held it

Christ's hot pounding heart—he held it

The earth, shrunk to the size of a hand grenade

And he held it he held it and held it and

BANG!

He was blasted to nothing.

As in most of these poems, the violence is closely linked to comedy.
The poem opens with a good joke about Proteus, and if explicit
verbal humour is suspended between 'the famous bulging Achilles'
and the end, we are obviously not meant to regard Crow's heroic
holding-on with unrelieved solemnity (in one aspect, of course, the
poem is a parody of ballads like 'Tam Lin'). The important question
is, what is the relation between the humour and the violence? In
other poems, particularly 'In Laughter' and 'Crow's Battle Fury',
Hughes successfully suggests that laughter is itself a manifestation
of violent, Dionysiac energy:

One of his eyes sinks into his skull, tiny as a pin,
One opens, a gaping dish of pupils,
His temple-veins gnarl, each like the pulsing head of a month-old
baby,
His heels double to the front,
His lips lift off his cheekbone, his heart and his liver fly in his
throat,
Blood blasts from the crown of his head in a column—
('Crow's Battle Fury')

113

This is simply a very good re-creation of the experience of helpless laughter, particularly forbidden laughter (Crow is laughing at 'the patient, shining with pain' et cetera); there is no problem about the relation between the violent images and actual experience, nor between the violence and the laughter.[4]

But there is a problem in 'Truth Kills Everybody', and in 'Crow and Mama', 'Oedipus Crow', 'Crow Improvises' and 'Magical Dangers'. If these are strong, serious and disturbing (though funny) poems, we must be able to regard them in something like the terms proposed by J. M. Newton:

> Humour isn't an opposite to tragedy and thus isn't a genuine alternative. It seems to require a similar reckless-shocking energy and largeness of spirit and at its purest and liveliest it, too, annihilates. Even when they are different paths of liberation, they nevertheless don't seem to lie far apart. In *Crow* they aren't different.
>
> (*Cambridge Quarterly*, vol. 5, no. 4, p. 377)

Such 'liberation' calls for something more than a reckless insouciance. 'Truth Kills Everybody' offers a series of neatly packaged (and sometimes rather hackneyed) images of elemental energy which can flatter the reader into believing that he is confronting something dangerous. It is possible to admire the intention behind the poem without succumbing to that delusion. The energy of the poem itself is confined to the mechanical accumulation of breathless excitement in 'he held it ... he held it.' The 'BANG!' at the end neither shocks nor relieves any very uncomfortable tension. Its triviality is underlined by the fact that it doesn't occur to anyone to wonder what has happened to Crow's built-in survival kit. The effect of the humour is to disguise the triviality by permitting the reader to see the poem as one which treats a serious subject in a 'reckless-shocking' way.[5]

Some of the violent-apocalyptic poems are better than this but the less good ones tend, like 'Truth Kills Everybody', despite their appearance of energy, to lack progression and rely on easy effects such as the phrase, 'Christ's hot, pounding heart'.

The number and homogeneity of these facile poems of violence and apocalypse is a weakness of *Crow*, but one which is magnified out of proportion by the fact that it is with reference to such poems (and parts of better poems that can be assimilated to them) that it

114

often seems easiest to discuss the book as a whole. For this reason we think it is critically useful and not just banner-waving to propose a list of poems that are more varied, and more linguistically and conceptually subtle. We shall be discussing more of these poems, and other good ones, in the rest of this chapter.

Poetry, Narrative and Myth

Anyone who attends a public reading from *Crow* by its author will find that he is experiencing a different kind of work from the book entitled *Crow: From the Life and Songs of the Crow*, or indeed from the record that Hughes has made of the book. In live performances Hughes tells a story about Crow's origin and the game in which God and Crow are engaged. Each poem is placed in the context of this narrative, which gives the poem a quite specific significance. In the published collection of Crow poems no narrative context is provided, although there are indications at every turn that a tale has been conceived, if not written. The first edition carried a note on the dust-jacket that the book 'contains the passages of verse from about the first two-thirds of what was to have been an epic folk-tale'. These words subsequently disappeared from the dust-jacket. In the year following *Crow*'s publication Hughes said in an interview: 'The story is not really relevant to the poems as they stand. Maybe I'll finish the story some day and publish it separately. I think the poems have a life a little aside from it' (*London Magazine*, January 1971, p. 18). In a letter to ourselves (September 1977) he said that he had intended to publish the whole background story, as well as many more poems, but that the work had been disrupted by circumstances out of his control.

The reader who did not know this, however, and who had heard the public readings, could be forgiven for thinking that Hughes had actually chosen to reserve the narrative for live story-telling, leaving it as unfixed material for spontaneous improvisation in the manner of a traditional teller of tales. While the unfinished nature of the project causes difficulties for the reader of the book, there are compensations for the audience at the poetry-readings, which are livelier and more compelling occasions than they would be if Hughes were reading from a published story. As a consequence of the improvisation the story takes on different qualities at each

115

performance. In the space of a month in 1975 Hughes gave performances at Ilkley and at Cambridge; two different styles of story-
telling could be distinguished. The basic narrative was the same:

> After having created the world God has a nightmare in the
> form of a Voice and a Hand which ridicules the creation and
> particularly God's masterpiece, Man. God claims that his
> creation has been a complete success and a debate ensues
> which is interrupted by a message from the world that Man
> wants God to take life back. God challenges the Nightmare to
> do better and the Nightmare's response is to create Crow.
> God, who regards Crow as a poor competitor for his creation,
> shows him round the universe and sets him various challenges
> and ordeals, in the course of which Crow becomes more
> intelligent and resourceful. This universe is one in which all
> history is happening simultaneously, so Crow is able to move
> freely from one era to another, from the beginning of the
> world to the end. He observes and is occasionally implicated in
> various aspects of the Creation. During his adventures he
> begins to wonder who his own creator is and he encounters
> various female figures who are avatars of his creator, but he
> never recognizes her and always bungles the situation.

At both Ilkley and Cambridge the poems were introduced as
episodes in this narrative or responses to it. The poems read on both
occasions were almost the same. But the style of narrative at Ilkley
was noticeably more poetic, more demanding of the imagination,
than the style of the story told at Cambridge. The latter was more
formalized and fully explained: for example the universe of Crow
was described as a physical entity in which the various stages of
history happened simultaneously 'in different compartments'. At
each performance Hughes read a different poem from *Cave Birds* as
part of the Crow story. At Ilkley the poem 'Bride and groom' was
read in this context, the night after it had been given its 'première' as
part of the *Cave Birds* sequence commissioned for the Ilkley Festival. In the *Crow* context it was introduced as Crow's answer to the
question 'Who gives most, him or her?': one of seven dilemma
questions about love set to Crow by his disguised creator. In *Cave
Birds* it is part of a quite different narrative.

It could be claimed, then, that the poet has left space for the
story-teller to create his different meaning. But has the story-teller
been left so much space that the book is incoherent? Have the

116

poems in the volume *Crow*, individually and collectively, enough internal unity to make useful sense?

That question obviously underlies this whole chapter and our answer, a qualified affirmative, needs the rest of the chapter to be made. But the difficulties that prompt the question can be exemplified by one poem, 'Lovesong'. This poem portrays a predatory, possessive and sadistic sexual love:

> Her smiles were spider bites
> So he would lie still till she felt hungry
> His words were occupying armies
> Her laughs were an assassin's attempts
> Her looks were bullets daggers of revenge
> Her glances were ghosts in the corner with horrible secrets
> His whispers were whips and jackboots
> Her kisses were lawyers steadily writing
> His caresses were the last hooks of a castaway
> Her love-tricks were the grinding of locks....

In *The Art of Ted Hughes* Keith Sagar remarks that 'it is a pity that readers are obliged to come to terms with Crow through only a selection of the poems about him and without the folktale context' which 'would make it impossible to assume, as David Holbrook does, that "Lovesong" gives us Hughes' fixed personal attitude towards sexual love' (1st edition, p. 167). At Ilkley 'Lovesong' was presented as Crow's answer to the question 'Who paid most, him or her?' and was followed by 'Bride and groom' which as we have seen is the answer to 'Who gives most, him or her?' Here is the conclusion of 'Bride and groom':

> She stitches his body here and there with steely purple silk
> He oils the delicate cogs of her mouth
> She inlays with deep-cut scrolls the nape of his neck
> He sinks into place the inside of her thighs
>
> So, gasping with joy, with cries of wonderment
> Like two gods of mud
> Sprawling in the dirt, but with infinite care
>
> They bring each other to perfection.

This effect of contrasting potentialities undoubtedly changes our response to 'Lovesong', but the effect was available only to the audience who heard the poems read together. To anyone else a comparison of the poems would suggest not a range of attitudes within *Crow* but a subsequent progression. It would be reasonable to see the reading of 'Bride and groom' as a *correction* to the emphasis of the published *Crow*; even to suspect that the question to which 'Lovesong' is an answer was not part of the poem's inspiration but a later attempt to qualify its effect.[6] In any case, Mr Sagar does not solve the problem of *Crow* the book by quoting the story and the extra poem.

Even in its published form, however, *Crow* is evidently more than a collection of Hughes's most recent poems, and the partially obscured narrative framework is only one of numerous characteristics that have led people to speak of it as a mythic work. It is useful to consider some of the implications of the word 'myth' in relation to *Crow*.

First, we think that there is a genuine resemblance between certain features of *Crow* poems and of primitive myths. Here are two such myths summarized by Mircea Eliade in *Patterns in Comparative Religion*. The first is an Australian version of the Deluge myth.

> One day all the waters were swallowed by an immense frog, Dak. In vain the parched animals tried to make her laugh. Not until the eel (or serpent) began to roll about and twist itself round did Dak burst out laughing, and the waters thus rushed out and produced the flood.
>
> (p. 160)

The second example is part of the Maori creation myth.

> The Maoris call the sky Rangi and the Earth Papa; at the beginning, like Ouranos and Gaia, they were joined in a close embrace. The children born of this infinite union—Tumata-nenga, Tane-mahuta and others—who longed for the light and groped around in the darkness, decided to separate from their parents. And so, one day, they cut the cords binding heaven to earth and pushed their father higher and higher until Rangi was thrust up into the air and light appeared in the world.
>
> (p. 240; a much fuller version can be found in Paul Radin's *Primitive Man as Philosopher*, pp. 303–20)

The most striking feature of these stories is their practicality: the crude but inspired simplicity of the answers they propose to cosmological questions. The animal or divine inhabitants of the early world are imagined as people finding solutions to practical problems resembling those encountered in everyday life. And, again as in everyday life, the solution to one problem creates another: the drought becomes a flood; the liberation of Tumata and Tane is the tragedy of Rangi and Papa.

Here is the opening of 'Crow Blacker than Ever':

> When God, disgusted with man,
> Turned towards heaven.
> And man, disgusted with God,
> Turned towards Eve,
> Things looked like falling apart.
>
> But Crow   Crow
> Crow nailed them together,
> Nailing Heaven and earth together—
>
> So man cried, but with God's voice.
> And God bled, but with man's blood.
>
> Then heaven and earth creaked at the joint
> Which became gangrenous and stank—
> A horror beyond redemption.

The particular resemblance to the Maori myth is unimportant; it is probably a coincidence. What is important is the general similarity: the way in which the problem, in this case a metaphysical one, is 'explained' in a story that bypasses metaphysics by representing it in practical terms, and seeing it as the consequence of a solution to another problem. The importance of the 'practicality' is that it is not (as it might seem) reductive, but something irreducibly and commonly human. We see the same pattern in 'A Childish Prank', when Crow solves the problem of man's and woman's soulless inertia by biting the worm in two and stuffing half of it into each of them. There is a resemblance to the slightly different feeling of the Australian myth in the delightful uncollected poem 'A Lucky Folly': Crow, in the role of St George, first panics then charms the dragon by cutting holes in his beak and playing a tune on this 'flute'. There is the same inspired improvisation and preference for psychological manipulation of the threat rather than militant confrontation.

The most noticed resemblance of *Crow* to pre-existing myths is to the widespread figure known as Trickster, and particularly to the classic text published by Paul Radin in *The Trickster*: the Winnebago Indian cycle of stories about Wakdjunkaga. In his adventures Trickster commits innumerable gross and comic outrages against tribal standards of morality and decency; he is completely amoral, or more accurately pre-moral. Although he has many human attributes he does not behave like an integrated human being, particularly in the early stages of the cycle: his hands fight against each other, for example. He is at the mercy of his instincts, particularly hunger and sex, in an extreme and literal way. This is graphically symbolized by his enormous penis which he keeps coiled in a box on top of his head: when he wants to copulate with a woman on the other side of the river he tells his penis to swim across the river and perform the act for him. The name Trickster is paradoxically glossed as Foolish One, and this is borne out in the story, for Trickster is, in Paul Radin's words, 'he who dupes others and is always duped himself' (*The Trickster*, p. ix). Despite the negativeness of the character (Jung in his 'Psychological Commentary' predictably identifies him with the 'shadow'), he is appealingly innocent in all his adventures. Radin summarizes the significance of the myth as follows:

It embodies the vague memories of an archaic and primordial past, where there as yet existed no clear-cut differentiation between the divine and the non-divine. For this period Trickster is the symbol. His hunger, his sex, his wandering, these appertain neither to the gods nor to man. They belong to another realm, materially and spiritually, and that is why neither the gods nor man knows precisely what to do with them.

The symbol which Trickster embodies is not a static one. It contains within itself the promise of differentiation, the promise of god and man. For this reason every generation occupies itself with interpreting Trickster anew. No generation understands him fully but no generation can do without him. Each had to include him in all its theologies, in all its cosmogonies, despite the fact that it realized that he did not fit properly into any of them, for he represents not only the undifferentiated and distant past, but likewise the undifferentiated present within every individual. This constitutes his universal and persistent attraction. And so he became and remained everything to every man—god, animal, human being, hero, buffoon, he who was before good and evil, denier, affirmer, destroyer and creator. If we laugh at him, he grins at us. What happens to him happens to us.

(pp. 168–9)

Crow is sometimes ('Crow on the Beach', 'Crow and the Sea') a fully human consciousness; sometimes the unfeeling mocker of human pain and perplexity ('A Childish Prank'). Occasionally he is the voice of humanitarian protest ('Crow's Account of the Battle') or affirmer of a tenderness for Nature ('Crow's Undersong'); he is also ('Crow's First Lesson', 'Crow Blacker than Ever') the originator of horrors. He is ignorant of and perplexed by his own being ('The Black Beast', 'Crow's Nerve Fails') and is the voice of ironic commentary on such ignorance and perplexity ('Crow's Account of St George', 'A Bedtime Story'). In fact, virtually all the categories that Radin lists at the end of the passage quoted could be applied to Crow. Furthermore, Radin claims that Trickster develops, through his adventures, towards a more integrated human condition, and Hughes has said in a radio interview that Crow is trying to become a man. There is, however, no consistent development through the poems published in the book. Crow lacks one prominent feature of Trickster: his uncontrollable sexuality. Although sex is often the subject of Crow poems, none of the poems collected in the book shows Crow as having any sexual feelings himself, though the other instinct that drives Trickster, hunger, is stressed in poem after poem.[7]

We should be cautious of an excessive preoccupation with primitive myth—Crow probably owes as much to Caliban as to Trickster—but there can be no doubt that certain characteristics of such myths have found their way into the poems. An unsympathetic reader might call this pastiche, but the 'primitive' is complicated by too many other elements for the poems to have the purely parasitic quality of pastiche. Hughes's own attitude is stated in a letter to Keith Sagar quoted in *The Art of Ted Hughes*:

My main concern was to produce something with the minimum cultural accretions of the museum sort—something

autochthonous and complete in itself, as it might be invented
after the holocaust and demolition of all libraries, where
essential things spring again—if at all—only from their seeds
in nature—and are not lugged around or hoarded as preserved
harvests from the past. So the comparative religion/mythology
background was irrelevant to me, except as I could forget it. If
I couldn't find it again original in Crow, I wasn't interested to
make a trophy of it.

(2nd edition, p. 107)

Whether this is literally true or not, it suggests that source-hunting is
a futile exercise (it is not part of our argument, for example, that
Hughes had in mind the Maori creation myth when he wrote 'Crow
Blacker than Ever'). The presence of pre-existing myths in *Crow* is
of a different kind from Eliot's use of the Grail legend, or the
exploitation of mythical and historical material for specifically cultural purposes by such poets as David Jones and Geoffrey Hill. It is
impossible to understand the references to fishing in *The Waste
Land* without knowing the story of the Fisher King. The reader may
well decide that this knowledge makes little difference to the poem's
effect, but he is only able to make that judgement after having
acquired the knowledge. 'Apple Tragedy' exemplifies the opposite
case with *Crow*:

So on the seventh day
The serpent rested.
God came up to him.
'I've invented a new game,' he said.

The serpent stared in surprise
At this interloper.
But God said: 'You see this apple?
I squeeze it and look—Cider.'

The serpent had a good drink
And curled up into a questionmark.
Adam drank and said: 'Be my god.'
Eve drank and opened her legs

And called to the cockeyed serpent
And gave him a wild time.
God ran and told Adam
Who in drunken rage tried to hang himself in the orchard.

The serpent tried to explain, crying 'Stop'
But drink was splitting his syllable
And Eve started screeching: 'Rape! Rape!'
And stamping on his head.

Now whenever the snake appears she screeches
'Here it comes again! Help! Help!'
Then Adam smashes a chair on its head,
And God says: 'I am well pleased'

And everything goes to hell.

This poem has its roots not only in Genesis but also in the Pelasgian creation myth which describes the coupling of Euronyme, the Goddess of All Things, with the great serpent Ophion, and her subsequent bruising of his head with her heel because he claims to be the author of the Universe (Robert Graves, *The Greek Myths*, vol. 1, p. 27). And, according to Mircea Eliade, it is a common primitive belief that women copulate with serpents (*Patterns in Comparative Religion*, pp. 164–7). But this does not mean that Hughes is being disingenuous when he says that his 'main concern was to produce something with the minimum cultural accretions of the museum sort'. Apart from the handful of familiar Biblical passages that are essential to the effect (and which are hardly, even today, 'cultural accretions of the museum sort') a knowledge of the poem's 'sources' is not more necessary than a knowledge of Shakespeare's sources. It might lead us to admire the wit with which Hughes has manipulated this material; it might help to lend a more-than-individual authority to the poem's vision, or it might interfere with the directness of the poem. But it will not help us to understand the poem any better. Even if we suspect that Hughes was consciously exploiting the mythical and anthropological material, the poem's success is not a matter of 'trophies' but of rediscovery.

Crow resembles genuine mythic material, but does it make sense to say that it *is* myth? In Chapter 2 we borrowed a passage from Malinowski, and in particular the phrase, 'a primeval, greater, and more relevant reality', in discussing the 'mythical' quality of some of the poems in *Wodwo*. That phrase characterizes the burden of nearly every poem in *Crow*, but despite the relentlessness of the book it is not a single, simple 'primeval reality' thumped out in poem after poem. In 'Apple Tragedy' we are told a story of jealousy and division among the inhabitants of the early world, the consequences of which reverberate at least through the Christian era. Two poems later, in 'Crow's Last Stand', Crow himself is the primeval, present and everlasting reality which is continuously surviving universal conflagration.

> Burning
>   burning
>   burning
>   there was finally something
> The sun could not burn, that it had rendered
> Everything down to—a final obstacle
> Against which it raged and charred
>
> And rages and chars
>
> Limpid among the glaring furnace clinkers
> The pulsing blue tongues and the red and the yellow
> The green lickings of the conflagration
>
> Limpid and black—
>
> Crow's eye-pupil, in the tower of its scorched fort.

But immediately after this, Crow is the helplessly inadequate observer of the greater reality outside himself:

> He tried ignoring the sea
> But it was bigger than death, just as it was bigger than life.
>   ('Crow and the Sea')

Then ('Truth Kills Everybody') he is subjected to the destructive shape-changing of Proteus, and ('Crow and Stone') engaged in an everlasting battle. The latter poem ends:

> *And still he who never has been killed*
> *Croaks helplessly*
> *And is only just born.*

All these poems (they are not equally successful—they have been quoted as a random sequence) are narratives or fragments of narrative.

The context of the Malinowski passage, however, brings into

focus the limits of the usefulness of 'myth' as a description of *Crow*. For he goes on to point out that myths, and particularly myths of origin, cannot be understood in isolation from the social context to which they belong (*Myth in Primitive Psychology*, pp. 45, 55). Primitive myth confirms and is confirmed by the experience of daily living in a particular social group; it is enacted in ritual. It is obvious that a deliberately invented literary 'myth', whatever its relation to social reality, cannot be part of the texture of society in this way. In fact, as Robert Graves points out in alluding to the absence of Biblical stories from the *New Larousse Encyclopaedia of Mythology*, if we believe something to be true we do not call it a myth (Introduction to *New Larousse Encyclopaedia of Mythology*, p. v).

Is there, then, an impossible contradiction in calling *Crow* 'mythic'? There is a contradiction, but it is one that points to the peculiar nature and strength of *Crow*. *Crow* offers no temptation whatever to play the game of alternative worlds. There is absolutely no invitation to 'make believe'. Despite the enormous popularity of the book, no cult of the Tolkien kind has grown around it. Although, in a review in the *Listener* (19 March 1964), Hughes referred to 'the realm of mythologies, the realm of management between our ordinary minds and our deepest life', he obviously does not contemplate a return to the kind of relation Malinowski's Trobriand Islanders had to their myths.

In the *London Magazine* interview he refers to Christianity as 'just another provisional myth of man's relationship with the creator and the world of spirit' (January 1971, p. 16). This view is amply corroborated in poems such as 'Apple Tragedy' and 'A Childish Prank'. But we are not to suppose that in *Crow* he is aspiring to replace a provisional or false myth with a permanent and true one. His cavalier handling of Biblical and classical stories, his use of what Robert Graves calls 'iconotropy' (rearranging the visual elements of a story to make a different story), imply an invitation to treat *Crow* in the same way. The self-consciousness of the project, its critical and ironic spirit, guards against the danger inherent in myth, of casting a spell that closes the mind. Nevertheless the power of *Crow* *is* partly the power of myth—of, in Mircea Eliade's words, 'exemplar history which can be repeated ... and whose meaning and value lie in that very repetition' (*Patterns in Comparative Religion*, p. 430). One reason why we cannot make a sequential narrative of it is that we imagine Crow always flailing through space after the

Black Beast, always marching away from the sea, always 'trying to remember his crimes', and we recognize the eternal repetition of these stories in human history and in ourselves.

Crow's Critique of Ideas

The relationship between language and reality, which was the starting point of *Crow*, in a sense becomes the subject of many of the *Crow* poems. Hughes's statement that the God of *Crow* 'bears about the same relationship to the Creator as, say, ordinary English does to reality', makes an interesting link between ordinary English and the God of *Crow* who is 'the man-created, broken-down, corrupt despot of a ramshackle religion' (record-sleeve of *Crow*). Many of the poems in *Crow* challenge the everyday assumptions of our language. Part of the project of *Crow* is the attempt to reveal that many concepts in the language which have come to be widely accepted as objectively real, are in fact 'man-created', false protections from reality.

The first published *Crow* poem made a direct confrontation with the power of a man-created Word to distort reality, and in its witty deflation of the Word on the rock of material reality the poem might be regarded as a declaration of intent. 'A Disaster' was published in the *Scotsman* in 1967.

> There came news of a word.
> Crow saw it killing men. He ate well.
> He saw it bulldozing
> Whole cities to rubble. Again he ate well.
> He saw its excreta poisoning seas.
> He became watchful.
> He saw its breath burning whole lands
> To dusty char.
> He flew clear and peered.
>
> The word oozed its way, all mouth,
> Earless, eyeless.
> He saw it sucking the cities
> Like the nipples of a sow
> Drinking out all the people
> Till there were none left,
> All digested inside the word.

Ravenous, the word tried its great lips
On the earth's bulge, like a giant lamprey—
There it started to suck.

But its effort weakened.
It could digest nothing but people.
So there it shrank, wrinkling weaker,
Puddling
Like a collapsing mushroom.
Finally, a drying salty lake.
Its era was over.
All that remained of it a brittle desert
Dazzling with the bones of earth's people

Where Crow walked and mused.

The ironic wit that accumulates its effects through the narrative of this poem arises from the exaggeration of a social process. Man creates words to symbolize his perception of reality. Sometimes he creates The Word which represents the core of his ideology or metaphysic, and that Word comes to be given an independent existence, as the objectified ideal of a social movement perhaps. Such a Word can kill people, and this is the starting point of the poem. Certainly the Word of the poem is dependent upon men, but its relationship is reversed. Instead of men having created the Word, it destroys men until they are 'all digested inside the word'. The choice of 'digested' is, of course, a witty reminder of this reversal. But because in reality The Word is dependent upon people for its original creation, it cannot exist without them. Physical reality teaches it the limits of its objectified existence. The end of the Word is the end of a social movement, and the shrinking of the Word is described in what might almost be called demographic terms. The mock sadness in the heavy rhythm is playfully underlined by the characteristic use of nouns as verbs. The death of a Word is, after all, the end of an era. In *Crow* Hughes systematically deflates a wide range of Words, some of which are at the height of their era in the latter half of the twentieth century. 'A Disaster' is not only a declaration of one part of the *Crow* project but is a model of the form and method of many of the poems.

Hughes's description of the method of Vasko Popa applies equally to his own work:

The air of trial and error exploration, of an improvised language, the attempt to get near something for which he is almost having to invent the words in a total disregard for poetry or the normal conventions of discourse, goes with his habit of working in cycles of poems. He will trust no phrase with his meaning for more than six or seven words at a time before he corrects his tack with another phrase from a different direction. In the same way, he will trust no poem with his meaning for more than fifteen or so lines, before he tries again from a totally different direction with another poem.

(Vasko Popa, *Selected Poems*, p. 15)

When Hughes 'tries again from a totally different direction with another poem' in *Crow*, the 'direction' is often another conception of reality, which the poem tests in a language improvised from the customary expression of the idea. The poem 'Lineage', for example, uses the Old Testament style of genealogy to place the invention of God and Eternity as the answer to a need to reconcile the tensions of living in the natural world. The language has exactly that 'air of trial and error exploration' as it improvises its parody towards the production of Crow:

In the beginning was Scream
Who begat Blood
Who begat Eye
Who begat Fear
Who begat Wing
Who begat Bone
Who begat Granite
Who begat Violet
Who begat Guitar
Who begat Sweat
Who begat Adam
Who begat Mary
Who begat God
Who begat Nothing
Who begat Never
Never Never Never

Who begat Crow

Screaming for Blood
Grubs, crusts
Anything

Trembling featherless elbows in the nest's filth

The organic relationship between 'fear' and 'wing', and 'granite' and 'violet' has been the subject of much of Hughes's earlier poetry: 'Crow Hill' and 'Still Life' for example. But in this poem the 'sweat' of these forces produces Adam, 'Who begat Mary/Who begat God/Who begat Nothing'. The wit of the appearance of God at this stage of the poem is inescapable. There is a subtler wit in the stages leading up to it, which conflate 'Adam begat Eve' and 'Mary begat Christ', reminding us of the traditional identities of Mary and Christ as the second Eve and Adam, and hinting that the begetting of God by Mary is another version of Eve's fall. Since God is man-made, or rather woman-made in this poem, he can of course produce nothing except the idea of nothingness, the mystical eternity of 'Never/ Never Never Never' out of which any mythical creature might be invented to satisfy a psychic need. Crow is not a fabulous beast, but he is an accurately described newly hatched crow (excusing 'elbow'). Indeed, it ought to be said that such undiscriminating ugliness does exist in the real nest's filth, lest one feel that Hughes is exaggerating the associations of 'Sweat' and 'Granite' at the expense of those of 'Guitar' and 'Violet'. The point is that Crow has his feet firmly on the ground, or rather his elbows firmly in the nest's filth, as does Hughes in his examination of the range of assumptions represented in *Crow*.

The use of the Biblical Creation story in several of the poems provides the opportunity for ironic accounts of some familiar Christian beliefs. In 'Crow's First Lesson', for example,

God tried to teach Crow how to talk.
'Love,' said God. 'Say, Love.'
Crow gaped, and the white shark crashed into the sea
And went rolling downwards, discovering its own depth.

'No, no,' said God, 'Say Love. Now try it. LOVE.'
Crow gaped, and a bluefly, a tsetse, a mosquito
Zoomed out and down
To their sundry flesh-pots.

'A final try,' said God. 'Now, LOVE.'
Crow convulsed, gaped, retched and
Man's bodiless prodigious head
Bulbed out onto the earth, with swivelling eyes,
Jabbering protest—

And crow retched again, before God could stop him.
And woman's vulva dropped over man's neck and tightened.
The two struggled together on the grass.
God struggled to part them, cursed, wept—

Crow flew guiltily off.[8]

In this poem the God of Love is challenged in the spirit of
Lawrence's essay 'Morality and the Novel':

> If the novelist puts his thumb in the pan, for love, tenderness,
> sweetness, peace, then he commits an immoral act—he *pre-*
> *vents* the possibility of a pure relationship, a pure relatedness,
> the only thing that matters: and he makes inevitable the
> horrible reaction, when he lets his thumb go, towards hate and
> brutality, cruelty and destruction.
>
> (*Phoenix*, p. 529)

Hughes's God in this poem is, as it were, Lawrence's novelist,
releasing horror where he intends to impose absolute 'LOVE'.
God's evasion of 'relatedness' to the evidence of predatory instincts
produces, ironically, a predatory kind of love. 'A Childish Prank'
gives a similarly ironic account of the relation between soul
and body.

The God of *Crow* emerges from the poems themselves as clearly
'the man-created, broken-down, corrupt despot of a ramshackle
religion'. But in the *London Magazine* interview Hughes goes
further in speaking of Eliot, Joyce and Beckett as portraying

> the state of belonging spiritually to the last phase of Christian
> civilisation, they suffer its disintegration. But there are now
> quite a few writers about who do not seem to belong spiritually
> to the Christian civilisation at all. In their world Christianity is
> just another provisional myth of man's relationship with the
> creator and the world of spirit. Their world is a continuation or
> a re-emergence of the pre-Christian world.... it is the world of

the little pagan religions and cults, the primitive religions from which of course Christianity itself grew.

(January 1971, pp. 15–16)

It seems probable that Hughes is speaking here of the generation of East European poets, Popa of Yugoslavia, Holub of Czechoslovakia and Herbert of Poland, whom he mentions in his Introduction to the *Selected Poems* of Vasko Popa. Each of these poets has an affinity with *Crow* and especially with its use of myth and irony. Popa's sequence entitled *Earth Erect*, for example, re-examines national legends through a folktale surrealism. Holub's ironic humour quietly reveals the limitations of social attitudes based on the certainties of positivist science and Marxist 'history' (see for example 'Suffering', 'Harbour' and 'The Lesson' in the Penguin selection). Perhaps the closest parallel to the wit and the seriousness of *Crow*'s critical and humane poems is to be found in the work of Zbigniew Herbert. One poem will have to serve as illustration, not only of its similarity to *Crow* poems but also of what we think Hughes is referring to as 'the re-emergence of the pre-Christian world'.

At the Gate of the Valley

After the rain of stars
on the meadow of ashes
they all have gathered under the guard of angels

from a hill that survived
the eye embraces
the whole lowing two-legged herd

in truth they are not many
counting even those who will come
from chronicles fables and the lives of the saints

but enough of these remarks
let us lift our eyes
to the throat of the valley
from which comes a shout

after a loud whisper of explosion
after a loud whisper of silence

this voice resounds like a spring of living water
it is we are told
a cry of mothers from whom children are taken
since as it turns out
we shall be saved each one alone

the guardian angels are unmoved
and let us grant they have a hard job

she begs
—hide me in your eye
in the palm of your hand in your arms
we have always been together
you can't abandon me
now when I am dead and need tenderness

a higher ranking angel
with a smile explains the misunderstanding

an old woman carries
the corpse of a canary
(all the animals died a little earlier)
he was so nice—she says weeping
he understood everything
and when I said to him—
her voice is lost in the general noise

even a lumberjack
whom one would never suspect of such things
an old bowed fellow
catches to his breast an axe
—all my life she was mine
she will be mine here too
she nourished me there
she will nourish me here
nobody has the right
—he says—
I won't give her up

those who as it seems
have obeyed the orders without pain
go lowering their heads as a sign of consent
but in their clenched fists they hide

132

fragments of letters ribbons clippings of hair
and photographs
which they naïvely think
won't be taken from them
so they appear
a moment before
the final division
of those gnashing their teeth
from those singing psalms
(Zbigniew Herbert, *Selected Poems*, Penguin)

This poem economically suggests its setting as a concentration camp afterworld in which the guards are angels. ('Anything Rather Than an Angel' is the title of a prose poem by Herbert which concludes, 'One should enter rock, wood, water, the cracks of a gate. Better to be the creaking of a floor than shrilly transparent perfection.') Not only is the mother unwilling to be separated from her child, but the lumberjack's attachment to his axe is given the same kind of dignity and value. In fact this kind of fetishism that expresses intense love of the material world is credited with a greater moral decency than the exclusive spirituality of Christianity. Those singing psalms at the end of the poem are already lost. This simple fetishism might be said to represent a 'little pagan religion or cult' that carries the human dignity of the poem.

The extraordinary balance of wit and pathos in this poem is caught in the best of the *Crow* poems. 'Crow's Account of the Battle' attacks the surrender of responsibility implicit in scientific determinism, with language which eschews the restraint in Herbert's method, but leaves the reader with an effect strikingly similar to that of Herbert's poem.

There was this terrific battle.
The noise was as much
As the limits of possible noise could take.
There were screams higher groans deeper
Than any ear could hold.
Many eardrums burst and some walls
Collapsed to escape the noise.
Everything struggled on its way
Through this tearing deafness
As through a torrent in a dark cave.

The cartridges were banging off, as planned,
The fingers were keeping things going
According to excitement and orders.
The unhurt eyes were full of deadliness.
The bullets pursued their courses
Through clods of stone, earth and skin,
Through intestines, pocket-books, brains, hair, teeth
According to Universal laws.
And mouths cried 'Mamma'
From sudden traps of calculus,
Theorems wrenched men in two,
Shock-severed eyes watched blood
Squandering as from a drain-pipe
Into the blanks between stars.
Faces slammed down into clay
As for the making of a life-mask
Knew that even on the sun's surface.
They could not be learning more or more to the point.
Reality was giving its lesson,
Its mishmash of scripture and physics,
With here, brains in hands, for example,
And there, legs in a treetop.
There was no escape except into death.
And still it went on—it outlasted
Many prayers, many a proved watch,
Many bodies in excellent trim,
Till the explosives ran out
And sheer weariness supervened
And what was left looked round at what was left.

Then everybody wept,
Or sat, too exhausted to weep,
Or lay, too hurt to weep.
And when the smoke cleared it became clear
This had happened too often before
And was going to happen too often in future
And happened too easily
Bones were too like lath and twigs
Blood was too like water
Cries were too like silence
The most terrible grimaces too like footprints in mud
And shooting somebody through the midriff
Was too like striking a match

Too like potting a snooker ball
Too like tearing up a bill
Blasting the whole world to bits
Was too like slamming a door
Too like dropping in a chair
Exhausted with rage
Too like being blown to bits yourself
Which happened too easily
With too like no consequences.

So the survivors stayed.
And the earth and the sky stayed.
Everything took the blame.

Not a leaf flinched, nobody smiled.

In this poem Hughes presents the classic image of man trapped by the uses made of his own constructions of the universe. When calculus and theorems are all that is used to interpret the universe, the results are self-destructive. But at the same time as presenting this thought the poetry achieves the pathos of the consequences:

The bullets pursued their courses
Through clods of stone, earth and skin,
Through intestines, pocket-books, brains, hair, teeth
According to Universal laws.

The arbitrary list evokes the pathetic fragility of humanity impaled by the prevailing philosophy, and unprotected by responsibility, which has been unloaded on to 'Universal laws' and calculus. The battle which 'outlasted/Many prayers, many a proved watch' is the practical lesson to be learned if reality is regarded only as a 'mishmash of scripture and physics'. As the tone of pathos grows to one of outrage, responsibility is implicitly demanded by a striking series of similes for the ease with which death is inflicted. The colloquial and even journalistic simplicity of this passage has been earned by the penetrating compression of such earlier effects as 'mouths cried "Mamma"/From sudden traps of calculus.' The irony of the last lines of the poem achieves a moral dignity comparable to that of 'At the Gate of the Valley'. It was of poets such as Herbert that Hughes said, in his Introduction to Popa: they do not despair 'to the point of surrendering consciousness and responsibility to their animal cells' (p. 10).

In two poems the psychological need for man to people the universe with his own conceptions is parodied with acute perception. In 'Owl's Song' owl rejects fictions about material reality, but then hears himself imposing on the universe his own 'clawtrack of star' and 'wingbeat of rock'. In 'Glimpse', however, Crow turns his lesson into a religious experience:

> 'O leaves,' Crow sang, trembling, 'O leaves—'
>
> The touch of a leaf's edge at his throat
> Guillotined further comment.
>
>   Nevertheless
> Speechless he continued to stare at the leaves
>
> Through the god's head instantly substituted.

Crow's trembling song is obviously a self-indulgent romanticizing of nature. The combination, in the poem's five lines, of parody, punning and witty juxtaposition is a concentrated example of the verve and intelligence of the book. The pun of 'guillotined' suggests that nature's revenge, while murderous, is a proper, authorized procedure, and the parliamentary sense of the word is echoed in the further pun of 'speechless'. The wit of 'guillotined' is heightened by its juxtaposition with (and disposal of) the leaden questionnaire diction of 'further comment'. This sense of contrasted diction is so strong in the poem that the glibness of 'instantly substituted' can hardly go unnoticed. Crow, in supposing that his proper and decent silence entitles him to godhead, has substituted another illusion for the glimpsed reality and is ready for yet another lesson. So is any reader who might have been betrayed into sharing the illusion.

The tendency we have been discussing in this section can fairly be called 'reductive'. Whether that word should have a derogatory force will depend on one's sense of *Crow*'s vision of the irreducible: whether it can be imagined, say, as a seed or as a cauterized stump. We believe that what most of the poems communicate when sensitively read is far from the nihilistic delight in reducing human life to a biologically determined survival instinct that critics such as David

Holbrook find in the book as a whole. This is clear from 'Crow's Account of the Battle' and will become more so when we come to discuss 'loss of self-importance'. But *Crow* is not exempt from such criticism. While it is absurd to demand 'balance' from a project such as this and, like Holbrook, to rewrite 'Examination at the Womb Door' in terms of human creativity, it is fair to remark that 'Lovesong' and 'Crow's First Lesson' *seem* to express a fixed and hopeless view of love because there is no hint of an alternative possibility. Such tenderness as *Crow* can boast (in 'Crow's Undersong' and 'Littleblood', for example) has a generalized object. Also Hughes is capable of cheapness (see 'Conjuring in Heaven').

On the other hand there is at least one myth/concept that escapes the kind of treatment we have been discussing: that of the 'Great Mother', the multivalent Goddess of nature who is the theme of Hughes's essay on Shakespeare, and who reigns explicitly over the worlds of *Gaudete* and *Cave Birds*. In *Crow* she features in a number of characteristically harsh poems (such as 'Crow and Mama' and 'Revenge Fable') as the inescapable to which Crow himself or the alienated 'person' of his stories is subjected. But she is most emphatically celebrated in the very *un*characteristic poem significantly titled 'Crow's Undersong'.

> She cannot come all the way
>
> She comes as far as water no further
>
> She comes with the birth push
> Into eyelashes into nipples the fingertips
> She comes as far as blood and to the tips of hair
> She comes to the fringe of voice
> She stays
> Even after life even among the bones
>
> She comes singing she cannot manage an instrument
> She comes too cold afraid of clothes
> And too slow with eyes wincing frightened
> When she looks into wheels
>
> She comes sluttish she cannot keep house
> She can just keep clean
> She cannot count she cannot last

She comes dumb she cannot manage words
She brings petals in their nectar fruits in their plush
She brings a cloak of feathers an animal rainbow
She brings her favourite furs and these are her speeches

She has come amorous it is all she has come for

If there had been no hope she would not have come

And there would have been no crying in the city

(There would have been no city)

This can be heard as the undersong to the immediately preceding
'Owl's Song' which rejects 'pretence', 'appearances' and 'hope'. But
more importantly it is surely the undersong to all of Crow's own
songs, the redemptive affirmation that links Crow back to 'Full
Moon and Little Frieda' and forward to *Season Songs* and *Cave
Birds*. We do not mean that without this poem Crow would be
unredeemed. Its strength is that despite its unironic lyrical beauty it
is still Crow singing: its innocence and directness are qualities we
already associate with him. His unillusioned plainness can be seen,
for example, in the way the gently rocking rhythm of the first two
lines is interrupted by the blunt 'no further'; in such practically-
minded diction as 'manage' and 'sluttish'; and in the rapid, un-
punctuated transitions from sentence to sentence within a line,
preventing the reader from dwelling self-indulgently ('O leaves') on
the lyricism. The goddess is like a beautiful female *enfant sauvage*
who has not 'come all the way' into the human plight of separation
from nature but who, in being recognizably human nevertheless,
reassures us that the plight is not hopeless. In the last lines we are
reminded that the city is a symbol both of that plight and of human
creativity, and the bracketing of the final affirmation subtly recalls
the earlier use of the device in Crow's meditation on the Christian
God, 'Crow Communes': '(Appalled)'.

This superb poem is, understandably, liked by some readers who
dislike *Crow* as a whole. However, like the more muted affirmative
poems at the end of the book (which we discuss in our next section),
it owes much of its authority to its relation to the spirit of the book as
a whole, to the continuity of this voice with that of the harsh,
reductive poems. To see it as opposed in spirit to those poems, and

even somehow invalidating them, is to risk making it seem a much slighter achievement than it is.

'Loss of Self-Importance'

Every stage of Crow's journey through this simultaneous universe 'is really an opportunity for more verses and more poems', Hughes explained at a reading (Loughborough, 12 March 1977). The verses are more important than the story or developing the character of Crow. Indeed, as we pointed out in the second part of this chapter, it is important to realize that Crow is not a consistent character in the sequence. He is used in different ways in different poems. In 'A Childish Prank' Crow ridicules God; in 'The Black Beast' Hughes ridicules Crow; in 'Crow's Account of the Battle' Crow represents Hughes the story-teller. The fact that Crow is used in several roles in the sequence does not mean that the sequence itself represents a kind of improvised survival at any price. Robinson and Sims accuse Hughes of advocating in *Crow* 'a retreat into *just* surviving' by a 'jettisoning of humanity' (*Human World,* no. 9, November 1972, p. 34). On the contrary, we feel there are a number of poems in the sequence that assert a fundamental humanity. For the duration of a poem Crow becomes human, questions his relationship with the universe and finally 'loses his self-importance' in Don Juan's phrase (Carlos Castaneda, *Journey to Ixtlan*, p. 35). These poems are not grouped together in the sequence, but in order to counter accusations such as that of Sims and Robinson these poems will be discussed together here as representing the affirmative achievement of the sequence.

Earlier in this chapter we quoted Paul Radin's description of the Winnebago Trickster and noted some striking similarities between this Trickster and Crow. We would now like to examine this parallel more closely in terms of Trickster's moral function. Radin's description pinpoints an important paradox:

> Trickster is at one and the same time creator and destroyer, giver and negator, he who dupes others and who is always duped himself. . . . He possesses no values, moral or social, is at the mercy of his passions and appetites, yet through his actions all values come into being.
>
> (*The Trickster*, p. ix)

It is not really accurate to say of Crow that he is entirely at the mercy of his passions and appetites. He is more often intelligently curious and wittily playful than blindly driven by passions and appetites. Certainly he has basic appetites, but more strong than these is the need to discover his creator, which leads him to search, test things out, and learn. It is in following these needs, the needs of his intelligence, that Crow is often the destroyer of false conceptions. But it is also true that in some of the most important poems Crow's learning leads to the discovery of human values.

Implicit in those poems which deflate arrogant human constructions of the universe is the need for a basic humility before the forces and the mystery of the natural world. This is made explicit in 'Crow and the Sea'.

He tried ignoring the sea
But it was bigger than death, just as it was bigger than life.

He tried talking to the sea
But his brain shuttered and his eyes winced from it as from open
flame.

He tried sympathy for the sea
But it shouldered him off—as a dead thing shoulders you off.

He tried hating the sea
But instantly felt like a scrutty dry rabbit-dropping on the windy
cliff.

He tried just being in the same world as the sea
But his lungs were not deep enough

And his cheery blood banged off it
Like a water-drop off a hot stove.

Finally

He turned his back and he marched away from the sea

As a crucified man cannot move.

Since Crow cannot ignore the huge mystery of the sea he attempts a human relationship with it. Some sort of metaphysic needs to be attempted, but the assumption that a relationship will be found in familiar human terms reveals a persistent human arrogance. The images which convey the practical results of this assumption render Crow increasingly insignificant and absurd. They represent Hughes's gift for expressing a metaphysical idea in a material way that is essentially poetic:

> And his cheery blood banged off it
> Like a water-drop off a hot stove.

He is being 'crucified' by the realization of his relative insignificance. Finally he acts with ironic firmness, turning his back and 'marching' away from the sea. Inevitably, this is also a movement towards another sea, so that, in relation to the sea, Crow 'cannot move', and Hughes characteristically introduces death (in this case, crucifixion) as the type of the inescapable (see Chapter 4).

In 'Crow and the Sea' and 'Crow on the Beach' a humility that is central to Hughes's conception of humanity is indirectly affirmed. This being the basis of Hughes's human values one does not find in *Crow* any confident positive assertions. Rather one sees the coming into being of a moral sense and a concept of self that is not divorced from the rest of the universe. Don Juan tells Carlos Castaneda that he must 'lose his self-importance' so that he is able not only to have respect for other living things as equals, but also to have the same respect for the inanimate natural world. 'As long as you feel that you are the most important thing in the world,' he tells Castaneda, 'you cannot really appreciate the world around you. You are like a horse with blinkers, all you see is yourself apart from everything else' (*Journey to Ixtlan*, pp. 39–40). Don Juan's technique for helping his apprentice to lose self-importance is to ask him to talk to some plants. Castaneda feels embarrassed and ludicrous but Don Juan ridicules his 'cleverness' and tells him, 'The world around us is a mystery and men are no better than anything else.' It is respect for the inanimate sea that is demanded of Crow, and his inability to speak to it reveals in a different way the need for him to lose his self-importance. It is a respect for life, on the other hand, that underlies the dignity and honest guilt of 'That Moment' (quoted in full on p. 94).

The moment captured in this poem is one of clear awareness of

the importance of a living being. It is precisely because one life is so
important that this face takes on the significance of 'the only face left
in the world'. It is precisely because one living awareness is so
important that at the moment of death it can be said that 'the trees
closed forever/And the streets closed forever.' This person has
'abandoned' the world and the world is the less for having been
abandoned. It is at this moment that Crow asserts the necessity of
eating. Suicide for Crow is unthinkable, so it is reasonable to see him
as that part of a man that demands to be kept going even when life
has become meaningless; who is both destroyer and preserver of
value, because, on the one hand, it seems an outrage and obscenity
to go on living and eating at such a moment but, on the other hand, if
Crow did not demand food we should all collapse into the hole dug
by our own high-mindedness and there would be no life left to create
value. In this way Crow is the agent of 'loss of self-importance', by
provoking into practical activity the full human consciousness of
which he is a part.

In the poem that followed in the first edition, 'Crow Tyrannosaurus', Hughes attempts to give Crow himself both the instinct
and the consciousness.

Creation quaked voices—
It was a cortege
Of mourning and lament
Crow could hear and he looked around fearfully.

The swift's body fled past
Pulsating
With insects
And their anguish, all it had eaten.

The cat's body writhed
Gagging
A tunnel
Of incoming death-struggles, sorrow on sorrow.

And the dog was a bulging filterbag
Of all the deaths it had gulped for the flesh and the bones.
It could not digest their screeching finales.
Its shapeless cry was a blort of all those voices.

142

Even man he was a walking
Abattoir
Of innocents—
His brain incinerating their outcry.

Crow thought 'Alas
Alas ought I
To stop eating
And try to become the light?'

But his eye saw a grub. And his head, trapsprung, stabbed.
And he listened
And he heard
Weeping

Grubs   grubs   He stabbed   he stabbed
Weeping
Weeping

Weeping he walked and stabbed

Thus came the eye's
                    roundness
                         the ear's
                              deafness.

The pompous diction of 'Alas Alas', the absurdity (at least for a crow) of considering stopping eating, the pretentiousness of 'the light', all indicate the unreality of Crow's question. Yet the question has been prompted by a sensitivity to the evidence that life is sustained by killing. It is the natural order of things, which man's superior intelligence enables him to rationalize away, his brain 'incinerating' the outcry from his own abattoirs. Crow's acceptance of responsibility for killing leads to his guilt, but in man this is usually rationalized or indulged so that it does not have to be taken seriously. Both responses are parodied in successive stanzas. At this point in the poem Crow's grand question is answered by the practical necessity of instinct. Whatever humanity Crow achieves in this poem is most powerfully revealed in the transfer of the weepings from grubs to Crow, from victims to killer who himself becomes victim of his guilt. The vertical arrangement of the 'weepings' avoids the effect of mere emotional emphasis through repetition. Certainly such emphasis is gained, partly by the contrast between the single-word lines and the rapidity of 'Grubs grubs He stabbed he stabbed'; but the arrangement draws attention to the grammatical progression (through which the 'transfer' is made) from noun via a kind of syntactical limbo to adverb, at the end of which the word that has for two lines held the stage alone is subordinated to the main verb 'stabbed': like Crow's head the syntax of the poem is 'trapsprung'.

For Crow, being a bird, the question, 'in a destructive-creative universe, is guilt absurd?' is answered by 'trapsprung' and the fateful step-by-step evolution of the last line. With a man, as in 'Thrushes', it is otherwise—human eating is not automatic—and the poem's irony and grim realism do not disguise a poignant sense of loss.

The same problem is the theme of 'Crow's Nerve Fails', which is a kind of companion-poem to 'Crow Tyrannosaurus' (both are among the very best poems in the book) and also portrays an advance in consciousness upon an earlier poem in the sequence, 'The Black Beast', in which Crow displayed a simple self-ignorance by looking for the beast everywhere but in himself.

> Crow, feeling his brain slip,
> Finds his every feather the fossil of a murder.
>
> Who murdered all these?
> These living dead, that root in his nerves and his blood
> Till he is visibly black?
>
> How can he fly from his feathers?
> And why have they homed on him?
>
> Is he the archive of their accusations?
> Or their ghostly purpose, their pining vengeance?
> Or their unforgiven prisoner?
>
> He cannot be forgiven.
>
> His prison is the earth. Clothed in his conviction,
> Trying to remember his crimes
>
> Heavily he flies.

The 'nerve' of the title is illuminated if we think back to 'Hawk Roosting'. In contrast to the hawk, Crow is burdened with what Sartre called 'the sin of existing': in other words, he is human. The guilt originates, not as in 'Crow Tyrannosaurus' with the consciousness of killing, but with the fact of physically existing. Existence, as felt by Crow in this poem, *is* guilt, and the identification is verbally knit up by the subtle pattern of alliteration which works, rather as in Donne's 'Thou hast made me', to convey a sense of inevitability. But the most subtle thing about the poem is that we don't feel this inevitability holds other than in Crow's consciousness. The existential paradoxes—'How can he fly from his feathers?', 'His prison is the earth', culminating in the superbly poker-faced final line—all half-ask to be interpreted as ironies at Crow's expense. At the same time we cannot afford to indulge in any such irony, since we are perhaps more deeply implicated with Crow in this poem than in any other. What weighs him down, and makes him cut such a sorry flight in comparison with the hawk's 'direct through the bones of the living', is introspection itself, without which we cannot think about the poem: the deadlock that occurs when we examine the objective evidence of ourselves and see ourselves as the attribute of something external, *their* archive, *their* purpose, *their* vengeance, *their* prisoner, while all the time the examining consciousness remains unaccounted for.

Because Crow is exploring the universe without preconceptions, discovering from direct experience what is needed for survival, his experiences are simply juxtaposed and the tensions between the poems are unresolved. But it is significant that many of the poems reveal the inevitability of and necessity for a basic humanity that is capable of humility, compassion, outrage, horror, guilt and responsibility in order to survive. Respect for life is related to respect for the material universe. Compassion for the suffering is juxtaposed with responsibility for causing death. The creative and destructive capacities in Crow are related to the creative-destructive nature of the universe. The inevitability of a moral awareness revealed in *Crow* is closely related to the inevitability of metaphysical questioning. Ultimately this is a matter of the concept of a self, both in relation to other creatures and in relation to the larger processes of the universe. The three poems which are placed at the end of the sequence seem to confront this issue in a summarizing, symbolic way.

145

The final poem, 'Littleblood', celebrates the persistence of the blood of life, hiding its vulnerability but strong as the elements, various in its forms from an elephant's nose to a gnat's feet, but finally wise in the full knowledge of its part in the forces of life and of death. The poem's paradoxes—'hiding from the mountains in the mountains', 'sucking death's mouldy tits'—recall 'Crow's Nerve Fails', but they are not caustically ironic. It seems as if, when freed from the burden of individual consciousness, when contemplated as the attribute of life itself, paradox is a source of wonder and tenderness, not of anguish. Certainly wonder and tenderness are the keynotes of the wholly delightful conceit with which the poem (and the volume) ends—like 'Crow's Undersong' putting Crow back in touch with the vision of 'Full Moon and Little Frieda':

> Sit on my finger, sing in my ear, O littleblood.

The two 'Eskimo Songs' explore further the relationship between the self and the processes of life and death. The first, 'Fleeing from Eternity', seems to reflect the kind of hubris defined by Paul Radin in *The World of Primitive Man*:

> From the point of view of the world of nature, human consciousness may be regarded as constituting initially, at least, a type of *hybris*, an act of defiance of the natural order and one which called for frequent atonement. This is, indeed, a conception not infrequently encountered in the myths and reflections of many aboriginal peoples. However, the cultural domestication of man necessitated the transformation of this *hybris*, very early, into a positive and creative force.
>
> (p. 6)

All of the elements of this process are evident in 'Fleeing from Eternity', although the narrative does not exactly follow the structure of Radin's description. The man's hubris, because he is trying to struggle into individual consciousness, leads him to experience the atonement of pain and blood as initiation into awareness of life. He finally fails because in transforming his hubris into the creative force of song he bargains away the very experience and awareness of pain that are life. The process of atonement should in fact diminish the hubris so that real positive creative forces can be released from a self of knowledge and acceptance. This is the process described in 'How Water Began to Play':

Water wanted to live
It went to the sun it came weeping back
Water wanted to live
It went to the trees they burned it came weeping back
They rotted it came weeping back
Water wanted to live
It went to the flowers they crumpled it came weeping back
It wanted to live
It went to the womb it met blood
It came weeping back
It went to the womb it met knife
It came weeping back
It went to the womb it met maggot and rottenness
It came weeping back it wanted to die

It went to time it went through the stone door
It came weeping back
It went searching through all space for nothingness
It came weeping back it wanted to die

Till it had no weeping left

It lay at the bottom of all things

Utterly worn out   utterly clear

When water has wept its way through experiences of the fragility and pain of life, it is ready to give up. But it is at that moment that it discovers itself. The gentle wit of the ending derives from the paradox that in having wept itself dry, with 'no weepings left', water in fact finds itself lying as it biologically does, 'at the bottom of all things'. It is therefore both literally clear as a basic element, and 'utterly clear' about its own nature. Its discovery is that it is water, and cannot have life or death. Without self-deceptions it 'comes clear' to its sense of itself and its place in the universe. And this metaphysic has been achieved through the experiencing of compassion, horror, outrage, and finally humble self-awareness.

This poem seems to us to symbolize both the process of *Crow* and its furthest point of development. It is not necessarily the best poem in *Crow*; it remains abstract and symbolic rather than locked in the tensions of a material experience such as 'Crow and the Sea' or 'Crow's Account of the Battle'. But it indicates the spirit of the entire volume in exposing self-deceptions by practical tests against material reality, in its quiet and tentative discovery of the need for the experience of basic human values, in its suggestion that the self may only find connection with the universe by the 'losing of self-importance', and in the recognition that the nature of the self (in man's case, his forces and his tensions) contains the elements that lie at the heart of all natural things.

There is nothing mystical about all this. To say, as Sagar does, that water 'weeps itself clear of both life and death' (*The Art of Ted Hughes*, 2nd edition p. 136) and then to claim that this is what Hughes is literally wanting man to achieve, is to deprive those words of any useful meaning. In the Sufi poem *The Conference of the Birds* by Farid ud-din Attar, thirty birds, after much prevarication and a long journey, finally reach the presence of the 'light of lights', the Simurgh. The poem continues:

> The sun of majesty sent forth his rays, and in the reflection of each other's faces these thirty birds (simurgh) of the outer world, contemplated the face of the Simurgh of the inner world. This so astonished them that they did not know if they were still themselves or if they had become the Simurgh. At last, in a state of contemplation, they realised that they were the Simurgh and that the Simurgh was the thirty birds. (p. 131)

This is surely the relationship between the tension in the self and the forces of the universe that Hughes is feeling towards in 'Fleeing from Eternity', achieves in 'How Water Began to Play', and celebrates in 'Littleblood'. The Sufi image represents precisely the achievement of the 'losing of self-importance' in *Crow*. Stripped of self-deceptive notions the moral man is ready to perceive the simple reality of his place in the universe. It is not in the spirit of *Crow* to make assertions such as this. The collection remains exploratory and questioning. Yet one must accept that poems placed at the end can be given some importance, and the evidence for such conclusions is to be found in the poems themselves.

The juxtaposition of various perceptions, explorations and results is an essential quality of the book: these perceptions, experiences, 'realities' co-exist as possibilities for the reader to evaluate. This does leave the book open to misunderstanding, and to the more crudely shocking poems overshadowing the subtler ones; but this inevitably follows from the tentativeness of the book's affirmations, resulting as they do from a starting-point at a level below or before that of moral choice and creative effort, rediscovering the need for such choice and establishing the conditions on which such effort must be made. Such a view of the book seems less indulgent in the light of *Cave Birds* than it might have seemed a few years earlier. And it is especially in the light of *Cave Birds* that we can see, as the very inspiration of *Crow*'s reductiveness, an affirmative spirit stated by Hughes himself thus:

> The infinite terrible circumstances that seem to destroy man's importance, appear as the very terms of his importance. Man is the face, arms, legs etc. grown over the infinite, terrible All.
> (Vasko Popa, *Selected Poems*, p. 16)

6

Gaudete

Gaudete is a major advance in Hughes's narrative achievement. In it he has developed some of the features of his early short stories, such as 'Sunday' and 'The Harvesting': in particular the treatment of situations in which an ordinary consciousness is invaded by natural or seemingly unnatural powers, and the subjection of the reader himself to the bewilderment undergone by the characters. But *Gaudete* is bolder than these prose tales. Its central character has a fully explored unconscious life that constitutes a 'spirit world', and its often moving treatment of ordinary people's experience develops the achievement of the stories to a much greater degree.

However, we do not agree that *Gaudete* has the pre-eminence among 'poetic work in English in our time' that Keith Sagar claims for it. At the end of his chapter on the poem he asserts that in it Hughes, unlike Eliot, Lawrence, Beckett or Brecht, 'has come close to achieving' a 'position that cannot be outflanked' (*The Art of Ted Hughes*, 2nd edition, p. 225). We believe it has crucial weaknesses that deprive it of the wholeness necessary to justify such a claim. At the same time we hope to give ample evidence of one of its major virtues that Mr Sagar ignores: the unsentimental, sympathetic insight it offers into minds disoriented by 'merciless' events.

We shall not enumerate our criticisms of the poem here—they will emerge in the course of the chapter—but we can propose a model and a guide to the kind of achievement Hughes is emulating. *Gaudete* can be seen as a deliberately distorted version of *The Bacchae* of Euripides, in which Dionysos, as a punishment for their denial of his divine birth, plagues the women of Thebes with madness and turns them into his skinclad, raw-flesh-eating devotees.

King Pentheus rigidly and violently opposes Dionysos but, like Shakespeare's Angelo, is fatally susceptible to that which he suppresses and is seduced by the god into spying on the Bacchae, as a consequence of which he is torn to pieces by his own mother. The Reverend Nicholas Lumb combines the role of Dionysos with the fate of Pentheus. He seduces all the women in his parish and turns the Women's Institute into a coven; he is hunted to death by the enraged men of the parish. Evidently both works are concerned with suppressed energies and their destructiveness when precipitately released. Evidently, also, Hughes does not follow Euripides' simple structure of opposing the triumphant Dionysos and the vanquished rational-puritanical suppressor. The final lines of *The Bacchae* express the Chorus's sense of life having been changed by the events of the play:

> Gods manifest themselves in many forms,
> Bring many matters to surprising ends;
> The things we thought would happen do not happen;
> The unexpected God makes possible:
> And that is what has happened here today.
>   (*The Bacchae and Other Plays*, tr. Vellacott, p. 228)

At the end of *Gaudete* the survivors burn the bodies of Lumb and two of his parishioners: 'All evidence goes up', implying that the potentialities revealed by the narrative will have no consequences.

The reader opening *Gaudete* for the first time finds a double page on which two epigraphs face an Argument. The interaction of these hints about themes, and information about the story, immediately challenges the reader to find meaning not only in *what* happens but in *how* the story is told. It is a challenge for the reader to examine his own responses to what he is to read.

> If it were not Hades, the god of the dead and the underworld, for whom these obscene songs are sung and festivals are made, it would be a shocking thing, but Hades and Dionysos are one.
>   Heraclitus[1]

> Their battle had come to the point where I cannot refrain from speaking up. And I mourn for this, for they were the two sons of one man. One could say that 'they' were fighting in this way if one wished to speak of two. These two, however, were one,

for 'my brother and I' is one body, like good man and good
wife. Contending here from loyalty of heart, one flesh, one
blood, was doing itself much harm.

PARZIVAL (Book XV)

Argument

An Anglican Clergyman, the Reverend Nicholas Lumb, is
carried away into the other world by elemental spirits. Just as
in the Folktale, these spirits want him for some work in their
world.

To fill his place in this world, for the time of his absence, the
spirits make an exact duplicate of him out of an oak log, and fill
it with elemental spirit life. This new Nicholas Lumb is to all
appearances exactly the same as the old, has the same knowledge and mannerisms, but he is a log. A changeling.

This changeling proceeds to interpret the job of ministering
the Gospel of love in his own log-like way.

He organises the women of his parish into a coven, a love-
society. And the purpose of this society, evidently, is the birth
of a Messiah to be fathered by Lumb.

While he applies himself to this he begins to feel a nostalgia
for independent, ordinary human life, free of his peculiar
destiny.

At this point, the spirits who created him decide to cancel
him. It may be that the original Lumb has done the work they
wanted him to do, and so the changeling's time is up. The
result is that all the husbands of the parish become aware of
what is happening to their wives.

The narrative recounts the last day of the changeling's life.

At the death of the changeling, the original Nicholas Lumb
reappears in this world, in the West of Ireland, where he roams
about composing hymns and psalms to a nameless female
deity.

The Argument prepares the reader for the Prologue's entry into the
visionary experience of the 'other world'. The Reverend Lumb is
uncertain about where he is going or, indeed, where he is, as he
walks the cobbles of an empty Northern town. 'He walks with
deliberate vigour, searching in himself for control and decision'
(p. 11). These last three words are to echo through the narrative as
character after character attempts to make sense of the situations in

which they find themselves. But throughout the Prologue the reader is made to share Lumb's difficulty in making sense of the events he suffers. We share his horror in finding that 'the whole town is a maze of mass-graves' (p. 12), his astonishment at the appearance of the laughing old man, and his confusion about the dead-alive woman into whose presence the old man brings him.

> Lumb bends low
> Over her face half-animal
> And the half-closed animal eyes, clear-dark back to the first
> > creature
> And the animal mane
> The animal cheekbone and jaw, in the fire's flicker
> The animal tendon in the turned throat
> The upper lip lifted, dark and clean as a dark flower
> Who is this woman
> And who is the ancient creature beside her?
>
> Lumb kneels to understand what is happening
> And what he is to do.
> He thinks most likely this woman also is dead.   (p. 14)

Lumb senses that he is called upon to do something for this animal-woman, but feels inadequate. 'He is not a doctor. He can only pray' (p. 15). Lumb appears to have failed the test of his response to this creature. What she seems to represent is the integrated animal self (beautifully caught in the description of her eyes as 'clear-dark back to the first creature'). Certainly she acts as an announcement of a preoccupation with the animal energies of characters in the narrative. Not only is she half-animal, half-human, she is both dead and alive. She is an embodiment of the identity of Hades and Dionysos. We begin to see the point of the poem's title ('Rejoice') with its ironic reference to the virgin birth:

> Gaudete, gaudete, Christus est natus
> Ex Maria virgine, gaudete.

It is Lumb's Christian separation of the spirit from Nature that makes him helpless in the face of the female who we come to realize is the Goddess of Nature. His seeing the roles of doctor and priest as

153

separate indicates the divisions he makes between the physical and psychological, the rational scientific and the Christian spiritual in his sense of self. 'Contending here from loyalty of heart, one flesh, one blood, was doing itself much harm.'

> He protests there is nothing he can do
> For this beautiful woman who seems to be alive and dead.
> He is not a doctor. He can only pray.

> He does not feel any blow. Only a sudden jagged darkness
> that rends him apart, from the top of his skull downwards.

Immediately Lumb expresses that division of roles he is struck, as if by a judgement. He finds himself admiring the detailed beauty of the skin of a gigantic man who 'squashes him dark'. Having emerged from this darkness into a wood Lumb is invited, by men whose faces are 'as alike as badgers', to select a tree. He tries to speak, but is struck hard across his skull by a whip. He expects to be crucified since the men lop the tree until its trunk has two arms to which Lumb is tied. In fact Lumb is flogged into unconsciousness and by the same action the tree is flogged into life. The Lumb who 'comes to' is the changeling. This is indicated to the reader by the new Lumb's lack of the whip-scar which he sees across his double's bald skull. From this point onwards in the narrative the name Lumb refers to the changeling who has adopted the memory of the Anglican priest, but interprets the role and doctrine of the priest in a 'rather wooden way' as Hughes described it at a reading. Not only is the parody of the doctrine of Christian Love thus launched, but the more important question of the connection between man, his animal self, and his natural environment is thus embodied in Lumb's tree-nature. The Lumb of the main narrative is not separated from the natural world and his animal self.

The changeling Lumb finds himself in an abattoir confronted by a huge white bull reminiscent of 'Bull Moses', 'dozily masticating, happy behind the walls of its curls'. But this bull is also a 'ceremonial image', it is suggested[2] (p. 17). Lumb is asked to shoot the bull which is then swung above him so that he can be drenched in its blood and guts by the men who hold him spreadeagled beneath it.

> They are trying to drown him with blood
> And to bury him in guts and lungs.   (p. 19)

But what appears to be a ritual drowning turns into a ritual birth as Lumb escapes through darkness into daylight, emerging from a cellar into the ordinary world of buses and shoppers.

Lumb re-enters this 'other world' at a later stage in the poem, and we shall be discussing some of the meanings it suggests later in the chapter. For the moment, we want to stress the kind of hold it takes on the reader's imagination. It is a mythic, ritualistic world. It is also violent, seemingly arbitrary and chaotic: so much so that the order of myth, its power to bestow meaning, is fragmented. Hughes's use of myth is not, like that of a modernist writer, explicitly self-conscious. Myth and ritual in *Gaudete* (in this part of it at least) are not applied to the experience of the poem but seem to be glimpsed through it. Our immediate concern is with the physical sensations of 'greasy pulps', 'heavy sloggings of cold water', the this-world actuality of 'electrified clubs' and 'screeching pulleys'. We are made to feel that if myth has any power to change life it must be attained through pain and humiliation.

The main narrative opens with a series of interlocking episodes that establish both the changeling Lumb's activities and the kind of world he inhabits. In each case we see, first through the eyes of a man, Lumb's effect on the women. We share the suspense of not knowing what is happening: as in the Prologue, we are made to interpret the evidence for ourselves. The men, looking through binoculars and telescopes, are explicitly voyeurs of their own and others' lives. The women are nearly all in a state of 'high-tension boredom'. The men are caricatures—

Paradeground gravel in the folded gnarl of his jowls.
A perfunctory campaign leatheriness.
A frontal Viking weatherproof
Drained of the vanities, pickled in mess-alcohol and smoked dark.
(pp. 23–4)

—their domestic interiors stereotypes of sterility:

> Rooms retreat.
> A march of right angles. Barren perspectives
> Cluttered with artefacts, in a cold shine.
> Icebergs of taste, spacing and repose. (p. 32)

Keith Sagar says of this world, 'It bears about the same relationship to nature, that is to say, to reality, as gravel to living rock' (*The Art of*

155

Ted Hughes, 2nd edition, p. 195). This would be more pertinent as a criticism of Hughes's art here than as what Mr Sagar intends, a comment on observed and recorded real lives.

One of the fascinating things about the poem, however, is that while Hughes falls back on stereotype to convey the quality of his characters' lives when undisturbed, his insight into their experience of the disturbance is astonishingly vivid, penetrating and sympathetic.

His skull, glossy, veined, freckled, bulges
Over the small tight ferocious hawk's face
Evolved in Naval Command. Commander Estridge
Is stricken with the knowledge that his dream of beautiful
daughters

Has become a reality.
Simply, naturally, and now inevitably, there by the open window.
The dream was as beautiful as the daughters.
But the reality
Is beyond him. Unmanageable and frightening.
Like leopard cubs suddenly full-grown, come into their adult
power and burdened with it.
(p. 41)

This is the kind of insight without which sociological analysis of the relations between parents and children is worthless. And the effectiveness of the insight is dependent on the poetry—especially on the unexpected and moving word 'burdened', coming when we think the sentence must have rhythmically exhausted itself, overburdening an already long line. Any complacent sense of superiority the reader might have about Estridge's inability to cope with these powers (manifested by his younger daughter's playing of a 'dragonish' Beethoven piano sonata) is immediately shattered by the suicide of his elder daughter Janet, pregnant by Lumb: we ourselves are given a merciless demonstration that Hades and Dionysos are one in the experience of these daughters.

Throughout these episodes, and the whole poem, Hughes sustains a continuous awareness of the landscape, a beautiful and dangerous presence, consistently undermining the merely picturesque.

> The parkland unrolls, lush with the full ripeness of the last week in May, under the wet midmorning light. The newly

156

> plumped grass shivers and flees. Giant wheels of light ride into the chestnuts, and the poplars lift and pour like the tails of horses. (p. 23)

The very terms of the natural beauty are those of its own dissolution, in verbs that are both active and transient, fugitive. The language of landscape merges with that of the characters' extremity: 'A purplish turbulence/Boils from the stirred chestnuts'; when Major Hagen loses control, 'an outrage too dazzling to look at ignites the whole tree of his nerves.' The final image takes us much deeper than metaphorical ingenuity. Hagen's wife, in the anguished disturbance wrought by her contact with Lumb, attempts a more positive connection by 'anointing her face' with leaf-mould and 'the bunched stems of squeaking spermy bluebells'. The ritual suggested by 'anointing' is an example of the level of healing needed, for which the priest admitted he could only pray. But it is still not effective: trapped in her separate self, 'She cannot get far enough down, or near enough' (p. 32).

Mrs Westlake, pregnant by Lumb and contemplating suicide, has made this contact despite herself:

> Her brain swoons a little, trying to disengage. The glistening tissues, the sweating gasping life of division and multiplication, the shoving baby urgency of cells. All her pores want to weep. She is gripped by the weird pathos of biochemistry, the hot silken frailties, the giant, gristled power, the archaic sea-fruit inside her, which her girdle bites into, which begins to make her suit too tight. (p. 39)

The range of language in this passage, passing from the scientific, through the archetypal, to the everyday, emphasizes the distance from which she observes her unalterable connection with the natural world.

Hughes consistently exploits paradox to convey the dislocation between the characters, including Lumb himself, and the world beyond them. We see the raging Hagen 'Controlling the explosive china with watchmender's touch'; having just killed his dog he 'kneels/Beside the stilled heap of loyal pet/Hands huge with baffled gentleness/As if he had just failed to save it' (p. 35). Lumb catches a dead pigeon thrown to him by Hagen 'as if to save it'. This sense of absurd helplessness in the face of their own lives introduces a poignancy into the harshest exposure.

157

Between the discovery of Janet Estridge's body and the explanation of the reasons for her suicide there is placed one of the most remarkable passages in the book. Lumb meditates on the material reality of the landscape, the processes at work in it, and his ambiguous connection with it. Lumb the changeling is continuing the consciousness of the original Lumb whose memory he has taken over. He is therefore not aware of himself as a changeling or as having a literal affinity with trees and the earth. Since the reader, on the other hand, is aware of this the whole passage works in two ways: a man is raising questions about his relationship with the forces of nature, and the implications of his tree-nature act as metaphorical hints at potential answers.

Lumb recognizes that the forces at work in trees and stones are also at work in himself, but he wonders to what degree he has control over them.

> He knows the blood in his veins
> Is like heated petrol, as if it were stirring closer and closer to
> explosion,
> As if his whole body were a hot engine, growing hotter
> Connected to the world, which is out of control,
> And to the grass under his feet, the trees whose shadows reach
> for him.
> (p. 49)

He senses that his own death is a timing device planted in his nature, connecting him to the natural processes of decay. But he fears that the world's processes are 'out of control', as in a real sense they are, although he is aware also of counterbalancing forces and processes, of the flux he sees as

> brightenings and darkenings, and rendings and caressings,
> With tiny crowded farness and near sudden hugeness
> And hot twisting roughness, and vast cantileverings of star-balance.
> (p. 50)

This is the 'music that lurches through him' against which he needs to 'fill his strength'. Beautiful as this passage might be in isolation, for Lumb it is a threat because he is uncertain about how much room this leaves for his own freedom of decision. Since he does not feel at

158

one with these processes he is still at the stage of seeking a sense of separate freedom.

This is his favourite meditation to which he yields. It is a concept of ever-receding openings on to alternative worlds waiting to be chosen. Lumb

> tries to imagine simple freedom—
> His possible freedoms, his other lives, hypothetical and forgone,
> > his lost freedoms.

But this is, he knows, a 'forlorn, desperate meditation' because it is a mental escape from material reality in which he must find his place:

> Between the root in immovable earth
> And the coming and going leaf
> Stands the tree
> Of what he cannot alter.

Any reader who had not been conscious of Lumb's tree-nature so far would be reminded of it here with a shock. The image clearly provides a metaphor for the self-awareness that is necessary in order to achieve unity with the natural universe. This image, then, reminds the reader of the Prologue, as do the subsequent 'crushing of himself from himself' and his rebirth in his vision. The emphasis in the Prologue was on his discovery of his animal self. In the present visionary sequence the emphasis is now on his search for those natural sources of energy that connect him with the landscape.

In a sequence of lines which echo 'Crow and the Sea' Lumb tries to pray himself into harnessing the natural powers of his environment into a decision for his future actions. He knows that any idea of his is subordinate to his natural processes. Finally, in an image that is both simply moving and metaphysically profound, Lumb discovers the unity of his physical nature and mental awareness with the natural world.

> He leans his forehead to an ash tree, clasping his hands over his
> > skull.
> He presses his brow to the ridged bark.
> He closes his eyes, searching.
> He tries to make this ash-tree his prayer.

He searches upward and downward with his prayer,
    reaching upwards and downwards through the capillaries,
Groping to feel the sure return grasp
The sure embrace and return gaze of a listener—

He sinks his prayer into the strong tree and the tree stands as his
                                                            prayer.
                                                        (pp. 52–3)

The humorous and profound implications of this passage are integrated in its emotional impact: the pathos of the search and its necessity, the absurdity of the idea and its celebration of a connectedness, the material representing the spiritual, the beauty of physical detail actually describing an effort of consciousness, and Lumb's final understanding being represented by the perfect natural image of himself.

It is significant that it is the women, as we have already seen in Mrs Hagen and Mrs Westlake, who attempt to exercise their own 'control and decision' by contact with nature. Those acts can now be seen as part of the metaphysical search conducted through the narrative. Perhaps the description of Mrs Holroyd, which follows soon after Lumb's meditations, can be seen as a rather bold attempt to represent an organic unity with the natural environment. She is sunbathing, but not in mystical sun-worship. She is listening to her transistor radio and squirming her toes. Her total contentment derives from straightforward sensuality of living. She suffers no traumas in her relationship with Lumb which is one of equally straightforward sensual delight. But there is also about this passage an over-simple escapism that is absurd:

> And she is like a plant.
> The sun settles the quilt of comfort
> Over her sleepy contentment with herself.   (p. 59)

She watches her bull who gets to his feet and rubs himself against a blossoming tree. 'The blossoms snow down, settling along his shoulders and loins and buttocks, like a confetti' (p. 60). In this incongruous image which concludes the section there is a more convincing truth: brute sexuality and delicate beauty are brought together in a brief moment of powerful celebration and praise.

One of the most important figures in the narrative is Lumb's

160

dumb, elderly housekeeper, Maud. The writing that concerns her raises acute problems of tone and is one of the major elements that, we think, damage the poem's wholeness. She is the stereotype of the devoted servant whose portentous manner is alarmingly at odds with her apparently domestic function.

> Her gaze, fixed and withdrawn,
> Glaucous, hyperthyroid,
> Glisteningly circumscribes
> The vicar's needs.
>
> And the full pale mouth
> Pursed in a compact nun stillness
> Is a sufficiency of speech
> Among the ivy shadows.   (p. 62)

She is the only character who is not an experiencing subject: the writing about her is designed purely to make an effect on the reader.

Her appearance in the narrative brings in, for the first time, conventional occult props: a crystal ball, 'Lumb's magical implements', 'the ebony hilted dagger'. Looking into the crystal ball, 'the hidden treasure', she sees 'trampling feet of cattle', 'the swivelling eye of a bull', a stag brought down by hounds in a river and the murder by stabbing of Lumb's bride. The bull recalls the Prologue and the cattle anticipate a later vision of Lumb's. Maud, in other words, appears to have access to Lumb's inner experiences. The death of the stag and the murder of the bride foretell Lumb's own death, hunted down by the husbands in the lake, and the murder of Felicity, Lumb's 'selected wife', by Maud herself. This gives Maud an authority which, unless we can take her seriously, is bound to diminish Lumb and the poem.

The problem of tone can be seen by looking at these lines:

> Maud puts everything back into the chest
> Where Lumb's magical implements lie folded in pelts of ermine.
> There lies the ebony hilted dagger,
> Blade sleeved in the whole pelt of an ermine.   (p. 64)

The details in this passage are such that their mere mention suggests a knowingly spine-chilling effect. They can occasion an easy kind of

161

humour, and there is in fact a touch of light comedy when Maud goes to the door, holding the dagger, to confront the breadman. Yet, as we have seen, these occult props are associated with real clair-voyance. The trouble is partly that in this particular passage they are 'merely mentioned': this is one of several passages of verse that read more like the screenplay that *Gaudete* started as than as poetry. It is consequently toneless. The same is true of Maud's next appearance when, in a graveyard, she follows a ghostly woman, and kneels and weeps by a grave on which the word 'Gaudete' is engraved (p. 94). Again the episode lends Maud authority, makes her seem close to the imaginative heart of the poem, but again the writing has nothing like the intensity or originality of Lumb's visionary experiences, or the normal if extreme experiences of the other characters. Keith Sagar suggests that Maud is a casualty of dualistic theology—'the maiden becomes old maid and murderous witch' (*The Art of Ted Hughes*, 2nd edition, p. 202)—and that the ghostly woman is the ghost of the Goddess. This is plausible at the level of intention, but at the level of achievement the writing about Maud is nothing like as compelling as Estridge's subjection to the reality of his daughters, or some of the similar, even more remarkable episodes we shall be discussing shortly; and the Goddess is more convincingly present in any of the evocations of landscape than in her tenuous appearance in the graveyard.

Maud, as we shall see, becomes increasingly important in the narrative. The problem of tone, of interpreting the occult atmos-phere that surrounds her, is accentuated by the fact that her first appearance is set in the midst of a series of the poem's most effec-tively comic episodes. Lumb is found sprawled between the legs, 'spread like a dead frog's', of Betty the barmaid, by the voyeuristic poacher Joe Garten, Lumb's rival for the love of Felicity and another key figure in the plot. Subsequently, in a scene of rich erotic farce, Garten just fails to surprise Lumb and his mother copulating in the garden hut, among escaped ferrets and rabbits. Meanwhile, in the pub, Felicity's grandfather gives his rambling interpretation of what Lumb is up to.

> Christianity's something about women....
> His eyes are seriously amazed
> At what such things evidently boil down to.

(pp. 65–6)

The speech is a mixture of comic vagueness and poignancy:

Christianity is Christ in his mammy's arms—
Either a babe at the tit
With all the terrible things that are going to happen to him
                                        hovering round his head like a halo,
Or else a young fellow collapsed across her knees
With all the terrible things having happened.

The whole passage has a penumbra of contexts, including the recurring figure of the mother in *Crow*, the argument of Hughes's essay on Shakespeare and, of course, *The White Goddess*. The world of the poem is presided over by a Goddess but, as in a later speech by Mrs Evans on pp. 113–14, Hughes seems to be offering the interpretation of Lumb's mission with a wicked grin, as if the reader who settles for this level of understanding will be missing the whole point.

The ambiguity of tone in the treatment of Maud and in Old Smayle's monologue seems crucial to the conceptual heart of the narrative. The imaginative heart, however, is more firmly established, as we see in the three superb episodes which almost immediately follow. Dr Westlake, after his visit to the Estridges, has drunk too much at lunchtime and is driving home. In so far as he is a character, he is an extremely unpleasant one but, while we never quite forget this, we are occupied for the next six pages not in making judgements but in sharing, with extraordinary intimacy and detail, the nexus of ideas, emotions and sensations that constitutes Westlake's state of being while he drives home, realizes that his wife too is having an affair with Lumb, and discovers them in a bizarre innocent-but-suggestive position.

The alcohol makes him clumsy, and oppressively hypersensitive to the sights and smells of the early summer's day. 'He searches for his car-keys, preoccupied, watching the mobs of young starlings struggling and squealing filthily in the clotted may-blossom, like giant blow-flies' (p. 71). Though only Hughes could have written that sentence, it is not his sensibility that is expressed, but the temporary condition of the unsettled and vulnerable doctor. The drink has also made him vulnerable to the erotic memory of 'Jennifer's insinuatingly amorous lamenting tones' which 'seem to have entered his blood, like a virus, with flushes of fever and shivers,

163

and light, snatching terrors'. Hughes's account of the feelings engendered by the spectacle of a woman sexually aroused by another man is shockingly vivid and apt:

But he has drunk too much.
And the finality of that dead girl lies at the centre of the day
Like an incomprehensible, frightful dream.
And her live sister is worse—all that loose, hot, tumbled softness,
Like freshly-killed game, with the dew still on it,
Its eyes still seeming alive, still strange with wild dawn,
Helpless underbody still hot. (p. 72)

This feeds directly into the sudden certainty that his wife and Lumb 'Fit together, like a tongue in its mouth'.

Throughout the episode there is a shifting relationship between what Westlake intends to do, what he thinks he is going to do and what he actually does. 'Numb-edged' and 'dark-edged', he 'aims himself at his car' but bangs his head on it twice, breaking his glasses. 'His body is still moving beyond him, its limits blurred.' This dislocation and loss of control are trivially explicable as the effects of alcohol, but their intensity and persistence manifest the disturbance of a new state of being that his mind has not caught up with and consequently cannot control. When Westlake 'deliberates control' the phrase is strikingly reminiscent of Lumb on the first page of the Prologue 'searching in himself for control and decision' and anticipates the assembled husbands in the Bridge Inn who 'continue to drink more forcefully in search of definition and action'. Control, decision and definition are for all the characters, including Lumb, imagined, striven-for possibilities, hardly ever actualities. When Westlake's disturbance finds its root in the knowledge of his wife's infidelity it ceases to be a random lack of co-ordination and becomes a compulsion to discover her *in flagrante delicto*.

> His alcohol dullness has settled
> To a hurtling lump, a projectile—
>
> He turns in at the gate of his home
> With the sensation of finding his trap at last tenanted.

But this sensation is of course completely illusory and when he arrives at the house he has to make 'a deliberate attempt/To realise afresh what he is about'.

Inside his house, he is described as standing 'Weightless, in the balance of decision', but again this is an illusion because his actions outstrip decision. He stands outside his bedroom door listening to 'the crying of his wife at some bodily extreme, which can have only the one interpretation', but while he is thinking about it 'his body has already moved convulsively, and the door bursts open.' What he sees is baffling, and he is forced to make an interpretation which, though absurd, will justify his convulsive and threatening presence in the room.

> His wife is lying fully clothed on the bed.
> She is being hysterical in her familiar style,
> Rolling from side to side
> As if to escape some truth which threatens to scorch her face.
> And the Reverend Lumb
> Is sitting at the foot of the bed, considerate as a baffled doctor.
> His calming hand detains her slim ankle.
>
> In one flash Westlake understands
> That his accurate intuition
> Has been forestalled and befooled
> By this goat-eyed vicar.
> In spite of what it looks like
> Something quite different is going on here,
> Even under his very eyes,
> And if he could only see clear
> Through the vicar's humbug solemn visage
> And his wife's actress tragedy mask
> It would be plain
> That her writhing and cries are actually sexual spasm,
> And that the Reverend Lumb, who seems to be gazing at him
> In such cool spiritual composure
> And mild secular surprise
> Is actually copulating with her
> Probably through that hand on her ankle
> In some devilish spiritual way.   (p. 75)

The joke is at Westlake's expense, but it is not just cruel mockery. This inability to trust the evidence of his senses is the consequence of a disorientation so vividly conveyed that for a moment we share it. We have to leaf back to earlier episodes (pp. 29–30 and 36–40) to realize that she might well be hysterical and Lumb attempting to soothe her.

After a perfunctorily narrated fight with Lumb, Westlake drives to the house of his friend Dunworth, an architect, where he sees Lumb's blue van. He phones Dunworth at his office, and the architect races home, fetches a target pistol and strides into the lounge, where he finds his own wife and Lumb naked on the couch.

His brisk executive plan evaporates confusedly.
The sight in front of him
Is so extraordinary and shocking
So much more merciless and explicit than even his most daring
fantasy

That for a moment
He forgets himself, and simply stares.
He gropes for his lost initiative,
But what he sees, like a surprising blow in a dark room,
Has scattered him.
He raises his pistol meanwhile.
He is breathing hard, to keep abreast of the situation.
He is trying to feel
Whether he is bluffing or is about to become
The puppet
Of some monstrous, real, irreversible act.

He waits for what he will do,
As a relaxed rider, crossing precipitous gulleys
Lets his horse find its way.
He levels the pistol at his wife's face and holds it there,
undecided.
(p. 85)

In Hughes's slow, detailed mapping of Dunworth's crisis the emphasis falls on the interstices between decision and action, perception and feeling: 'Her nakedness has outstripped his reaction, incredible,/Like the sudden appearance of an arrow, sticking deep in his body,/Seconds before the pain.' In these gaps, these moments in which everything seems decided and one only has to await the outcome, even though the outcome will be one's own action, the mind, unimpeded by 'brisk executive plans', enters a condition like that which the Sufis call 'heedfulness'. In such a moment Westlake observed

166

with a self-mesmerising stillness,
The peeled-back gorges of his rose-blooms, leaning poised in
space.
He marvels again that they are precisely where they are,
Neither an inch this way nor an inch that way,
But exactly there, with their strict, fierce edges.

(p. 74)

Dunworth has a more significant revelation.

Dunworth gazes back at his wife
Almost forgetting where he is or what he is doing.
He is helplessly in love.
He stands there, in his child's helplessness,
As if he had searched everywhere and at last somehow he had
found her.
An irresponsible joy chatters to be heard, somewhere in the back
of his head, as he gazes at her,
Feeling all his nerves dazzle, with waftings of vertigo,
As if he were gazing into an open furnace.
At the same time he tightens on the butt and trigger of the pistol,
readjusting his grip,
As if the terrible moment were approaching of itself.
In the remaining seconds
He studies her lips and tries to separate out the ugliness there,
Which he remembers finding regrettable.
He tries to isolate the monkey-crudity of her hairline,
Her spoiled chin, all the ordinariness
That once bored him so much,
But he feels only a glowing mass.
He stands there, paralysed by a bliss
And a most horrible torture—
Endless sweetness and endless anguish.   (p. 87)

The vision of his wife as a 'glowing mass' resembles the experiences
that Carlos Castaneda's Don Juan calls 'seeing'. We shall be quoting
such an experience later when we consider another instance of
'seeing' in *Gaudete* (p. 180).

Later, when Dunworth is sitting drinking with Westlake, we are
told that he 'is afraid that if he is left alone he might well kill himself
in a light-minded effort to be sincere' (p. 130). In fact his immediate
reaction to this vision of his wife is to put the pistol-muzzle into his

own mouth. One lesson that we learn from the men in *Gaudete* is perhaps that no action can be a sincere response to experiences as 'merciless and explicit' as they are subjected to. Like Dunworth when he points the pistol at his wife they are either bluffing or 'puppets of an act' that afterwards they could not take responsibility for. The perfect matching of consciousness and action that is a condition of sincerity is precisely what their experience robs them of. The climax of the narrative is an act of mass insincerity by all the men. But Dunworth's vision of his wife shows that this experience does make available discoveries which we can imagine enriching their future lives.

That last point, however, raises the obvious limitation in Hughes's 'characterization'. His portrayal of experience in moments of crisis cannot be matched by many novelists, but *Gaudete* suggests that Hughes could not write a novel. The characters are alive only at such moments—alive with astonishing vividness—and their creator does not seem to have tried to imagine, or to be interested in, the continuity of their lives. This would perhaps not matter if it were not for the feeble gestures towards that continuity: Pauline Hagen's marriage represented by the parquet and cut glass, the crude symbolism of the 'grey sterility' of Westlake's lounge.

The crises of Westlake and Dunworth represent one genuine imaginative centre of the poem: the psychological. They are separated by an episode that is occult and metaphysical in nature, but quite superior in imaginative quality to those in which Maud figures. Lumb is bathing a skin-wound inflicted by Westlake. He hears voices, of which the clearest is his own, calling his name. The sun is shining but thunderclouds are approaching. Felicity, in a boat on the lake, is frightened and wants to go home but Lumb has seen a fish that he wants to catch. While he is concentrating on the fish a naked figure, identical to Lumb, emerges from the water and pursues Felicity. With some reluctance Lumb abandons his fish and goes to her aid. By this time thunder, lightning and rain have turned the scene into one of chaotic elemental violence. A horrifying fight ensues, in which the hands of the two Lumbs become locked together, that of the intruder is torn off and he disappears back into the water. Lumb throws the hand after him and he is left comforting the sobbing Felicity in the now icy downpour. Here is part of the description of the fight:

168

The mountains have disappeared in a twilight mass of foggy rain.
Their pyramids leap in and out of blue-blackness,
Trembling in violet glare, like shadow puppets, and vanishing
                                                            again.
And thunder trundles continually around the perimeter of the
                                        deeply padded heaven
And through the cellars of the lake
With splittings of giant trees and echoing of bronze flues and
                                                mazy corridors,
And repeated, closer bomb-bursts, which seem to shower hot
                                                    fragments.

Suddenly under a long electrocuted wriggler of dazzle
That shudders across the whole sky, for smouldering seconds,
Their attacker glistening and joyous
Bounds over the turf bank and on to them.
Laughing like a maniac, he grabs Felicity's arm.
With clownish yells and contortions, he starts dragging her again
                                                toward the lake.
Again Lumb knocks him down and the two men wallow
                                                pummelling,
Plastered with peat-mud, under the downpour.
Finally, gasping and immobilised, they lie face to face, gripping
                                            each other's hands,
One grinning and the other appalled.   (pp. 81–2)

The recreation of the splendour of the elements is an excellent
example of Hughes's 'utility general-purpose style'. It seems casual,
made up of materials lying at hand, but achieves a remarkable
coherence. Matter seems to be unleashed and converted into
energy; and this co-exists with cellars, flues and corridors that evoke
the claustrophobia of the thunderstorm with hints of Gothic nightmare. The bold clash of diction has its triumph in 'a long electrocuted wriggler of dazzle', which vividly evokes the lightning and at
the same time merges it (through 'wriggler') with the double whom
it illuminates.

The double is clearly a part of this splendour and violence, even to
the point of being its personification. But there is, indeed, a multi-
plicity of clues to his identity—or rather the duality figured in the
fight—which need to be followed through, even though they may
seem to conflict with each other. The fight very obviously recalls the
epigraph from *Parzival*: 'One could say that "they" were fighting in

169

this way if one wished to speak of two', but they are two only for the purposes of the fiction and here, also, 'one flesh, one blood' is 'doing itself much harm'. When the two Lumbs 'lie face to face, gripping each other's hands', they reproduce the posture in which Lumb was 'created'. Lumb is, perhaps, being reminded of his origin and, since Felicity represents the temptation of an ordinary human destiny, warned. It doesn't seem very profitable, however, to try to identify the double with the 'original' Lumb—this clownish, demonic, grinning apparition has little in common with the protagonist of the Prologue or the gentle Orpheus of the Epilogue. His hold on the imagination is partly the consequence of his sudden, inexplicable appearance and disappearance.[3]

At the end of the narrative Lumb is killed in a lake (perhaps this one), and by that time Felicity, too, has been murdered. Might this episode, then, be a premonition of their deaths? The glistening, joyous clownishness of the double seems to link him with Dionysos but his apparent determination to drag first Felicity then Lumb into the underworld of the lake tempts us to see him equally as Hades. 'Hades and Dionysos are one', and if his designs on Felicity are ambiguously sexual and murderous we may recall that Hades, like other Olympians, paid occasional visits to this world for the purpose of rape and that his most famous rape, that of Persephone, was the origin of the nature that we live in—the world of interdependent life and death. At the mysteries of Eleusis, which were based on this myth, the initiates learned that 'death was not an evil, but a blessing.' Not in the sense, as at the end of *Oedipus the King*, that 'none can be called happy until that day when he carries his happiness down to the grave in peace', but because death and life, Hades and Dionysos, are one.[4]

If this is an interpretation of the episode it does not solve all the problems raised by it. If the assailant is Hades/Dionysos manifesting his vehement, 'glistening and joyous' nature and forewarning Lumb of his death, does it make sense to say that the incident is also a reminder to Lumb of his 'birth' and a punishment for wanting to be an 'ordinary man' with Felicity?[5] One reason why it is difficult to say is that the relationship with Felicity is one of the weakest elements in the poem. We are given no insight into his feelings for her and no indication, beyond Maud's word 'ordinary', of the nature of the proposed marriage. This is perhaps the most serious symptom of the poet's lack of interest in continuity and extension of experience.

The episode of the double should not of course be thought of in isolation from Lumb's other encounters with 'spirits'; we have made links with the Prologue and now we need to look at the third episode of this kind. While Lumb is driving along, a pair of 'stub-fingered hairy-backed hands' wrench the steering wheel from him and crash the car. He thinks he is in the river but finds himself in a cattleyard, in pouring rain, among lurching cattle, and that men in oilskins are attacking him with sticks, 'with intent to kill him'. During a pause in the assault he is handed a paper 'as if it were some explanation' but he cannot read it and it disintegrates. The assault is renewed and he is floored and trampled by the hooves of cattle. When he comes to 'He lies buried in mud,/His face into mud, his mouth full of mud', on a muddy plain where lie the crushed bodies of the men of his parish and where the women of his parish are buried alive to their necks, screaming. He catches sight of a 'mud being' squirming 'with horrible reptile slowness', which calls to him. 'Thinking this one creature that he can free' he pulls it out and when the rain washes the mud from its face he sees 'a woman's face,/A face as if sewn together from several faces./A baboon beauty face'. This woman clamps him in an embrace like cutting wires and he is made to enact her birth from his own body:

Flood-sudden, like the disembowelling of a cow
She gushes from between his legs, a hot splendour
In a glistening of oils,
In a radiance like phosphorous he sees her crawl and tremble.

He is covered in blood, and her face is now 'undeformed and perfect'. He crawls away, and finds that he is crawling out of the river into a sunlit day where his van is 'sitting out in a meadow' surrounded by men who vanish leaving the van 'empty, the doors wide open, as if parked for a picnic' (pp. 98–106).

Like Lumb's double rising out of the lake, this woman emerges from the mud; like the double again she holds Lumb in a painful and unbreakable clasp, and after the 'birth' she is, like him, 'glistening'. Her 'baboon beauty face' obviously recalls the 'half-animal' face of the woman in the Prologue, the Goddess to whom the final poems are addressed. In all three episodes Lumb is treated with extreme violence, in two of them by a group of anonymous and sinister men. This episode and the encounter with the double take place in

171

pouring rain. Cattle figure prominently here and in the Prologue. Here, as in the Prologue, he is bathed in blood, and the similarity of language underlines the parallel.

> He fights in the roping hot mass.
> He pushes his head clear, trying to wipe his eyes clear.
>
> (p.18)

> He fights in hot liquid . . . .
> He frees his hands and face of blood-clotted roping tissues.
>
> (p. 106)

The first time, of course, it is the bull's blood, the second time his own. The vision of the Prologue begins with Lumb seeing the town as a 'mass-grave'; in this episode he sees the men of his parish dead and the women undergoing a living death.

Although these experiences are extremely disturbing, and constitute or portend some kind of breakdown, they don't seem to us neurotic symptoms, nor to turn Lumb (nor Hughes) into a psychiatric case. There are none of the characteristic fears, guilts or anxieties that we associate with neurosis, and the pattern of significance, though hard to rationalize, seems to be a generally relevant one. The piece of paper on which the supposed explanation of the assault in the cattleyard was written disintegrated in Lumb's hand, 'weak as a birth membrane', sodden in the same downpour that soaked Lumb himself. This is an obvious warning, but we hope that the paper on which we write will not disintegrate if we say that for Hughes the world of the spirits is the world of the body, which is continuous with all other existence and which will die. The repeated soakings in water, mud and blood are like a ferocious demonstration of the literally and metaphysically fluid nature of the body's existence, the illusoriness of separation from the world of the animals and the elements.

This 'inner world of the body' is not however 'an extension of the outer world' in the sense that it can be perceived and understood by 'the sharp, clear, objective eye of the mind'. In the revised version of his essay 'Myth and Education' (*Times Educational Supplement*, 2 September 1977) from which these quotations come, Hughes argues that the inner world has always been interpreted by religion and mythology—that the stories into which the great religions

172

crystallize are imaginative instruments for handling the inner world—and that since the discrediting of Christianity and triumph of 'the sharp, clear, objective eye of the mind', that world has become 'elemental, chaotic, continually more primitive and beyond our control. It has become a place of demons' (p. 13). Since 'our real selves lie down there. Down there, mixed up among all the madness, is everything that once made life worth living', entry into this world is essential to life; but 'a faculty developed specially for peering into the inner world might end up as specialised and destructive as the faculty for peering into the outer one.' Hughes's paradigm of this latter faculty is the camera, and his symbolic story of its destructiveness concerns a photographer who went on taking shots while a tiger mauled a woman to death. The problem of entry into the inner world cannot be tackled in isolation, because 'the outer world and inner world are interdependent at every moment. We are simply the locus of their collision. Two worlds, with mutually contradictory laws, or laws that seem to us to be so, colliding afresh every second, struggling for peaceful coexistence.' The last sentence is strikingly reminiscent of the phrase in which Lumb's crisis is to be summarized: 'two worlds,/Like two strange dogs circling each other' (*Gaudete*, p. 125).

'Elemental, chaotic and primitive' are apt words to describe Lumb's inner world. The figures he encounters in the Prologue, we recall, had 'primitive, aboriginal faces' (p. 15). Could this be the 'demonized' inner world that Hughes speaks of in his essay? The peculiar combination of chaotic, apparently meaningless violence with fragments of ritual and myth is, perhaps, what we might expect such a world to be like. But if the men in oilskins are demons, spirits crazed with deprivation, Lumb also encounters women who need his help: the animal/human, dead/alive woman of the Prologue for whom, not being a doctor, he 'could only pray'; and the disfigured baboon woman who turns into 'a hot splendour/In a glistening of oils' through her rebirth out of his body. 'Down there, mixed up among all the madness, is everything that once made life worth living.' Moreover, the spirits do not merely terrorize Lumb. It is they, after all, the men with 'primitive, aboriginal faces ... alike as badgers', who are responsible for the birth of the changeling through the ritual of the tree, and they also, as the 'men in oilskins', who force the creative if agonizing birth of the baboon woman. And the Lumb-Hades-Dionysos of the lake, if 'like a maniac', is also 'glistening and joyous' and, in so far as he foretells Lumb's death, might be regarded as a 'helping spirit'.

The last phrase is the language of shamanism, which is one of the important imaginative contexts of *Gaudete*. Although none of the specific details of shamanic experience make their appearance—flight, dismemberment, seeing one's own skeleton, animal helpers, etc.—Lumb's career bears an unmistakable general resemblance to what Hughes has called 'the shamanic flight and return' (*London Magazine* interview, January 1971, p. 17). The sudden, psychotic-seeming breakdown, the cessation of ordinary reality and entry into a spirit world, the threats, violence and symbolic teaching undergone there, the provision of a new body and the transformed return (whether as the changeling of the narrative or the 'changed' man of the Epilogue) all correspond to the basic pattern.

We should hope to find that this is something more than a scholarly exercise, and in particular we should hope to find some connection between the shamanistic elements in *Gaudete* and the argument of 'Myth and Education', since it is precisely the shaman, or the man of shamanic temperament, who will make 'the attempt to re-enter that lost inheritance', to regain 'the lost awareness and powers and allegiances of our biological and spiritual being' ('Myth and Education', *Times Educational Supplement*, 2 September 1977, p. 13).

That connection can perhaps best be formulated in the question, 'What is the relation of shamanism to myth?' In other words, of the individual spiritual explorer to the common religious heritage? Mircea Eliade asserts that

> The shamans did not create the cosmology, the mythology, and the theology of their respective tribes; they only interiorized it, 'experienced' it, and used it as the itinerary for their ecstatic journeys.
>
> (*Shamanism*, p. 266)

Joseph Campbell appears to take a different view:

> the group rites of the hunting societies are, *au fond*, precipitations into the public field of images first experienced in shamanistic vision, rendering myths best known to shamans and best interpreted by shamans.
>
> (*The Masks of God: Primitive Mythology*, p. 254)

It is not our place to adjudicate between these views, merely to observe that the connection between shamanism and myth is in either case a vital one.

Joseph Campbell describes the 'basic form of the shamanistic crisis' in three stages:

A. A spontaneously precipitated rupture with the world of common day, revealed in symptoms analogous to those of a serious nervous breakdown: visions of dismemberment, fosterage in the world of spirits, and restitution

B. A course of shamanistic, mythological instruction under a master, through which an actual restitution of a superior level is achieved

C. A career of magical practice in the service of the community, defended from the natural resentment of the assisted community by various tricks and parodies of power

(p. 265)

Lumb undergoes A, there is no equivalent whatever for B, and (in consequence?) C goes disastrously wrong. Campbell's phrasing of B is a bit obscure, so it will be doubly useful to have Hughes's own version: 'he begins to study under some shaman, learning the great corpus of mythological, medical, and technical lore of the particular cultural line of shamanism he is in: this stage takes several years' (review of Eliade, *Listener*, 29 October 1964, p. 677).

To emerge from this anthropological hinterland, and summarize the impressions gained from seeing the poem in the light of 'Myth and Education' and Hughes's interest in shamanism: Lumb enters the inner world which has been demonized by the lapse of religion, which for the same reason he has to cope with without an established mythology or ritual, and without any formal teaching or initiation. Being a Christian he produces a distorted version of Christian love, in an attempt to reconcile the demands of his 'masters' with the existing religious tradition—but with results that are on the whole comic or horrific. He also takes other measures, for which we must return to the narrative.

In its second half the narrative becomes complicated: we realize that what we are reading is not a simple sequence of events but a developing plot which must ultimately reach a crisis. Three separate threads are interwoven: Joe Garten, Lumb's rival for the love of

175

Felicity, photographs him making love to Mrs Evans the black-smith's wife, goes to town to have the photograph developed, and shows it first to Evans, then to Felicity and the other husbands, whose separate motives for violent retribution begin to cohere; we see Maud, Mrs Davies and other women preparing for the Women's Institute meeting, at which Lumb will preside, and about which speculation is rife among the men; and we see Lumb recovering from his last encounter with the 'spirits', having a further vision or perhaps in this case fantasy, faced with Felicity's demand that he go away with her immediately, and forced to agree to her attending (for the first time) the W.I. meeting. The rapid cinematic cutting between the episodes that constitute these threads accentuates the feeling that Lumb, despite the impression given through the eyes of the husbands, is not in control of things. Practical control has passed to the vindictive voyeuristic photographer Garten, and spiritual or imaginative control (less certainly because of the mystery that always surrounds her) to the increasingly prominent and bizarre Maud. Lumb's loss of control is explicit when, back in his room after his last shamanic encounter, Maud looks after him in an almost ritualistic manner and when she has left him

> His only effort now
> Is pushing ahead and away the seconds, second after second,
> Now this second, patiently, and now this,
> Safe seconds
> In which he need do nothing, and decide nothing,
> And in which nothing whatsoever can happen.   (p. 108)

He is as much a passive victim as the husbands have been in their crises. He lies in this debilitated condition while Garten collects his photograph and begins showing it, and while Maud, in the room below, wrenches the head off a pigeon and smears her naked body with its blood. He drifts into a dream: thousands of women are streaming into a Cathedral in which he is throned and, beside him,

> An apparition, a radiance,
> A tall blossoming bush of phosphorous
> Maud has become beautiful.   (p. 121)

He kisses her—'Their kiss deepens./In a bush of flames they are burning'—while the Cathedral drums with the voices of the women who continue to stream in despite the fact that the Cathedral is burning. The fantasy of piling women and blazing church becomes increasingly phantasmagoric until 'only a hard banging remains.'

> Lumb
> Lies unconscious on the carpet, face crawling with sweat
> In front of the burned-out fire.

> Maud
> Striped with the dove's blood, which has now dried,
> Lies face upwards on the bare boards
> Of the room beneath, still gripping
> The blood-rag of the bird.

> Her eyes flicker open.

> She listens
> To the banging on the door downstairs.   (p. 123)

The ironic contrast between Lumb's fantasy of pentecostal transfiguration and the reality of Maud's gruesome rites is enough to justify the use of the word 'fantasy' to distinguish this dream from Lumb's other visionary experiences.

The banging is not, this time, the breadman but Felicity, wanting an explanation for the photograph. 'She begs him to tell her it was faked./He tells her it was faked', and she believes him. 'She wants to leave now, this moment' and urges him to cancel the meeting. His response is to start undressing her but 'She wants him to save it/Till they have escaped right away from all this and from everybody.' When he says that he cannot cancel the meeting she insists on going to it 'So she can be completely sure/That the rumour about those meetings is a lie', and it is at this point that Lumb

> Gazes blankly toward a reassessment
> Impossibly beyond him. Two worlds,
> Like two strange dogs circling each other.   (p. 125)

Maud enters the room and Lumb asks her to 'prepare' and 'instruct' Felicity for the meeting. Felicity overcomes a sudden terror and goes with Maud.

It is in this episode most of all that Hughes's failure to realize Felicity and Lumb's relationship with her is damaging. The words that describe Lumb's reaction to her entrance—'He is cleansed and renewed'—have a glibness that makes one suspect irony without being confident of its presence, still less of its point. This is followed by, 'His arms close round her, as if joyfully'. *As if* joyfully? Is he not really 'cleansed and renewed' then? What is the relation between what he appears to be feeling and what he is feeling? Lumb's feelings about Felicity (as distinct from his feelings about his dilemma) are given no more articulation than this, and the extent of Felicity's individuation is the conventional naïvety of 'She wants him to save it ...' The important lines about the 'reassessment', which seem close to the heart of Lumb's situation and therefore of the poem, have little purchase as a consequence. Their most immediate reference is to the world of 'an ordinary man and his ordinary wife' and that implied by the W.I. meeting. We have just explained our problem with the former; about the nature of the latter we have had only lurid hints so far, and even when we have read to the end of the poem its relation to Lumb's shamanic experience (in which it presumably originates) remains problematical. We remarked earlier that we were reminded of 'Two worlds,/Like two strange dogs' by Hughes's account in 'Myth and Education' of the interdependence and conflict between the 'outer' and 'inner' worlds. The representation of Lumb's inner world being one of the poem's triumphs, it is very tempting to make this link, but a leap to that level of generality from the lines' vague and unsatisfactory immediate context would violate any sensitive reading of the poem and put an enormous strain on one of its weakest elements. If Hughes intended such a meaning, the intention is unrealized.

All we can confidently say about this episode is that Lumb, by his dishonesty, his attempt to use sex as an escape from an awkward situation, and his handing Felicity over to Maud, abandons even ordinary human responsibility. Still less does he seem capable of meeting the difficult and dangerous social responsibilities of a shaman. Our sense that he has lost control is confirmed.

Soon we are taken to the church basement where women are assembling for the W.I. meeting. A comic note is immediately struck with the 'dainty triangular sandwiches' into three of which Mrs Davies slips a slice of fly agaric. Music is playing, 'archaic music of pipes and drums,/An inane cycle of music, hoarse and metallic'.

The eyes of the women are 'glazed like young cattle./They are waiting for the first shiver of power', but 'Something is obstructing it.' The atmosphere is anxious and apprehensive.

Maud, wearing black lace, black shawl and a white bridal dress, has doped Felicity who perceives that Maud is crazy but follows her will-lessly. We catch a glimpse of Lumb rummaging through his 'magical apparatus'—he cannot find his dagger, 'his weapon of weapons'. Again the occult properties, again the portentous tone that might just be humorous. This time the portentousness is reinforced by an explicit manifestation of 'power': Lumb knows by listening that the dagger is not in his room. Maud delivers Felicity at the church basement, 'pausing impressively/Like a slightly tipsy actress', and slips out to steal Lumb's car-keys from his car and drop them in a 'freshly-dug not yet occupied grave'.

The description of the ritual itself begins with a powerful evocation of the music and the women's response to it:

Lumb
Is walking in a circle. The room is a maze of smoke
From smouldering piles of herbs in ashtrays.
He is holding something up, it is a stag's antlered head on a pole,
Heavy and swaying and shag-maned.
The pipe and drum music is a tight, shuddering, repetitive
machine
Which seems bolted into the ground
And as if they were all its mechanical parts, the women are
fastened into it,
As if the smoke were the noise of it,
The noise of it raucous with the smoke and the smoke stirred by
it.
A hobbling, nodding, four-square music, a goblin monotony,
The women in a circle clapping to the tread of it.
Their hair dangles loose, their eyes slide oiled, their faces oiled
with sweat
In the trundling treadmill of it.
It is like the music of a slogging, deadening, repetitive labour.
They have left their faces hanging on the outside of the music as
abandoned masks.
They no longer feel their bodies.
They have been taken deep into the perpetual motion of the
music
And have become the music.   (p. 139)

179

This is a point at which the reader is likely to be especially alert to tone, and to signs of an attitude to what is being described. The closely mimetic rhythm, on which the success of the passage as a piece of evocative writing rests, does not permit any distance, and the suggestions of the language are ambiguous: there is a kind of transcendence in the women's experience (in the last three lines) but the music that they have 'become' is 'slogging, deadening, repetitive'.

Felicity's mind has been blown by the magic mushroom ('In the lottery of the mushroom sandwich/Everything was arranged for her'):

What she has eaten and drunk
Is flying her through great lights and dropping her from gulf to
                                                                    gulf.
Wings lift through her and go off.
A tiger
Is trying to adjust its maniac flame-barred strength to her body.
And it seems natural
That she should be gazing at the surprisingly handsome breasts
The surprisingly young body of Mrs Davies,
And the luminous face which is now revealed to her as an infinite
                                                                    sexual flower.
She can see Mrs Davies is infinitely beautiful
And Mrs Garten is a serpentiné infinite wreath of flowing light.
                                                                    (p. 140)

This is the experience described by Carlos Castaneda's Mexican shaman as 'seeing'. Here is Castaneda's account of one such experience:

> When I stood up and turned around I definitely saw don Juan; 'the don Juan I know' definitely walked towards me and held me. But when I focused my eyes on his face I did not see don Juan as I am accustomed to seeing him; instead, I saw a large object in front of my eyes.... What I was looking at was a round object which had a luminosity of its own. Every part of it moved. I perceived a contained, undulatory, rhythmical flow; it was as if the flowing was enclosed within itself, never moving beyond its limits, and yet the object in front of my eyes was oozing with movement at any place on its surface. The thought that occurred to me was that it oozed life.
> (*A Separate Reality*, p. 164)

180

We should not quote this, however, without also quoting don Juan's reaction to Castaneda's account of his experience: 'You saw a glow, big deal' (p. 166). This succinctly gives our own reaction to Felicity's experience: still more so, since Castaneda's careful and restrained narration contrasts favourably with the facile injection of significance given by the repeated 'infinite'. The important contrast, however, is with the earlier experience of Dunworth, who discovering his wife naked with Lumb tries to find in her 'all the ordinariness/That once bored him so much,/But he feels only a glowing mass'. The difference is not just that Dunworth's experience isn't drug-induced but that it is significant: the 'merciless' shock of the experience releases something that has presumably been at the bottom of his life as long as he has been married and which the critical everyday eye has obscured. The recovery of this most precious thing in such horrible circumstances is, understandably, a cause of 'Endless sweetness and endless anguish'. Felicity's vision by contrast is automatically switched on and leads nowhere.

The ritual continues to be presented through its effect on Felicity:

Lumb is suddenly standing in front of her looking at her.
He is holding something shaggy and terrible above her.
Felicity understands that she is a small anonymous creature which
is now going to be killed.
She starts to cry, feeling the greatness and nobility of her role.
She starts to sing, adoring whatever the terrible lifted thing in
front of her is,
Which needs all she can give, she knows it needs her.
She knows it is the love animal.
The clapping hammers her head, her body has given up trying to
move.

Now she becomes aware that Lumb is holding some slender thing
towards her.
He touches her navel with it, it seems to her to be a foxglove.
Fleetingly she cannot understand how she came to be naked.
But it is too late to do anything about anything.
She is already drowning in the deep mightiness of what is about
to happen to her.
She knows she herself is to be the sacramental thing.
She herself is already holy
And drifting at a great depth, a great remoteness, like a spark in
space.

181

She is numbed with the seriousness of it, she feels she is vast,
Enlarging into space from a withering smoulder of petty
voices. . . .

Somehow she has become a goddess.
She is now the sacred doll of a slow infinite solemnity.
She knows she is a constellation very far off and cold
Moving through this burrow of smoke and faces.
She moves robed invisibly with gorgeous richness.
She knows she is burning plasma and infinitely tiny,
That she and all these women are moving inside the body of an
incandescent creature of love,
That they are brightening, and that the crisis is close,
They are the cells in the glands of an inconceivably huge and
urgent love-animal
And some final crisis of earth's life is now to be enacted
Faithfully and selflessly by them all.

(pp. 141–2)

Felicity's passivity, her readiness to adore 'whatever the terrible
lifted thing in front of her is', is that of an exploited innocent. The
conventional religious language—'greatness and nobility', 'deep
mightiness', 'sacramental', 'holy', 'seriousness', 'infinite solemnity',
'faithfully and selflessly', as well as the earlier repetition of
'infinite'—produces an effect of religiosity, of corrupt acquiescence
in a vague and bogus atmosphere of profundity and solemnity:
'*some* final crisis of earth's life'. The lowering of social and rational
defences reveals, not only in Felicity but in all the women, a
stultified paralysis of the inner life.

As the ritual reaches its climax the horror is acted out. Everyone
is now wearing animal skins and masks, and Felicity 'understands
that she has become a hind' (p. 145). Maud grips her neck between
her thighs, and Lumb, wearing antlers and stag's pelt, 'mounts
Felicity from behind, like a stag' (p. 146). All the women participate
in the orgasm and immediately after it Maud stabs Felicity in the
neck with Lumb's dagger (his 'weapon of weapons'). She then
explains herself.

She is announcing
That this girl is not one of them
That she is his selected wife

182

That he is going to abandon them and run away with this girl
Like an ordinary man
With his ordinary wife.

The fuddled women grope for what has happened
And for what is being said
But their brains are still in the music
And nothing will separate.
They receive Maud's words as the revelation of everything.

(p. 147)

Lumb, in one of the poem's most poignant moments, is reduced to a passive, helpless tenderness:

> With all his gentleness
> He pulls on the hilt of the dagger,
> As if gentleness intense enough
> Could force a miracle
> And unmake the black-mouthed slot
> From which the frightening taper of steel
> Continues to glide
> Like a snake's endless length gliding from a hole.

(p. 148)

The women attack him, Maud 'flogging him over his bald skull with the cable-hard, twisted, horny stag's pizzle'. Lumb escapes and, back in his room, reveals the bankruptcy of his mission with the wish that everyone might be put 'back into their clothes and their discretion' (p. 150).

What meaning can we attach to this horrible débâcle? In 'Myth and Education', speaking of access to the 'inner world', Hughes writes:

> Drugs cannot take us there. If we cite the lofty religions in which drugs did take the initiates to where they needed to go, we ought to remember that here again the mythology was crucial. The journey was undertaken as part of an elaborately mythologized ritual. It was the mythology which consolidated the inner world, gave human form to its experiences, and connected them to daily life. Without that preparation a drug carries its user to a prison in the inner world as passive and

183

isolated and meaningless as the camera's eye from which he escaped.
(*Times Educational Supplement*, 2 September 1977, p. 13)

There is a ritual of sorts going on, but can it be said to give 'human form' to the experiences of its participants and 'connect them to daily life'? If the ritual has a meaning it is not articulated in the poem and not understood by Felicity—clearly her 'preparation' at the hands of Maud has not been of the kind Hughes is referring to here. As for the other women, doesn't their reaction to Maud's speech perfectly exemplify the 'passive and isolated and meaningless' imprisoned condition of the unprepared drug-user? Furthermore, doesn't the response of most of them to sex with Lumb show the same condition? The most remarkable characteristic of the various mystical works and traditions in which Hughes has shown an interest—Sufism, the Bardo Thodol, Castaneda's books—is the degree of discipline to which their participants subject themselves. Compared to these lamas, sufis, sorcerers and shamans Lumb is an amateurish bungler.

Again, we may speculate that the lack of a tradition, the lapse in the continuity of 'religious' consciousness, debars Lumb from effectively practising the public and social function of the mystagogue: with a few distorted Christian and pagan fragments he can disrupt but not enlighten the lives of his parishioners. 'Myth and Education' certainly exonerates Hughes of irresponsible devil-worship, but is this sufficiently evident without such external help? Is there any excuse for the complete failure to understand the poem of, for example, Martin Dodsworth: 'Hughes can't and won't think.... Gaudete, simply, is a fantasy that has enslaved its creator' (*Guardian*, 19 May 1977)?

The language of the ritual episode is one reason for this problem. Hughes has found a corrupt language to convey a corrupt experience, and mixed in with it lines that have his own unique summoning power ('A tiger/Is trying to adjust its maniac flame-barred strength to her body'). Terry Eagleton, in his review in *Stand* (vol. 19, no. 2), complains that 'one never has the feeling . . . that Hughes's language self-reflectively takes the measure of its own limits and capabilities.... Hughes's language . . . is insufficiently *inflected* and *articulated*.... Hughes's language fails to assume any *attitude* to what it speaks of' (pp. 78–9). The examples he quotes, this episode and Maud's crystal-gazing, are precisely those in which we ourselves are troubled by an ambiguity of perspective. Eagleton's complaint clearly indicates a radical hostility to Hughes's art, a demand that the poet submit the language of his imagination to the judgement of the rational intellect. It remains true that Hughes is making unusual demands on the reader: it is we who are required to make the judgement, which is rational in that it involves distinguishing between creative and parodistic language, but which if excessively rational will fail to see that anything significant is happening at all. Our own response is that a genuine power is unleashed, which the women are utterly unprepared to cope with. Such a response involves, as nowhere else in Hughes, speculating about the poet's *intention* (the 'intentional fallacy' cannot be a fallacy where parodistic language is concerned); it involves trusting not only the poet's creative powers but also his critical judgement—we have to reflect that, while Hughes can write badly, he nowhere writes badly in just *this* way. Such judgements are extremely delicate and difficult. In this particular case it is made more difficult by Hughes's stereotyped rendering of these people's normal lives, and the problems concerning Maud and the use of conventional occult properties. We have no secure grasp of a whole within which this episode, powerful though it is, can be seen to have a general significance.

It is not true that Hughes's language *never* assumes an attitude to what it speaks of, as we shall see in turning to the revenge of the men that has been accumulating during the preparations for the ritual. As Garten goes the rounds with his photograph Hughes takes the opportunity to observe the husbands at a further stage in their crises. Most of these episodes are strikingly better written than those which we have just been examining (see, for example, pp. 126–7). The men gather in the bar at the Bridge Inn, where Hughes gives us the chaos of individual violent feelings welded by drink into a murderous whole.

Nobody quite knows what to do.
They continue to drink more forcefully in search of definition and
                                                                    action.
They all know what they want to happen
And they drink to make it more likely
So that the criss-cross push and pull of voices works steadily in
                                                              one direction.
                                                                  (p. 137)

185

'Definition and action' are beyond them, just as 'control and decision' were beyond Lumb on the first page of the Prologue and 'control' something that Westlake could only 'deliberate' in his crisis. Dunworth tries to introduce 'a fuddled reasonable attitude'; earlier he and Westlake are seen 'trying to imagine logicality' (p. 130). In Estridge 'the recurrent idea to kill Lumb keeps foundering in the proliferating concerns for what ought rightly to be done, in a civic and rational manner' (p. 128). In each case the familiar means of control are out of reach or subject to interference, they have become like a dim memory or an inexplicably lost skill. The likely reason for this is that those means of control are inappropriate to the crisis that each man faces in his inner life. They have no other, more appropriate resources and, anyway, Garten's camera has translated each man's private, inner experience into the outer, public, 'civic' sphere: hence a 'squabble of unlistened-to voices/Trying to become a meeting' (p. 137). We have no way of knowing how the men would have fared in their individual crises without Garten's interference; there is no indication of what those more appropriate resources might be, though Dunworth's vision of his wife suggests what the foundation might be. Now they are committed to public action, to 'decision' and 'definition'; but this is impossible. Hence the drinking.

Action is precipitated by the arrival in the pub of Commander Estridge.

> He does not know what he will do now. He knows that anything will have to be forgiven him.
> He enters the Bridge Inn for the first time in his life, remembering, as he pushes the door, the wren in Macbeth.
>
> (p. 143)

The wren was cited by Lady Macduff in her complaint against her husband's desertion:

> He loves us not:
> He wants the natural touch; for the poor wren,
> The most diminutive of birds, will fight,
> Her young ones in her nest, against the owl.
>
> (*Macbeth*, IV. ii. 8–11)

It is Estridge's 'young ones', of course, that he is concerned about. One is already dead, the other rendered strangely both demonic and imbecilic by her dealings with Lumb. There is, then, some justification for his seeing Lumb as a predator, though there is a sinister self-pity in his identification with the wren when it means that 'anything will have to be forgiven him.' We are given an immediate ironic reminder of Estridge's 'bulbous hawk's eye'.

His arrival 'Is like permission', and the men march 'in a tight group up the middle of the evening street'.

> They are solemn, possessed by the common recklessness, not speaking above the odd murmur. Overawed by their own war-path seriousness. In the armour of alcohol, they feel safe. And new satisfactions open. The single idea of revenge shuffles its possible forms. Now Lumb will somehow pay for everything. Their decision has released them. It has outlawed him. Sentenced him. All they have to do is carry out the sentence.
>
> (p. 143)

The way in which the men o'erleap decision is one of the most brilliantly perceptive touches in the poem. For no decision, of course, has been taken. But they need to believe they have decided in order to act, for they cannot act without disguising the anarchic, criminal nature of what they are going to do. The exceptional event of Estridge's first appearance in the pub—the appearance of the man whose daughter has died—is an emotional catalyst that serves in place of decision. The illusion of a decision absolves the men from responsibility. The 'decision' *was* their act of responsibility, but now it is in the past and they can relax into being the instruments of their decision.

This is psychologically convincing and, like the ritual, horrible. But there is no doubting, in this case, that the reaction is intended. Here the language does assume 'an attitude to what it speaks of', though not exactly by means of inflexion and articulation. What is the difference in the language of the two episodes? The short, clipped sentences and non-sentences recognizably imitate the tight-lipped spirit of a group of men bent on some grim enterprise. But no more than the loose verse and vague religious language of the earlier episode imitates a stoned passivity and credulity.

A comparison of two brief phrases will, we hope, make our point.

> She is numbed with the seriousness of it   (p. 141)

> Overawed by their own war-path seriousness   (p. 143)

187

The first phrase (or rather sentence) is a simple statement. What is stated may be thought deplorable but the statement does not in any way embody the thought. We can imagine Felicity herself, had she survived the experience, saying without any irony, 'I was numbed with the seriousness of it.' On the other hand if a man spoke of having been 'overawed by my own war-path seriousness' we should strongly suspect that his valuation of the experience had changed. There is, if not a contradiction, at least a tension between 'over-awed' and the reflexive 'own', that suggests something worked-up and self-indulgent. More overtly, the use of the word 'war-path' in any but the most literal, anthropological sense is bound to be funny, especially (considering its associations of ritually-controlled frenzy) in this context.

In this condition of irresponsible release the men march to the church, discover the aftermath of the ritual and follow Lumb to his room. He is unable to escape in his car because of Maud's trick with the keys, and a cross-country chase on foot ensues, which alone would be enough to redeem the poet's faults. The landscape, whose presence has given the poem so much of its life, comes into its own here. What is described is a man running, wounded, becoming exhausted, getting his second wind, becoming exhausted again and finally shot dead in the lake, but it is described in terms of Lumb's changing relationship with the landscape, the most moving and dramatic relationship in the poem. The passage is full of ways of using the imagination, controlling mental processes, to conserve and acquire sources of physical energy; within limits, Lumb's bodily resources can be controlled by techniques of consciousness, but beyond those limits the laws of physical nature take over.

He starts out 'Easy and strong', but by the bottom of p. 155 his knees 'tangle with their chemical limits', 'The miles of otherworld rootedness weigh in against him.' The landscape becomes bleak, prisonlike, inescapable. Reminding us again of his origin he embraces a tree—'With fixed imagination he sinks nerves into the current of the powerline'—but he only 'feels his separateness'. Twice he manages to rest, consciously summoning energy and will, 'the inrush of renewals and instructions'. The second time he is discovered by Evans who spears him with a pitchfork, but he is still able to run and the ensuing passage exemplifies the essential drama of the whole chase.

He runs with freed limbs.
He bounds down the new-grassed slope toward the long flat of
                                                    the lake,
Gold-hot and molten, under the late sky.
And toward the skyline beyond, and the tree-lumped frieze which
                                                is the highway.

He runs imagining
Mountains of golden spirit, he springs across their crests.
He has plugged his energy appeal into the inexhaustible earth.
He rides in the air behind his shoulders with a whip of hard will
Like a charioteer.
He imagines he is effortless Adam, before weariness entered,
                                            leaping for God.

He safeguards the stroke of his heart
From the wrenching of ideas.
He hoards his wasteful mind like a last mouthful.

He runs
In a balancing stillness
Like a working gleam on the nape of a waterfall,
And he is exulting
That the powers have come back they truly have come back
They have not abandoned him.

At the same time
He runs badly hurt, his blood inadequate,
Hurling his limbs anyhow
Lumpen and leaden, and there is no more air. . . .

And he knows
He has lost every last help
Of the grass and the trees,
He knows that the sky no longer ushers towards him glowing
                                    hieroglyphs of endowment,
That he is now ordinary, and susceptible
To extinction.

                                            (pp. 163–4)

The passage is one of the best examples of the style of *Gaudete*, its
relaxed freedom, and rhythmical and metaphorical vitality.
Hughes's mastery of the long line is again apparent in 'He imagines
he is effortless Adam, before weariness entered, leaping for God.'

189

The line enacts, with the light anapaestic rhythm of its opening, the juxtaposed drawn-out syllables of the middle, and the mimetic stress-pattern of the final phrase, the alternation of energy and weariness that it describes. Containing this variation of effect within (in Blake's phrase) one 'wiry bounding line', Hughes achieves a Blake-like vivid innocence, and an inspiring reinterpretation of the myth of Paradise. In the 'working gleam on the nape of a waterfall' he finds a metaphor for Lumb's experience that, though superbly visualized, is only marginally visual in its significance and remarkably comprehensive: brightness, bodilessness, stillness-in-movement, above all being the manifestation of 'powers' not oneself.

Here we have perhaps a hint of the 'shamanistic affinity with nature' which is, according to Campbell, 'of a deeper, more occult *God: Primitive Mythology*, p. 250). To an impressive though limited degree (and the more convincingly for the limitation) Lumb, alone and facing death, displays the 'powers' that are notably absent from his dealings with the community. We have just a glimpse of that imagination which, Hughes says quoting Goethe, 'keeps faith with the world of things and the world of spirits equally' (*Times Educational Supplement*, 2 September 1977, p. 13).

In the end the exhausted Lumb is left seeing the world as 'A spiritless by-product/Of the fact that things exist at all'. 'He knows at last' why the land has become 'an ignorance, waiting in a darkness'. He also 'understands quite clearly at last'

> Why he has been abandoned to these crying beings
> Who are all hurrying towards him
> In order to convert him to mud from which plants grow and
> > which cattle tread.
> > (p. 165)

Is this the grim and paradoxical final triumph of imagination, or its failure? Does what Lumb 'understands' and 'knows' have to do with the events of the whole narrative, or just with the fact that he is about to die, and that when converted to mud he will have nothing to do with 'spirits'? These questions, which reach deep into the heart of the poem, we have no answer to.

Finally Lumb is shot in the lake by Hagen, who once again leaps into vivid and perverse life as he aims his rifle:

Germanic precision, slender goddess
Of Hagen's devotions
And the unfailing bride
Of his ecstasies in the primal paradise, and the midwife of Eden's
          beasts,
Painlessly delivered, with a little blood,
And laid at his feet
As if fresh from the Creator's furnace, as if to be named.
With her, only with her
Hagen feels his life stir on its root.   (p. 167)

As Lumb is dragged from the lake we are briefly reminded of the imagery of his visions: 'The blood from his burst head washes his face and neck/In thin solution and ropy lumps,/And puddles black the hoofprints under his head.' His body is carried to the church. Maud stabs herself and the three corpses are immolated with the church itself. 'All evidence goes up.'

In the Epilogue a man who the Argument informs us is the original Lumb turns up in Ireland and summons an otter out of a lough, telling three little girls that this is a miracle. He drives off, leaving a book full of 'densely corrected' poems. The girls take the book to a priest and tell him about the 'miracle'. 'If that is a miracle,' the priest replies, 'then what must that poor man think of the great world itself, this giant, shining beauty that God whistled up out of the waters of chaos?' He is 'suddenly carried away by his words' and delivers a rhetorical speech describing 'the first coming of Creation ... an infinite creature of miracles, made of miracles and teeming miracles'. The girls become dull and disappear but the priest 'thought something supernatural had happened'.

It is unlikely that we are meant to take the priest's rhetoric seriously. Lumb's 'miracle' has been a modest but beautiful display of human 'power', an exceptional 'affinity with nature'. The priest's reaction , beginning with an orthodox depreciation of human power and natural affinity, is merely words: his use of 'miracle' to describe the creation itself is meaningless, since there is no non-miraculous against which to define it. He talks himself into the belief that his own emotion is supernatural. His account of creation is also, of course, at odds with the evidence of the narrative, in which the world is both 'Heavens opening higher beyond heavens' and 'A spiritless by-product/Of the fact that things exist at all'.

The Lumb we see here seems intended as a suggestion of what the harmonious exercise of the powers gained through entry into the 'inner world' might be like. He is a kind of Orpheus, who seems to have reconciled the inner and outer worlds. But he operates on such a modest scale, and he is such a fanciful figure, so much less intensely imagined than the Lumb of the narrative, that he can't be said to weigh in any balance.

The question of how the Epilogue—both the prose introduction and the poems—relates to the narrative is crucial to the coherence of *Gaudete*. Keith Sagar believes that the positive achievement represented by the Lumb of the Epilogue does balance and even outweigh the calamity of the narrative. His view entails giving a great deal of weight to the summoning of the otter, and interpreting, against the evidence of the language and the girls' reaction, the priest's emotion as a genuine spiritual revelation. It also entails a very high valuation of the poems—he regards them collectively as 'forty-five of the finest poems Hughes has yet written' (*The Art of Ted Hughes*, 2nd edition, p. 209).

We do not believe they are as good as this, and we think that to place such emphasis on these poems misrepresents Hughes's achievement. They are the closest Hughes has come to being literally a devotional poet. They uniformly have a solemn preoccupied intensity, like the words of a man possessed, and most of them are addressed to the Goddess who, in the 'spirit world', was eventually reborn through Lumb. An obvious starting-point, therefore, and measure of the achievement, is 'Crow's Undersong', and one of the poems in particular invites the direct comparison.

I know well
You are not infallible

I know how your huge your unmanageable
Mass of bronze hair shrank to a twist

As thin as a silk scarf, on your skull,
And how your pony's eye darkened larger

Holding too lucidly the deep glimpse
After the humane killer

And I had to lift your hand for you

192

While your chin sank to your chest
With the sheer weariness
Of taking away from everybody
Your envied beauty, your much-desired beauty

Your hardly-used beauty

Of lifting away yourself
From yourself

And weeping with the ache of the effort   (pp. 190–1)

This is one of the best of the poems. It has a beautifully sustained and expressive rhythm, and the images of the hair and the pony's eye create a tenderness very like that of 'Crow's Undersong'.

She comes dumb she cannot manage words
She brings petals in their nectar fruits in their plush
She brings a cloak of feathers an animal rainbow
She brings her favourite furs and these are her speeches

The achievement of the earlier poem, however, is to sustain its imaginative embodiment throughout, not lapsing into abstraction, which is, surely, just what this poem *does* lapse into with the lines 'lifting away yourself/From yourself'.

Mr Sagar, in rightly praising the marvellous poem 'Waving good-bye', refers to 'Hughes's ability to ground his larger themes, which could so easily become abstract, cold or contrived, in very moving common experience in the contemporary world' (*The Art of Ted Hughes*, 2nd edition, p. 217). 'Waving goodbye' is indeed a triumph of particularity and naturalness, but the drift into abstraction, of which the end of 'I know well' is a mild example, is precisely the problem we have with most of these poems. Only rarely is a whole poem abstract—

Every day the world gets simply
Bigger and bigger

And smaller and smaller

Every day the world gets more
And more beautiful

193

And uglier and uglier.

Your comings get closer.
Your goings get worse.　　　　(pp. 198–9)

More typical is this one:

Calves harshly parted from their mamas
Stumble through all the hedges in the country
Hither thither crying day and night
Till their throats will only grunt and whistle.

After some days, a stupor sadness
Collects them again in their field.
They will never stray any more.
From now on, they only want each other.

So much for calves.
As for the tiger
He lies still
Like left luggage

He is roaming the earth light, unseen.

He is safe.

Heaven and hell have both adopted him.　　　　(p. 197)

The first eight lines are superb: they have the same unsentimental pathos and tenderness as the 'Moortown' poems. The tiger, in whose favour the calves are dismissed from our attention, has nothing like the same presence. Hughes seems to have been drawn, as by a fatal whirlpool, to Blake, whose dialectic becomes a bald yoking of opposites. Other poems lapse into self-parody:

Music, that eats people
That transfixes them
On its thorns, like a shrike
To cut up at leisure ...

Is the maneater
On your leash.　　　　(p. 182)

194

The sea grieves all night long.
The wall is past groaning.
The field has given up—
It can't care any more.

Even the tree
Waits like an old man
Who has seen his whole family murdered.

Horrible world

Where I let in again—
As if for the first time—
The untouched joy.   (p. 194)

Many of the poems derive their images from episodes and
metaphors in the Prologue and narrative. Thus the tiger is like a
parody of its genuinely imaginative evocation in the ritual (p. 141),
'Music that eats people', of the effect of the Beethoven sonata in the
Estridge episode (pp. 41–4). But such variations do not always
suffer in comparison with the original statement of the theme, as the
following superb poem shows.

Your tree—your oak
A glare

Of black upward lightning, a wriggling grab
Momentary
Under the crumbling of stars.

A guard, a dancer
At the pure well of leaf.

Agony in the garden. Annunciation
Of clay, water and the sunlight.
They thunder under its roof.
Its agony is its temple.

Waist-deep, the black oak is dancing
And my eyes pause
On the centuries of its instant
As gnats
Try to winter in its wrinkles.

The seas are thirsting
Towards the oak.

The oak is flying
Astride the earth.   (p. 199)

If we are reminded of Yeats's 'great-rooted blossomer' we must also
notice (in line 3 for example) Hughes's utterly distinctive vivid
colloquial diction, the specificity of observation that keeps the tele-
scoping of time from being too abstract, the way (in 'my eyes pause')
the observer is drawn into the oak's temporal dimensions. The final
couplet is like an involuntary cry, releasing the sense of wonder that
has been built up in the poem's imaginative intensity.

This poem, and 'Waving goodbye', are indeed among the best
Hughes has written, and the sequence as a whole is absorbing, but
the achievement is put in perspective if we imagine the effect of
finding, among them, 'Crow's Undersong', 'After there was nothing
there was a woman' (from *Cave Birds*), 'The stone' (from *Moortown*) or even some of the more adult *Season Songs* (which 'Your
tree—your oak' somewhat resembles). Those are the poems in
which Hughes, more than in the *Gaudete* Epilogue (with the excep-
tions noted), grounds his larger themes in common experience,
without a hint of abstraction, coldness or contrivance.

We have said enough to indicate our belief that *Gaudete* has many
magnificent qualities, some of them new in kind or degree to
Hughes's work: the limited but uniquely vivid psychological observation, the explicit and convincing dealings with the 'inner world',
the relaxed but continually startling style. It would be ungrateful
and ungenerous to call the poem a failure. But Hughes is rightly
preoccupied with the imaginative power and coherence of the story
as such, and the most generous reading cannot evade the judgement
that certain crucial weaknesses obscure the meaning of the narrative
itself. A brief comparison will clarify our point.

In 1977 the BBC broadcast a play by Peter Redgrove, *The God of
Glass* (published as a novel in 1979 by Routledge), in which an
outbreak of demonic 'possession' among teenage girls is controlled
by an African, Geoffrey Glass, whose method entails the invocation
of the suppressed and half-forgotten witch-culture. Glass has served
a long prison sentence for flaying a man alive, most of which he
spent sitting at a table in his cell, repeating the words, 'Mr Glass sat

at a table'. His shamanic power to 'reflect' the energies of women releases new creative forces into the male-dominated (and masculine-spirit-dominated) society. Redgrove's play is violent and disturbing, but it is a harmonious and coherent, if excessively didactic, fable. It is significant that the function of his male shaman is to 'reflect', bring to consciousness and recognition a knowledge and energy latent in women, whereas Lumb is the aggressive masculine conveyer of energy to a group of women who have little magic of their own.[6] A similar comparison can be made with *The Bacchae*, whose relationship to *Gaudete* we have outlined at the beginning of this chapter.

We are not demanding a neat interpretative formula for *Gaudete*. It seems to us to be concerned with the necessity of establishing communications with the 'inner world' and creating some public, social embodiment of them, in a secularized world to which 'myth' has become synonymous with 'falsehood'. It must therefore be profoundly connected not only with the concerns of Hughes's other poetry but with his private and public identity as a poet. The reconciliation of the inner and outer worlds, and of the shamanic function with a fully, ordinarily human life, are essential parts of this preoccupation.

'A child takes possession of a story as what might be called a unit of imagination', Hughes says in 'Myth and Education' (*Times Educational Supplement*, 2 September 1977, p. 11). We think that Hughes, who has created some wonderful 'units of imagination' for children, and many of whose best short poems for adults have a strong narrative quality, has not in *Gaudete* succeeded in his evident aspiration to create a large-scale 'unit of imagination'. Certain vital parts of the imaginative organism are fatally undeveloped. If, as we believe, the poem requires us to understand something of our society's exile from the inner life, its presentation of a social world, and of the lives of its people beyond intensely observed moments, is grossly reliant on caricature and the stereotypes of an outdated popular fiction. The drama of Lumb's crisis is considerably weakened by the insipidity and vagueness of his relationship with Felicity. Everything to do with Maud and Lumb's disastrous attempt at a public religion is tainted with a portentousness which, since it is not on any account possible to take it seriously, threatens to diminish the poem's genuine dealings with the 'inner world'.

It is a remarkable testimony to Hughes's genius (not, as Martin

197

Dodsworth thinks, just 'careless strokes of genius', but sustained and disciplined imaginative work) that despite all this the poem's healthy organs take a stronger hold on the imagination with each reading. Hughes's narrative skill, and the range and depth of imaginative exploration, promise that the ambition represented by *Gaudete* (and implied in all his work since *Wodwo*) to write a long, connected work is not in itself misguided.

7

Cave Birds

Cave Birds is, we believe, Hughes's finest book to date. It is certainly his most consistent—only a few of the twenty-eight poems are open to radical criticism—and several poems, certainly 'The executioner', 'The knight', 'Bride and groom' and 'The risen', are among Hughes's greatest achievements. The terror that is essential to its subject, the hero's transformation, is never far removed from a sense of splendour, and a promised or actual joy. Hughes permits himself a much greater richness and sensuousness of language than in *Crow*, yet the poems are more disciplined than many in the earlier sequence. The 'living, suffering spirit, capable of happiness' (Introduction to Vasko Popa's *Selected Poems*) emerges from the reductive questioning of *Crow* as a subject of celebration, and the metaphysical discovery hinted at in *Crow*'s final poems, such as 'How Water Began to Play'—the discovery of the universal in the self—is the basis of *Cave Birds*. The authenticity of this celebration is the fruit of the rigours of Hughes's earlier 'adventure'.

Cave Birds was first presented to the public in a 'performance' at the Ilkley Literature Festival in May 1975, shortly followed by a broadcast on BBC Radio 3. Ten of the poems, with accompanying drawings by Leonard Baskin, were published in an expensive limited edition at the same time, and most of the other poems appeared in various magazines, often with revisions, between 1974 and 1976. The text published by Faber in October 1978 contains two fewer poems than the broadcast version, and also lacks the brief narrative links that Hughes provided for the broadcast. With one exception, each poem is accompanied by a Leonard Baskin drawing. As we shall be demonstrating shortly, this form of publication

199

enables a wide audience to understand the true character of the poems for the first time, in a way not possible in the broadcast or magazine publications.

The Faber edition also informs the reader that *Cave Birds* is an 'Alchemical Cave Drama'. Each one of these words is likely to be puzzling to many readers. We are not deeply read in alchemy but it seems safe to say that Hughes's use of the word refers to the aspect of alchemy explored by C. G. Jung in his numerous writings on the subject: the mystical transformation, or rebirth, that occurred within the alchemist in the course of the outward operation. This idea of transformation is the most important link, though there are also more detailed correspondences with alchemical writings, such as the symbolic flaying ('A flayed crow in the hall of judgement') and dismemberment ('The accused') and, most prominently, the symbolic marriage of body and soul.

The word 'cave' is also likely to puzzle readers as it does not occur anywhere in the text. To us it suggests both the inwardness of the drama, its location in the 'cave' of the protagonist's being, and the mysterious, frightening character of caves—the likelihood, perhaps, of encountering in them just such awesome mutations as we see in Baskin's drawings.

Thirdly, in what sense is a sequence of poems, however much written in character, a 'drama'? It is perhaps helpful to remember that most of Hughes's plays have been written for radio, and that in his two published adult plays, 'The Wound' and 'Eat Crow', the suitability of this medium is evident, since almost the entire action takes place within the protagonists. *Cave Birds* is a drama of inner voices, not of action but of reaction, taking place as much between individual poems as within them. It might usefully be seen as the development of a form to accommodate the 'drama of consciousness' that we detected (Chapter 3) in Hughes's early poetry.

Although at Ilkley the drawings were projected on to a screen during the performance, what is most difficult to reconcile with the dramatic character of the work is the vital relationship between poems and drawings. Most of the drawings were done before the poems, and the poems originated as responses to the drawings. Dates are written on many of the drawings, and these help the reader to distinguish the early ones which inspired their accompanying poems from those which were done later as illustrations. These later drawings, we think, are inferior (the illustration to one of the finest poems, 'Bride and groom', is particularly disappointing) but the earlier ones, such as 'The summoner', 'The interrogator', 'The plaintiff', 'The gatekeeper' and 'The owl flower', provoke directly in the reader the awe and terror that are expressed in Hughes's poems. In some cases the poems cannot be understood without the drawings. Unless one recognizes Baskin's interrogator as a vulture, for example, it is impossible to understand the sustained metaphor of the poem. In the most extreme case, 'The owl flower', the poem has to be seen, in the first place, as a poem *about* the drawing.

Big terror descends.

A drumming glare, a flickering face of flames.

Something separates into a signal,
Plaintive, a filament of incandescence,

As it were a hair.

In the maelstrom's eye,
In the core of the brimming heaven-blossom,
Under the tightening whorl of plumes, a mote
Scalds in dews.

A leaf of the earth
Applies to it, a cooling health.

A coffin spins in the torque.
Wounds flush with sap, headful of pollen,
Wet with nectar
The dead one stirs.

A mummy grain is cracking its smile
In the cauldron of tongues.

The ship of flowers
Nudges the wharf of skin.

The egg-stone
Bursts among broody petals—

And a staggering thing
Fired with rainbows, raw with cringing heat,

Blinks at the source.

This is perhaps the most magnificent of all the Baskins, and drawing and poem work as a single imaginative unit. Baskin's luminous figure suspended, off-centre, in blackness, seems to be hurtling towards the looker from the depths of space: 'Big terror descends.' The poem, which in isolation would be an incomprehensible accumulation of arbitrary images, is in fact focused unremittingly on this disturbingly ambiguous figure. It dramatizes the poet's response, its images suggesting his attempts to control the terror by fixing the figure with familiar natural images. Flames, blossom, plumes, a leaf, wounds, tongues: all these things can be seen in the figure but none suffices, and in the end their proliferation draws attention to the ambiguity. This attempt to control the power of the figure is most evident in the lines

> A leaf of the earth
> Applies to it, a cooling health.

It is of course the poet who is 'applying' the outline of a leaf to the figure, and applying it also to his own heated and disturbed imagination.

This is not to say that the poem is just a series of notes in the margin of the drawing. The contradictory attributes that Hughes sees in the figure are those of nature itself: the creative and destructive heat of the sun, the coolness of a leaf, the softness of petals and the hardness of stone, the fruitfulness of sap and pollen, the deathliness of wounds. The figure seems at one moment comforting, the next frightening; it even seems to be scared itself by its own radiance. In the context of the 'drama' (it is the penultimate poem) it is both the transformed protagonist and what, as a consequence of his transformation, he sees in the world.

We begin to see that the poems characteristically work at more than one level, and that these 'levels' are linked. In most cases a reading begins by tracing the poet's response to the drawing, but one's final understanding is enhanced by the fact that this is also the experience of a persona who has undergone several stages of a transformation, in which changes in himself are paralleled by changes in his awareness of the nature of things. Other poems are simultaneously accounts of real experience—in particular death and sexual love—and stages in a symbolic adventure.

The sequence begins with a kind of psychic trauma in which the

hero's complacent view of the world and his place in it is shattered
by the visitations of various terrifying bird-beings who confront him
with the evidence of his material nature and mortality. His own ego
is symbolized (in the drawing of 'The accused') by a cockerel. He is
taken on a journey into himself, the first stage of which is a classic
process of death and rebirth. This death is both the destruction of
the complacent ego and a full conscious realization of his own actual
physical death. He is changed from a cockerel to a 'flayed crow in
the hall of judgement'. After an interlude in which he is offered and
rejects various illusory heavens he enters the second major stage,
the symbolic marriage with a female who is both his hitherto imprisoned daimon or inner self and the spirit of material nature. The last
poem, an apotheosis of the transformed hero as a falcon, is followed
by a brief Finale which undermines any complacent sense of finality
the reader may have about the process he has been taken through.

The *Cave Birds* sequence opens with a striking poem which
immediately confirms that this book is an extension of the central
concerns of Hughes's work.

The scream

There was the sun on the wall—my childhood's
Nursery picture. And there was my gravestone
Which shared my dreams, and ate and drank with me happily.

All day the hawk perfected its craftsmanship
And even through the night the miracle persisted.

Mountains lazed in their smoky camp.
Worms in the ground were doing a good job.

Flesh of bronze, stirred with a bronze thirst,
Like a newborn baby at the breast,
Slept in the sun's mercy.

And the inane weights of iron
That come suddenly crashing into people, out of nowhere,
Only made me feel brave and creaturely.

When I saw little rabbits with their heads crushed on roads
I knew I rode the wheel of the galaxy.

Calves' heads all dew-bristled with blood on counters
Grinned like masks, and sun and moon danced.

And my mate with his face sewn up
Where they'd opened it to take something out
Raised a hand—

He smiled, in half-coma,
A stone temple smile.

Then I, too, opened my mouth to praise—

But a silence wedged my gullet.

Like an obsidian dagger, dry, jag-edged,
A silent lump of volcanic glass,

The scream
Vomited itself.

The tone of the opening lines suggests that the first-person voice of the poem is a persona. What is caught in that tone is a too-easy acceptance of the nature of things that amounts to a glib complacency in its expression. The happy acceptance of the hero's own death is childishly expressed, indicating no distinction between his response to this and his response to what he sees as the world at work without tensions. Lines like 'All day the hawk perfected its craftsmanship', and 'Worms in the ground were doing a good job' might appear to be close to the spirit of unironical celebration found in a *Season Songs* poem such as 'Swifts':

> And they've made it again,
> Which means the globe's still working.

In fact a sense of the universe at work in all its complementary processes is at the heart of *Cave Birds*, but these early expressions of the hero betray a complacency of inaction implying that there is no need to look further. The detail of 'Swifts' demands that the reader achieve a sense of the world working by looking attentively at the evidence of a swift.

The swifts
Materialise at the tip of a long scream
Of needle. 'Look! They're back! Look!' and they're gone
On a steep

Controlled scream of skid
Round the house-end and away under the cherries. Gone.
Suddenly flickering in sky summit, three or four together,
Gnat-whisp frail, and hover-searching, and listening

For air-chills—are they too early? With a bowing
Power-thrust to left, then to right, then a flicker they
Tilt into a slide, a tremble for balance,
Then a lashing down disappearance

Behind elms.

In comparison with such discipline the blind faith of the hero in 'The scream' is clearly naïve. What begins as naïvety becomes callousness at the point when the hero's response to violent death is a self-satisfied cosmic generalization. His easy praise is prevented by that part of his nature that he has failed to take account of and which therefore appears to be autonomous:

The scream
Vomited itself.

What is released by the scream in this first poem is to be the evidence and the focus of the accusation in the trial which is heralded by the appearance of the summoner in the following poem. The confidence that Hughes has in this first poem, which we feel to be entirely justified, is indicated by the omission of the narrative intro-duction to the broadcast of *Cave Birds*: 'The hero's cockerel inno-cence, it turns out, becomes his guilt. His own self, finally, the innate nature of his flesh and blood, brings him to court.'

The first six lines of 'The summoner' are clearly a response to Baskin's drawing, although this is not to suggest that the images work only in a visual way:

Spectral, gigantified,
Protozoic, blood-eating.

205

The carapace
Of foreclosure.

The cuticle
Of final arrest.

When Hughes uses a technical word like 'foreclosure' it is usually in a quite precise way. In this case it indicates the threat of disposses-sion, since a foreclosure is a barring of the right of mortgage redemption upon non-payment of dues. The threat has clear implications for the hero, whose complacency has been a non-payment of dues to the material world and to that part of his own material nature which surfaced in the scream. Thus the threat of the summoner has always been there, if only at the fringe of the hero's consciousness.

> Among crinkling of oak-leaves—an effulgence,
> Occasionally glimpsed.
>
> Shadow stark on the wall, all night long,
> From the street-light. A sigh.
>
> Evidence, rinds and empties,
> That he also ate here.
>
> Before dawn, your soul, sliding back,
> Beholds his bronze image, grotesque on the bed.
>
> You grow to recognise the identity
> Of your protector.
>
> Sooner or later—
> The grip.

If the hero is to see these hints as the identity of a protector who is also a fearfully grotesque image found only in the most deep and most vulnerable kind of sleep, the incongruity suggests a gangster protectionist, a sinister protector who sooner or later will demand his dues.

There follows a poem which begins the pattern of describing the hero's response to the previous figure. The poem is a weak one in which the hero's appeals to convention are crudely met with the summoner's physical ripostes:

When I said: 'Civilisation,'
He began to chop off his fingers and mourn.
When I said: 'Sanity and again Sanity and above all Sanity,'
He disembowelled himself with a cross-shaped cut.

('After the first fright')

These sorts of defence have been better deflated in *Crow*, and perhaps it is an indication of *Cave Birds'* advance on *Crow* that this poem is inadequate and even redundant in this sequence.[1]

'The interrogator' is one of those poems which derive their wit from the image on the page opposite. When the reader sees that this bird is a vulture the wit of the title can be seen at work in the precision of the poem's images:

Small hope now for the stare-boned mule of man
Lumped on the badlands, at his concrete shadow.

This bird is the sun's key-hole.
The sun spies through her. Through her

He ransacks the camouflage of hunger.

Investigation
By grapnel.

Some angered righteous questions
Agitate her craw.

The blood-louse
Of ether.

With her prehensile goad of interrogation
Her eye on the probe

Her olfactory x-ray
She ruffles the light that chills the startled eyeball.

After, a dripping bagful of evidence
Under her humped robe,

She sweeps back, a spread-fingered Efreet,
Into the courts of the after-life.

In stripping a body the vulture is, of course, doing the sun's work of reduction, and what is revealed is the material nature of man, unprotected by claims of 'civilisation'. In lines eight and nine Hughes typically uses a description of a physical action to wittily suggest a thought about it, establishing the bird's symbolic role in terms of its real nature. It is the word 'righteous' which makes the very literal insistence on the hero's mortality so powerfully suggestive. His response to the interrogator (in 'She seemed so considerate'), however, is to be morbidly obsessed with the fact of death, although the only 'fellow creature' he still cares for is his pet fern, an inanimate creature. The fern is dead, evidence that in the words of the interrogator, the protagonist's 'world has died'. These words have a double meaning. His illusion of reality (expressed in 'The scream') has been destroyed, and for him the death that he formerly shrugged off has become a horrific, ever-present reality: 'their heads sweated decay, like dead things I'd left in a bag/And had forgotten to get rid of.' The 'cancelling' of his world produces an apathy that incidentally foreshadows his own death and rebirth: 'Whether dead or unborn, I did not care.'

Obviously judgement is what the hero is now waiting for, and the judge is appropriately the next figure in the sequence. But who is to sit in judgement and what can the concept of judgement mean in the material universe? Hughes's meditation on Baskin's fine drawing sets up a dense maze of paradoxes:

The judge

The pondering body of the law teeters across
A web-glistening geometry.

Lolling, he receives and transmits
Cosmic equipoise.

The garbage-sack of everything that is not
The Absolute onto whose throne he lowers his buttocks.

Clowning, half-imbecile,
A Nero of the unalterable.

His gluttony
Is a strange one—his leavings are guilt and sentence.

Hung with precedents as with obsolete armour
His banqueting court is as airy as any idea.

At all hours he comes wobbling out
To fatten on the substance of those who have fouled

His tarred and starry web.

Or squats listening
To his digestion and the solar silence.

This poem must present something of a shock for the reader, in that it is clearly different from the other legal figures. This figure is an abstraction ('The pondering body of the law') who is at the same time a physical denial of abstractions. Previous figures have represented aspects of the natural world that demand fear and awe, but this parody appears to challenge the narrative. It is not until one recognizes the voice of the hero in 'The scream' that this poem's place in the narrative can be seen. This figure results from an attempt to reconcile two conceptions of nature. First there is the idea that a figure presiding over the universe is preserving equilibrium. The concept of pure balance lies behind the sort of expression the hero used in 'The scream' ('I knew I rode the wheel of the galaxy'), just as it underlies 'web-glistening geometry' and 'cosmic equipoise'. Against this conception is the voracious view of nature represented by the judge's gluttony. The judge seems to think that his fat buttocks will sit with dignity on the throne of the Absolute. The capital letter betrays the grand illusion at the centre of the parody.

The wit of the poem draws attention to the fact that these two conceptions of nature cannot be reconciled. A concise phrase like 'Nero of the unalterable' sums up the poem's parody of a presiding figure maintaining balance over what are in fact the unalterable workings of physical processes. In effect the poem is saying that there can be no judge since 'judgement' is irrelevant to a description of material processes. The poem acts as a warning early in the sequence that the figures be seen, not as independent controlling forces but as representatives of the hero's own physical nature.

This is true of the figure who appears in the next poem, 'The plaintiff', who is presented entirely through a sequence of precise and pregnant metaphors embodying a burning core of vitality:

> This bird
> Is the life-divining bush of your desert
>
> The heavy-fruited, burning tree
> Of your darkness.

Hitherto imprisoned in the darkness of the self unacknowledged by the protagonist, it has been roused by the trial:

> Your heart's winged flower
> Come to supplant you.

This creature is significantly female, anticipating a later stage in the hero's experience.

The hero is aware that this process of supplanting or cancelling has started, since his next speech is begun in what he knows to be his 'fading moments' and ends in a powerful image of his rejection by the world.

In these fading moments I wanted to say

> How close I come to a flame
> Just watching sticky flies play
>
> How I cry unspeakable outcry
> Reading the newspaper that smells of stale refuse
>
> How I just let the excess delight
> Spill out of my eyes, as I walk along
>
> How imbecile innocent I am
>
> So some perfect stranger's maiming
> Numbs me in freezing petroleum
> And lights it, and lets me char to the spine
>
> Even the dead sparrow's eye
> Lifts the head off me—like a chloroform

But she was murmuring: Right from the start, my life
Has been a cold business of mountains and their snow
Of rivers and their mud

Yes there were always smiles and one will do a lot
To be near one's friends

But after the bye-byes, and even before the door closed, even
while the lips still moved
The scree had not ceased to slip and trickle
The snow-melt was cutting deeper
Through its anaesthetic
The brown bulging swirls, where the snowflakes vanished into
themselves
Had lost every reflection.

The whole earth
Had turned in its bed
To the wall.

The hero's claims to be living a life that is the opposite of complacent are transparently desperate exaggerations that betray their
own falsity. The special pleading of his claim to be an 'imbecile
innocent' only draws attention to his guilt. In fact the voice of the
plaintiff seems to prevent the hero from saying these things because
she is murmuring the evidence of his guilt from the depths of his
inner life. Her metaphors indicate her unity with the material world
and suggest that the warming moments of his outer life are no
protection against inward processes. As in 'The plaintiff' Hughes
finds images that suggest many dimensions to the connection
between the inner life of the hero's material reality and the processes at work in the natural world. The forces of the hero's material
nature now cut through the anaesthetic of his own outer life, swell
like the waters of snow-melt, and close it. The pathos of this moment
is beautifully caught in a reversal that presents his death from his
own perspective. For him it is the natural world that has died and
rejected him.

We have already discussed the next poem, 'The executioner', in
our chapter 'Knowledge of Death' in which we showed how the
poem's rhetorical structure invites the reader to contemplate his
own non-being. In the context of the *Cave Birds* sequence it can be

seen that the poem works simultaneously at more than one level, and that the overwhelming sense of non-being that the poem communicates in isolation is balanced by the developing use of the word 'filling' (with its hint of fulfilling) towards the moment at which death is also rebirth: 'It feels like the world/Before your eyes ever opened.' In context the significance of these lines is heightened by the conclusion of the earlier poem 'She seemed so considerate': 'Whether dead or unborn, I did not care.' It is, however, only by so convincingly suggesting the experience of actual death that the poem can work effectively as part of a symbolic drama of death and rebirth.

In the momentum of poems that move the hero towards the complete submission of 'The knight' the next two poems are rather simple stages of the narrative which are each distinguished by a striking image and also confused by obscure phrases. The first poem begins 'The accused/Confesses his body' and traces the hero's confession of the nature of each part of his body as it is dismembered. He confesses in a telling image,

> his hard life-lust—the blind
> Swan of insemination.

What seems less inspired, and certainly less clear, is what is intended by:

> his atoms are annealed, as in x-rays,
> Of their blood-aberration—

It is hard to believe that Hughes is suggesting that the hero's blood itself is an aberration unless in some sense that is not made clear by the poem.

'First, the doubtful charts of skin' starts as a perfunctory journey through the hero's body, parts of which seem deliberately obscure, but the hero then moves into a landscape which recalls the archetypal landscape of the folklore of quest, evoked by Eliot in the latter stages of *The Waste Land*:

> In this decayed hole among the mountains
> In the faint moonlight, the grass is singing
> Over the tumbled graves, about the chapel
> There is the empty chapel, only the wind's home.

212

> It has no windows, and the door swings,
> Dry bones can harm no one.
> Only a cock stood on the rooftree.

The cockerel-hero of *Cave Birds* enters, via his own body, a strikingly similar place:

> I came to loose bones
> On a heathery moor, and a roofless church.
>
> Wild horses, with blowing tails and manes,
> Standing among graves.
>
> And a leaning menhir, with my name on it.
> And an epitaph, which read:
> 'Under this rock, he found weapons.'

This discovery, and the concept it represents, is central to the magnificent and pivotal poem 'The knight', which we have already found the need to refer to in earlier chapters and to quote in full on page 15. If the hero's finding weapons in his own grave suggests that he must discover his own subjection to death and that this knowledge strengthens his life, it is the quality of that subjection and completeness of that power which constitute the achievement of 'The knight'.

The discipline of the poem's central metaphor permeates the tone of the poem so that complete submission to the process of death achieves a still knowledge of unity with the material universe:

The knight

> Has conquered. He has surrendered everything.
>
> Now he kneels. He is offering up his victory
> And unlacing his steel.
>
> In front of him are the common wild stones of the earth—
>
> The first and last altar
> Onto which he lowers his spoils.
>
> And that is right. He has conquered in earth's name.

213

The 'conquest' of the knight (actually a dead bird) is without irony: the simple statement and its dignity of 'rightness' expresses the achievement of accepting his own death as an actual contribution to the earth itself. The quiet celebration of his own body's physical decay is here the product of a discipline of consciousness. It is in this sense that the knight's bones are his weapons. In the final stanzas the implications of this achieved state of consciousness are indicated in the completeness of the self and the sense of oneness with the processes of the universe:

> the skull's beauty

> Wrapped in the rags of his banner.
> He is himself his banner and its rags.

> While hour by hour the sun
> Strengthens its revelation.

To the knight the sun's revelation is that he is unified with the material universe. In the alchemical sequence such a revelation will become embodied in a new persona for the hero. Perhaps this is what is glimpsed in the form of the eagle-hunter at the end of the next poem.

In the *Crow* poem 'Criminal Ballad', the life of a man is haunted by the suffering of other people of which he gradually becomes aware until he finds his own hands bloodied. At one point his children's songs in the garden are made inaudible by machine guns and prisoners' screams.

> And he could not turn towards the house
> Because the woman of complete pain rolling in flame
> Was calling to him all the time
> From the empty goldfish pond.

This might well be the basis of the following poem which has a quite different tone and effect:

> *Something was happening*

> While I strolled
> Where a leaf or two still tapped like bluetits

214

I met thin, webby rain
And thought: 'Ought I to turn back, or keep going?'
Her heart stopped beating, that second.

As I hung up my coat and went through into the kitchen
And peeled a flake off the turkey's hulk,
                                    and stood vacantly munching
Her sister got the call from the hospital
And gasped out the screech.

And all the time
I was scrubbing at my nails and staring
                                    through the window
She was burning.

Some, who had been close, walked away
Because it was beyond help now.

They did not stay to watch
Her body trying to sit up, her face unrecognisable
As she tried to tell
How it went on getting worse and worse
Till she sank back.

And when I saw new emerald tufting the quince, in April
And cried in dismay: 'Here it comes again!'
The leather of my shoes
Continued to gleam
The silence of the furniture
Registered nothing

The earth, right to its far rims, ignored me.

Only the eagle-hunter
Beating himself to keep warm
And bowing towards his trap
Started singing

(Two, three, four thousand years off key.)

The man in the earlier poem appeared to be doing nothing rep-
rehensible, yet he suffered a complete alienation and breakdown
because he had failed to reconcile others' suffering with his own

daily life. This is not unreasonable or inconceivable, but the tone of the poem seems arbitrary and casually shocking. The deep compassion underlying the present poem derives in part from the suggestion of the juxtapositions that the hero was implicated by his complacency, beginning in the opening sentence. The other source of the sense of compassion in the poem is the way it follows through different aspects of this single death. The stanza describing the woman's final agony is followed by that in which the hero's dismay at the onset of spring turns himself into as unresponding an object as his shoes or his furniture. But this poem concludes with an enigmatic image that can only be interpreted as a positive voice.

So far the poem has been considered as a naturalistic report from the hero's earlier life which ends with a voice of hope. As such it is a moving and powerful poem. It can also be read as a stage of the sequence if the woman is seen as the female who haunts the narrative in one aspect as the interrogator, in another as the plaintiff, and who is most fully identified in 'A riddle' in which, among other accusations, she says 'As you saved yourself/I was lost.' In fact this poem can be seen as the relationship of 'A riddle' exemplified in an actual incident which is also a summary of the narrative so far. Having ignored the suffering of the female figure the hero finds himself cancelled by the world. The song of the eagle-hunter hints at the hero's transformation—finding the voice of the self that is in tune with the elements to which he is also subjected—his 'bowing towards his trap' suggests a nature that is both reverent and practical. It is not until later in the sequence that the new form of that song can be discovered for the hero. At this stage, it must remain archaic, '(Two, three, four thousand years off key)', in tune with the primeval dimension in which the resilient natural self of the eagle-hunter lives.

The process of rebirth, then, is begun in the poem 'The gatekeeper' which repeats in a series of generalizations the points established in a less dogmatic way in earlier poems. In the next poem the hero is flayed, a transformation motif that Jung remarks on in his commentary on the visions of the alchemist Zosimos the Divine. In the words of Lawrence's Birkin: the hero must 'cease to be, for that which is perfectly himself to take place in him'. The opening of this poem 'A flayed crow in the hall of judgment', superbly re-creates the sensations suggested by Baskin's drawing:

216

Darkness has all come together, making an egg.
Darkness in which there is now nothing.

A blot has knocked me down. It clogs me.
A globe of blot, a drop of unbeing.

Nothingness came close and breathed on me—a frost
A shawl of annihilation has curled me up like a new foetus.

I rise beyond height—I fall past falling.
I float on an air
As mist-balls float, and as stars.

A condensation, a gleam simplification
Of all that pertained.

The complete integration of images of non-being with the spark of
re-creation they contain is perfectly suggested by the womb-
darkness, the bloodclot that is also the 'globe' of life, the frost that
curls leaves and creatures into a foetal shape, and the water-drop
image of reduction and source. The questions which the hero then
starts to ask develop the consciousness which is at the mercy of
processes outside itself.

Where am I going? What will come to me here?
Is this everlasting? Is it
Stoppage and the start of nothing?

Or am I under attention?
Do purposeful cares incubate me?
Am I the self of some spore?

In this white of death blackness,
This yoke of afterlife?
What feathers shall I have? What is my weakness good for?

The final questions of the poem strongly recall Hamlet's famous
speech:

If it be now, 'tis not to come; if it be not to come, it will be now;
if it be not now, yet it will come. The readiness is all. Since no

man has aught of what he leaves, what is 't to leave betimes?
Let be.

(Hamlet, V. ii)

Hamlet's condition in the final act of the play is perhaps a useful
analogue to this stage in the cockerel's transformation. If we can see
the condition of Shakespeare's hero not as a paralysed fatalism but
as a recovered and enlarged sense of self, deriving from an acknowledgement of his subjection to forces outside himself, it should be
possible to respond similarly to the fatalistic implications in this
stage of Hughes's sequence.

> A great fear rests
> On the thing I am, as a feather on a hand.
>
> I shall not fight
> Against whatever is allotted to me.
>
> My soul skinned, and the soul-skin laid out
> A mat for my judges.

This sense of 'readiness' will certainly be reinforced if we are alert
to the suggestions of the imagery in the fine little poem that
follows:

> ### The baptist
>
> Enfolds you
> In winding waters, a swathing of balm
>
> A mummy bandaging
> Of all your body's puckering hurts
>
> In the circulation of sea.
> A whale of furtherance
>
> Cruises through the Arctic of stone,
> Carrying you blindfold and gagged.
>
> You dissolve, in the cool wholesome salts
> Like a hard-cornered grief, drop by drop

218

    Or an iceberg of loss
    Shrinking towards the equator

    Or a seed in its armour.

The achievement of this poem is that whilst dissolution is associated with the easing of pain and grief by death, it also produces images of continuity. The poem derives both depth and directness from the biblical reference and folktale style that are used to address the reader himself.

    The hero's rebirth is followed by a pair of poems in which a figure who claims to be his 'guide' offers him a choice of illusory heavens which he experiences and rejects.

    Here is the heaven of the tree:
    Angels will come to collect you.
    And here are the heavens of the flowers:
    These are an everliving bliss, a pulsing, a bliss in sleep.

    And here is the heaven of the worm—
    A forgiving God.
    Little of you will be rejected—
    Which the angels of the flowers will gladly collect.
                        ('A green mother')

This is a paradisal vision that de-natures earth and blurs the distinction between the this-worldly and the other-worldly. The poem's irony is evident in a splendid example of Hughes's mordant wit:

    In none of these is the aftertaste of death
    Pronounced poor.

In the following poem the hero actually finds himself in one of these heavens, which is reminiscent of the *Songs of Innocence* and Shelley's visions of a regenerated earth in *Queen Mab* and *Prometheus Unbound*:

They were so ecstatic
I could go in among them, touch them, even break pieces off them
Pluck up flowers, without disturbing them in the least.
The birds simply flew wide, but were not for one moment distracted

219

From the performance of their feathers and eyes.
And the animals the same, though they avoided me
They did so with holy steps and never paused
In the glow of fur which was their absolution in sanctity.

('As I came, I saw a wood')

This illusion offers as a redemption a return to the state of complacency with which he started. We are reminded of the repeated
warnings in the *Tibetan Book of the Dead* that the various deities
encountered in the Bardo state are illusions created out of the dead
person's 'thought-forms'. What enables the hero of *Cave Birds* to
recognize and turn away from the illusion is the remembrance of his
own carnivorous nature:

I could see I stood in a paradise of tremblings

At the crowded crossroads of all the heavens
The festival of all the religions

But a voice, a bell of cracked iron
Jarred in my skull

Summoning me to prayer

To eat flesh and to drink blood.

These are perhaps the most straightforward of the *Cave Birds*
poems. They serve as a warning that the transformation is not an
abolition of nature's predatoriness and destructiveness. They form
an interlude between the rebirth and the second stage of the transformation, which begins with 'A riddle':

Who am I?

Just as you are my father
I am your bride.

As your speech sharpened
My silence widened.

As your laughter fitted itself
My dumbness stretched its mouth wider

220

As you chose your direction
I was torn up and dragged

As you defended yourself
I collected your blows, I was knocked backward

As you dodged
I received in full

As you attacked
I was beneath your feet

As you saved yourself
I was lost

When you arrived empty
I gathered up all you had and forsook you

Now as you face your death
I offer you your life

Just as surely as you are my father
I shall deliver you

My firstborn
Into a changed, unchangeable world
Of wind and of sun, of rock and water
To cry.

The female who speaks here dominates the rest of the sequence. She is clearly identical to the plaintiff—'the life-divining bush of your desert', who informed the hero that 'Right from the start, my life/Has been a cold business of mountains and their snow/Of rivers and their mud.' Here she appears both as accuser and as corrective to the illusions of the Green Mother: the world into which this mother will deliver the hero is 'a changed, unchangeable world/Of wind and of sun, of rock and water', and he will be delivered into it 'To cry' (whereas the Green Mother 'has wiped her child's face clean/Of the bitumen of blood and the smoke of tears'). This world is changed only to the hero's perception, and what he perceives is, in fact, that it is unchangeable.

This figure who, for want of a precise word, we call the hero's

daimon, is the compensatory sufferer for the triumphs of the conscious self; she is what pays the price for the hubristic claims of the
ego ('As you chose your direction/I was torn up and dragged'). But
since she is also nature itself she is indestructible, and always available to take over after such a process of ego-destruction as the hero
has undergone. 'A riddle' is the first of a group of four poems which,
in the context of the sequence, celebrate a symbolic marriage
between the hero's conscious self and a female who represents the
natural processes both within and outside him. To a certain extent
this poem is dependent on the sequence, and some readers may
think that, in isolation, the speaker's assertion that she is daughter,
bride and mother to the protagonist is a pretentious pseudo-
mystical paradox. These relationships can be articulated however. It
is the hero's task to bring this being to conscious birth, but he is
obviously dependent on her for his existence and, moreover, the
birth of the daimon is for the hero himself a rebirth from which he
emerges radically changed. The 'marriage' between the two is the
achievement of wholeness: both a union between the divided parts
of himself and a sense of belonging in the world. In the superb poem
'Bride and groom lie hidden for three days' the lovers 'bring each
other to perfection': both a real act of love and an achievement of
this twofold wholeness. In the union celebrated in this poem each
creates the other, so that the marriage is a synthesis of the
mother–son and daughter–father relationships.

The success of Hughes's treatment of this 'symbolic marriage' can
be demonstrated by looking in detail at the two best poems in the
group.

After there was nothing there was a woman

Whose face had reached her mirror
Via the vulture's gullet
And the droppings of the wild dog, and she remembers it
Massaging her brow with cream

Whose breasts had come about
By long toil of earthworms
After many failures, but they were here now
And she protected them with silk

Her bones
Lay as they did because they could not escape anything
They hung as it were in space
The targets of every bombardment

She had found her belly
In a clockwork pool, wound by the winding and unwinding sea.
First it was her toy, then she found its use
And curtained it with a flowered skirt.
It made her eyes shine.

She looked at the grass trembling among the worn stones

Having about as much comprehension as a lamb
Who stares around at everything simultaneously
With ant-like head and soldierly bearing

She had made it but only just, just—

The juxtapositions in this poem will seem crude only until the reader
recognizes that there is no irony. To reconcile such tenderness for
the feminine, and for delicacy and innocence, with such insistence
on its origins in carrion and excrement is a remarkable achievement.
But 'reconcile' is the wrong word. The tenderness actually derives
from the recognition that the femininity, delicacy and innocence are
not a posture or a withdrawal: 'she remembers' her origins, 'Her
bones/Lay as they did because they could not escape anything.' The
poem is a celebration of wholeness. The achievement is highlighted
when we remember Hughes's early love poems and in particular the
crude and self-defeating irony of 'Fallgrief's Girl-Friends':

> 'Whilst I am this muck of man in this
> Muck of existence, I shall not seek more
> Than a muck of a woman'....
>
>   The chance changed him:
> He has found a woman with such wit and looks
> He can brag of her in every company.

'After there was nothing there was a woman' is quite self-sufficient
as a love poem, and it is because we can imagine this wonder
and tenderness having a real human object that the symbolic

meaning—the arousal of these feelings by the hero's hidden self or daimon—does not seem evasive or excessively abstract.

The same is true of the poem with which the symbolic marriage culminates.

Bride and groom lie hidden for three days

She gives him his eyes, she found them
Among some rubble, among some beetles

He gives her her skin
He just seemed to pull it down out of the air
                         and lay it over her
She weeps with fearfulness and astonishment

She has found his hands for him,
                 and fitted them freshly at the wrists
They are amazed at themselves,
                    they go feeling all over her

He has assembled her spine
                he cleaned each piece carefully
And sets them in perfect order
A superhuman puzzle but he is inspired
She leans back twisting this way and that,
                  using it and laughing incredulously

Now she has brought his feet, she is connecting them
So that his whole body lights up

And he has fashioned her new hips
With all fittings complete and with newly wound coils,
                    all shiningly oiled
He is polishing every part, he himself can hardly believe it
They keep taking each other to the sun,
                they find they can easily
To test each new thing at each new step
And now she smooths over him the plates of his skull
So that the joints are invisible
And now he connects her throat,
             her breasts and the pit of her stomach
With a single wire

She gives him his teeth, tying their roots
                                    to the centrepin of his body

He sets the little circlets on her fingertips
She stitches his body here and there
                                    with steely purple silk
He oils the delicate cogs of her mouth
She inlays with deep-cut scrolls the nape of his neck
He sinks into place the inside of her thighs

So, gasping with joy, with cries of wonderment
Like two gods of mud
Sprawling in the dirt, but with infinite care

They bring each other to perfection.

This is even more obviously a self-sufficient love poem celebrating, in a delicate and original way, the sense of coming into possession of a new body through sexual union. The sustained mechanical metaphor is not, of course, reductive, any more than Donne's famous lines, 'If we be two we are two so/As stiff twin compasses are two . . .' or even the Song of Songs: 'the joints of thy thighs are like jewels, the work of the hands of a cunning workman.' What Hughes has done is to find a fresh language with which to treat what might have been thought an overworked subject. He escapes the sentimental, quasi-religious, tired poetic effect of limiting the treatment of love to metaphors drawn from the organic world. He shows that it is possible to describe the human body as a machine and still find it a thing of wonder. He undermines, in short, the conventional habit of regarding machinery as something the very thought of which threatens one's most intimate experience. Such imagery is common in Hughes's accounts of the world at work, and this poem will seem less of a singular *tour de force* if we place beside it his description of spiders mating in the marvellous observation-poem (so far available only in limited edition) 'Eclipse':

Under his abdomen he had a nozzle—
Presumably his stumpy little cock,
Just as ginger as the rest of him, a teat,
An infinitesimal nipple. Probably

225

Under a microscope it is tooled and designed
Like some micro-device in a space-rocket.
To me it looked crude and simple. Far from simple
Though, were her palps, her boxing-glove nippers—
They were like the mechanical hands
That manipulate radioactive matter
On the other side of safe screen glass.
But hideously dexterous. She reached out one,
I cannot imagine how she saw to do it,
And brought monkey fingers from under her crab-nippers,
And grasped his nipple cock.

The spiders look grotesque, but the mechanical language does not diminish them. They are 'unbelievables' like the wonderful creatures whose extermination Hughes laments in another excellent uncollected poem, 'The Last Migration'.

In 'Bride and groom' this language is also much more resonant than might be expected. It contributes to the simplicity and innocence of newly-created beings discovering themselves, and to the sense of the lovers as craftsmen surprised and delighted by their own skill. The poem's only weakness is the forcible and in context incongruous reminder, with the phrase 'Sprawling in the dirt', of what the earlier poem has already established about the nature of the bride.

In these poems it is impossible and unnecessary to make a rigid distinction between the levels of meaning. Sexual union is a metaphor for wholeness of being and oneness with the world; it is also both a cause and a consequence of wholeness and unity. Interlocking, as it were, with this group of poems is another group that deal directly, in individual terms, with the transformed nature of the protagonist. The reader's attention is made to alternate between these complementary groups so that the way one reads 'The guide', for example, is influenced by the marriage group, and influences our reading of that group in turn. This poem was earlier titled 'A true guide', emphasizing the contrast with the false guide of 'A green mother'.

When everything that can fall has fallen
Something rises.
And leaving here, and evading there
And that, and this, is my headway.

Where the snow glare blinded you
I start.
Where the snow mama cuddled you warm
I fly up. I lift you.

Tumbling worlds
Open my way

And you cling.

And we go

Into the wind. The flame-wind—a red wind
And a black wind. The red wind comes
To empty you. And the black wind, the longest wind
The headwind

To scour you.

Then the non-wind, a least breath,
Fills you from easy sources.

I am the needle

Magnetic
A tremor

The searcher
The finder

This is the first of the bird-figures that has nothing terrifying, absurd
or equivocal about it. Its straightforwardly beneficent nature indicates, of course, the change that has taken place in the hero. The
guide seems to represent the achievement of an intuition, a sure
instinct for living, that starts from subjection to the elements. We
are reminded of the hero's delivery, by the speaker of 'A riddle',
into 'a changed, unchangeable world/Of wind and of sun, of rock
and water' and, from much earlier in the sequence, the plaintiff's
words, 'Right from the start, my life/Has been a cold business of
mountains and their snow/Of rivers and their mud.' This transformed condition is further expressed in 'Walking bare':

> What is left is just what my life bought me
> The gem of myself.
> A bare certainty, without confection.
> Through this blowtorch light little enough
>
> But enough.

He is integrated into the world in the sense that he does not interrupt its processes; he is a channel for messages that have nothing to do with him; he no longer egotistically considers himself the privileged recipient of every sign:

> Hurrying worlds of voices, on other errands,
> Traffic through me, ignore me.

The poem also seems to be trying to express a patient waiting for predetermined moments of revival by forces outside the self, but there is an obscurity in the way 'corolla' has also to suggest 'corona' in the astronomical metaphor in the final lines:

> A one gravity keeps touching me.
>
> For I am the appointed planet
> Extinct in an emptiness
>
> But a spark in the breath
> Of the corolla that sweeps me.

'Walking bare' seems to be straining to find images for a condition that is both human and fully at one with the non-human. A much more satisfactory poem is 'The risen', but its success as a poem entails an ironic reflection on the way the sequence has seemed to develop.

> He stands, filling the doorway
> In the shell of earth.
>
> He lifts wings, he leaves the remains of something,
> A mess of offal, muddled as an afterbirth.
>
> His each wingbeat—a convict's release.
> What he carries will be plenty.

He slips behind the world's brow
As music escapes its skull, its clock and its skyline.

Under his sudden shadow, flames cry out among thickets.
When he soars, his shape

Is a cross, eaten by light,
On the Creator's face.

He shifts world weirdly as sunspots
Emerge as earthquakes.

A burning unconsumed,
A whirling tree—

Where he alights
A skin sloughs from a leafless apocalypse.

On his lens
Each atom engraves with a diamond.

In the wind-fondled crucible of his splendour
The dirt becomes God.

But when will he land
On a man's wrist.

The effect of this superb poem depends on the most subtle relation
between levels of meaning to be found anywhere in the sequence.
Like so many of the best poems, it starts out as a response to the
Baskin, which is also one of the best in the book. A falcon stands on
broad talons and trunk-like legs, his wings raised but not spread.
Behind him, less broad than himself, is a black background, like a
doorway that he seems to have come through. In isolation the
poem's subject would seem to be simply the falcon, with the shift at
the end to the question, whether the bird's splendour and control
can ever be attained by a human being. The poem captures, in an
almost naturalistic way, the bird's speed, his sudden inexplicable
disappearance and emergence somewhere else, and above all the
electrifying alteration that takes place in everything within his range
of vision, so that he really does resemble a God, altering nature by
simply being there. (The line, 'Under his sudden shadow, flames cry

out among thickets' is a brilliant condensation of the effect of these naturalistic lines from the poem 'Funeral' in *Moortown*:

> Twice a day
> The brain-flaying ratchet of the storm-cock
> Announces the hawk here
> With his implements.

> Then for some minutes every bird in the neighbourhood tolling
> the alarm

> Then a silence—
> The odd starling crossing
> Like a convict escaping,
> The odd blackbird
> Hurtling to better hiding, low.

> And for the next half-hour
> A prison-state curfew execution silence, horrific.)

'The risen' exemplifies a characteristic style and structure of several of the best poems in the sequence. It moves not so much by development as by accretion. Each couplet has a haiku-like compression and completeness, as if the poet were striving for his subject to be fully present at every point. Consider for example the lines:

> In the wind-fondled crucible of his splendour
> The dirt becomes God.

The density of suggestion, reaching back into the sequence, makes the word 'splendour' more substantial than an admiring gesture. 'Fondled' suggests that the falcon is the minion of nature's tenderness, but the agent of the tenderness is the wind that also 'scours' and 'empties' (in 'The guide'). And the fondling cannot be separated from the implications of 'crucible'—the subjection to the 'burning unconsumed' of the bird's own nature, which in turn, of course, brings to mind the phoenix. 'Crucible' also recalls the alchemical transformation, and the syntactical ambiguity suggests that the crucible is not merely the receptacle in which the splendour is created, but is the splendour itself. The bird achieves its divinity by being subjected to its divinity—just as the bird-beings to whose terrors the hero was subjected were all aspects of his own nature.

This reminds us that the falcon, too, is an apotheosis of the transformed hero. Or is it? Despite the pervasive bird imagery, the reader becomes accustomed to thinking of the hero as a man, and of the sequence's development as the transformation of a man. This being so, the final couplet

> But when will he land
> On a man's wrist

must come as a shock. It is clearly a challenge to the reader, as much an imperative as a question, a warning against any complacent assumption that reading or writing a poem is a substitute for reality. It is also perhaps a reminder to the poet himself of how natural to him it is to write a poem—however great—about a bird as the culmination of a human drama. In the text 'The risen' is immediately followed by a Finale:

> At the end of the ritual
> up comes a goblin

which one cannot help reading as a comment on that final couplet. Hughes has used these words before, in the *London Magazine* interview.

> You choose a subject because it serves, because you need it. We go on writing poems because one poem never gets the whole account right. There is always something missed. At the end of the ritual up comes a goblin. Anyway within a week the whole thing has changed, one needs a fresh bulletin. And works go dead, fishing has to be abandoned, the shoal has moved on. While we struggle with a fragmentary Orestes some complete Bacchae moves past too deep down to hear. We get news of it later.... too late. In the end, one's poems are ragged dirty undated letters from remote battles and weddings and one thing and another.
>
> (January 1971, p. 15)

It is encouraging and awe-inspiring that a writer should feel like that about a work as complete and ambitious as *Cave Birds*.[2]

᠅ 8 ᠅

Remains of Elmet and *Moortown*

Landscape, in the poetry of Ted Hughes, has always been active, alive with the universal processes that shape it. The landscape described in 'Wind' and 'Crow Hill' actually came alive through personification in the fables of 'Still Life' and 'Sugar Loaf'. For Hughes, landscape has always been the material reality in which he has rooted his metaphysical adventure. It provides in his poems the measure of man's unity with and separation from the natural world. The processes at work in landscape are the touchstones of the revelation of *Cave Birds*, in 'The knight', for example:

> Skylines tug him apart, winds drink him,
> Earth itself unravels him from beneath—

and the enquiry of *Gaudete*, which is perhaps best exemplified by the remarkable section in which Lumb tries to overcome his separation from the living earth (pp. 49–53).

Until the appearance of some of the poems in *Season Songs* Hughes had moved away from the pursuit of his adventure in personal terms. Also the landscapes of his early poems were often unpeopled. But all his life Ted Hughes has had a personal interest in the landscape in which he was born and grew up.

The Calder Valley, west of Halifax [he writes, introducing *Remains of Elmet*], was the last ditch of Elmet, the last British Celtic kingdom to fall to the Angles. For centuries it was considered a more or less uninhabitable wilderness, a notorious refuge for criminals, a hide-out for refugees. Then in the early 1800s it became the cradle for the Industrial Revolution

232

in textiles, and the upper Calder became 'the hardest-worked river in England'.

Throughout my lifetime, since 1930, I have watched the mills of the region and their attendant chapels die. Within the last fifteen years the end has come. They are now virtually dead, and the population of the valley and the hillsides, so rooted for so long, is changing rapidly.

Fay Godwin's photographs, which accompany Hughes's poems in the book, capture not just the physical images of this area now, but the feel of the elements at work between 'the long swell of land' and 'the long/Press of weather'. There is a tension in the air of these black and white photographs that provides a visual complement to the tensions between man and landscape, the industrial and the organic, childhood and present, social and natural processes, that are explored in the poems.

So here is a peopled landscape of personal significance to the writer, through which he can continue with unique directness his interest in the relationship between human and elemental processes. The result is a language which can suggest unity whilst describing decay:

When Men Got To The Summit

Light words forsook them.
They filled with heavy silence.

Houses came to support them,
But the hard, foursquare scriptures fractured
And the cracks filled with soft rheumatism.

Streets bent to the task
Of holding it all up
Bracing themselves, taking the strain
Till their vertebrae slipped.

The hills went on gently
Shaking their sieve.

Nevertheless, for some giddy moments
A television
Blinked from the wolf's lookout.

233

Some poems in the sequence celebrate the pioneering spirit with which these hills and their valleys must have been settled by successive waves of people. 'Hill Walls' takes the sustained metaphor of a ship setting out on the hills, when 'Even the grass/ Agreed and came with them', such was the confidence of these people that the landscape was allowing itself to be domesticated. But 'When Men Got To The Summit' opens with a sense of awe and seriousness which, in the transfer from 'heavy' to 'hard', develops into rigid puritan determination, in as natural a way as houses seem to spring up in spontaneous support. The effect of describing their houses and streets as suffering in human terms is twofold. It links human ageing with material decay in a delicate balance of humour and pathos, and secondly it places the decay of settlements in a reduced timescale, thereby subjecting them to the perspective of the landscape itself.

Perhaps the central idea of *Remains of Elmet* can be summed up by 'The hills went on gently/ Shaking their sieve.' Hughes observes both the remains and the shaking process itself. Just as walls set out to tame the hills, the mills attempted to domesticate the river, and civilize the valley. Part of the mills' remains are 'Lumb Chimneys' and opposite this poem Fay Godwin's photograph shows a tree-trunk chimney growing out of ferns beside tree-trunks. The photograph visually represents the final image of the poem:

> Before these chimneys can flower again
> They must fall into the only future, into earth.

This organic image for industrial decay, with its startling implication, is typical of the language of *Remains of Elmet*. Indeed industrial loss in the valley hangs over even the natural silences in 'Hardcastle Crags':

> But here the leaf-loam silence
> Is old siftings of sewing machines and shuttles,
> And the silence of ant-warfare on pine-needles
> Is like the silence of clogs over cobbles.

The alliterative sounds of the second and fourth lines re-create the sounds that are absent in the reclamation of leaf-loam and pine-needle accumulations. Not that this represents a nostalgia. A number of poems emphasize the dehumanizing experience of the mills.

In 'The Sheep Went On Being Dead' human senses are dulled by the apparently 'happy work-hum of the valley mills' to the extent that people cannot smell the death of the sheep or perceive 'earth such a fierce magnet/Of death' (including their own). 'Hill-Stone Was Content' implicitly raises the question whether people should also have been as 'content' as stone was to 'let itself be conscripted/Into mills'.

> It forgot its wild roots
> Its earth-song
> In cement and the drum-song of looms.
>
> And inside the mills mankind
> With bodies that came and went
> Stayed in position, fixed like the stones
> Trembling in the song of the looms.
>
> And they too became four-cornered, stony.

The song of the looms, whilst representing a certain kind of creativity, is actually the drum-song of slavery that is reality for workers who have been dehumanized into a generalized 'mankind/With bodies that came and went'. Once again the landscape provides the image for what the people have become. In the poem 'Heptonstall' the reverse is the case.

The photograph of Heptonstall on the book's cover indicates the visual source of the poem's sustained metaphor.

Heptonstall

> —old man
> Of the hills, propped out for air
> On his wet bench—
> Lets his memories leak.
>
> He no longer calls the time of day
> Across to Stoodley, soured on that opposite ridge.
> And Stoodley has turned his back
> On the Museum silence.
>
> He ignores Blackstone Edge—
> A huddle of wet stones and damp smokes
> Decrepit under sunsets.

He no longer asks
Whether Pecket under the East Wind
Is still living.

He raises no hand
Towards Hathershelf. He knows
The day has passed
For reunion with ancestors.

He knows
Midgley will never return.

The mantel clock ticks in the lonely parlour
On the heights road, where the face
Blue with arthritic stasis
And heart good for nothing now
Lies deep in the chair-back, angled
From the window-skylines,
Letting time moan its amnesia
Through the telegraph wires

As the fragments
Of the broken circle of the hills
Drift apart.

We find this poem as moving as the poem about actual old people, 'Crown Point Pensioners'. The effect is a remarkable unity between human experience of ageing and the ageing of settlements that is achieved in a more deeply personal way than in 'When Men Got To The Summit' where the same technique was used. 'Heptonstall' gains pathos from the observed details of actual places and of individuals (such as Hughes's uncle in the marvellous dedicatory poem of the book). The final image of the poem, then, works as a psychological perception of an old man, as a geographical image of lapsing communication, and of physical change in the landscape itself. But to state this is almost to crush its subtle emotional effect, concluding as it does a deceptively simple achievement of the language of the book.

This language which celebrates connection while describing separation is not such a prominent feature of all the poems, although one often discovers connections being made almost casually. Many poems rejoice in an absence of people: 'Heather', 'Moors' and the title poem, for example. Yet 'Heather' opens with an image from early industry:

> The upper millstone heaven
> Grinds the heather's face hard and small.
> Heather only toughens.

The simple force of the celebration of that toughness makes the human connection of the millstone image inconspicuous. 'Moors'

> Are a stage for the performance of heaven.
> Any audience is incidental.

So when the drama of the clouds concludes with sunset the human origin of the phrase 'working late tonight' is again inconspicuous because it is so appropriate to a snipe's drumming hard at dusk:

> Shattered, bowed armies, huddling leaderless
> Escape from a world
> Where snipe work late.

As also with 'Moors' Fay Godwin's photograph accompanying the title poem provides evidence for the accuracy of the sustained metaphor. Beside 'Remains Of Elmet' one can see 'the long gullet of Calder' in the photograph, which captures the magic quality of the landscape.

> Now, coil behind coil,
> A wind-parched ache,
> An absence, famished and staring,
> Admits tourists
>
> To pick among crumbling, loose molars
> And empty sockets.

The remarkable power of 'A wind-parched ache' can be felt in the throat of the reader as it is suggested that the valley gullet feels it.

Some of that 'ache' must be felt by the writer at a personal level judging by the sharply detailed excitement of the childhood experiences in the book. 'The Canal's Drowning Black', 'The Long Tunnel Ceiling' and 'Sunstruck' each create a sense of exhilaration that is the living spirit of the book. The actual word 'exhilaration' cannot be prevented from surfacing in a number of poems ('Hill Walls', 'There Come Days To The Hills') and it is the invigorating quality of such celebrations as 'Cock-Crows' (discussed in Chapter 2) and 'Football At Slack'.

> Between plunging valleys, on a bareback of hill
> Men in bunting colours
> Bounced, and their blown ball bounced.
>
> The blown ball jumped, and the merry-coloured men
> Spouted like water to head it.
> The ball blew away downwind—
>
> The rubbery men bounced after it.
> The ball jumped up and out and hung on the wind
> Over a gulf of treetops.
> Then they all shouted together, and the ball blew back.
>
> Winds from fiery holes in heaven
> Piled the hills darkening around them
> To awe them. The glare light
> Mixed its mad oils and threw glooms.
> Then the rain lowered a steel press.
>
> Hair plastered, they all just trod water
> To puddle glitter. And their shouts bobbed up
> Coming fine and thin, washed and happy
>
> While the humped world sank foundering
> And the valleys blued unthinkable
> Under depth of Atlantic depression—
>
> But the wingers leapt, they bicycled in air
> And the goalie flew horizontal
>
> And once again a golden holocaust
> Lifted the cloud's edge, to watch them.

This poem has a fineness of touch and evident affection that recall 'Full Moon and Little Frieda'. The danger of any discussion of the poem is that its gently mocking, quietly admiring humour might be overwhelmed. In fact the humour derives not only from the slight exaggeration of 'rubbery men' and 'the goalie flew horizontal' but also from the absurdity that results from viewing the players as a group at a distance, as the landscape is viewed—in the third stanza for example. Part of the fun of the poem is in the way the rhythm of the lines reflects the action, as in the run-on second line of that stanza, the banging third line, and the rush of 'Then they all shouted together, and the ball blew back.' The point is that the men are enjoying playing with the large-scale forces of wind on landscape. The relationship between man and the elements in this unusual poem is both a celebration of the vitality and an acceptance of the absurdity of this human activity in these conditions. Because of the lack of pretensions in the game there seems something more valuable and ironically more permanent in this exhilaration than in the exhilarations of colonizing the hills and valleys. It might come as something of a shock to find (as Hughes informed the audience at a reading) that this football pitch has long since gone and that this vivid picture is a reminiscence, until one realizes that each weekend just such a mixture of absurd vitality is evident throughout the country.

A poem such as 'Football At Slack' is evidence that in *Remains of Elmet* Hughes is writing at the height of his powers. In a very different way 'Walls' is also one of Hughes's finest poems.

> What callussed speech rubbed its edges
> Soft and hard again and soft
> Again fitting these syllables
>
> To the long swell of land, in the long
> Press of weather? Eyes that closed
> To gaze at grass-points and gritty chippings.
>
> Spines that wore into a bowed
> Enslavement, the small freedom of raising
> Endless memorials to the labour
>
> Buried in them. Faces
> Lifted at the day's end
> Like the palms of the hands
>
> To cool in the slow fire of sleep.
> A slow fire of wind
> Has erased their bodies and names.

239

> Their lives went into the enclosures
> Like manure. Embraced these slopes
> Like summer cloud-shadows. Left
>
> This harvest of long cemeteries.

That final line is neither glib nor cynical. It is the climax of a respect for an effort which created an achievement as local, practical, yet mutable as regional speech. Indeed this effort contributes the syllables of the visual language of the landscape, as in other poems stones are associated with speech ('For Billy Holt', 'Wild Rock' and 'Churn-Milk Joan' for example). It is the rhythm of work as much as the dense associations of the imagery that gives this poem its power. Each sentence is broken by a line-ending, just as within a sentence there may be a straining of paradoxical imagery: 'soft' and 'hard', 'swell' and 'press', 'bowed' and 'raising', 'raising' and 'buried', 'cool' and 'fire' all move towards 'This harvest of long cemeteries'. In a precise and unsentimental way the poem celebrates a language, a brief 'embracing' of the hillsides, and the 'manuring' decay these 'cemeteries' also represent.

'Churn-Milk Joan' is a fine poem about an actual stone and its various folklore associations. Hughes's interest here is in the possible 'wrenching' of the word 'Joan' from 'jamb' and the doubt this throws on the truth of the legend, together with the way the stone stands as a memorial to the need for a legend of death behind this place-name. It is an explicit indication of the implicit project to find a language to explore the mystery of man's interaction with this place. This is the achievement of Hughes's own legend, 'Heptonstall Old Church':

> A great bird landed here.
>
> Its song drew men out of rock,
> Living men out of bog and heather.
>
> Its song put a light in the valleys
> And harness on the long moors.
>
> Its song brought a crystal from space
> And set it in men's heads.

Then the bird died.

Its giant bones
Blackened and became a mystery.

The crystal in men's heads
Blackened and fell to pieces.

The valleys went out.
The moorland broke loose.

Again the photograph beautifully provides the evidence to support the verbal image. This great bird is the spirit that is the cause of the whole book. The elation of Hughes's response, in other poems, to the moorland's liberation here recedes to an undertone of the menace derived from the powerful images of disintegration and decay. The co-presence of these feelings in the phrase 'broke loose' makes the poem central to the sequence's vision and linguistic achievement.

The deeply personal significance of this place is articulated through a notably related metaphor in 'Heptonstall Cemetery'.

Wind slams across the tops.
The spray cuts upward.

You claw your way
Over a giant beating wing.

And Thomas and Walter and Edith
Are living feathers

Esther and Sylvia
Living feathers

Where all the horizons lift wings
A family of dark swans

And go beating low through storm-silver
Toward the Atlantic.

The experience of the wind seems to suggest the image of the hill-top as 'a giant beating wing' out of which the inspired idea of

241

characterizing those buried there as 'living feathers' grows quite naturally. These 'feathers' are dead but part of a living organism as are real feathers. And out of this personal association grows the universal image which encompasses the same 'living feathers' in other horizons of other regions. One feels after reading this poem that the writer has sung a very personal song of his relationship with the landscape as with these people.

The ongoing beating of wings at the end of this poem is like the vision of 'In April' with which it might be paired.

> The black stones
> Bear blueish delicate milk,
>
> A soft animal of peace
> Has come a million years
> With shoulders of pre-dawn
> And shaggy belly
>
> Has got up from under the glacier
> And now lies openly sunning
> Huge bones and space-weathered hide
>
> Healing and sweetening
> Stretched out full-length for miles—
> With eyes half-closed, in a quiet cat-ecstasy.

'Healing and sweetening' in 'quiet cat-ecstasy' may only happen briefly in April in this landscape but it has 'come a million years' and it is the hero of this book. But the drama that has taken place on its back has been the subject of the poems, just as they represent a personal engagement with it. Ted Hughes has written a social history as a natural history, and in so doing has created a densely suggestive language that can relate social to natural processes in the timescale of a landscape.

The use of organic images for industrial remains, and human images for natural processes, is not merely technique; it is a vision which is articulated in *Remains of Elmet* in such a respectful, exhilarating and ultimately personal way that this book represents an important chapter in the continuing adventure.

. . . . .

One of the outstanding features of Hughes's poetry in the seventies is the range of form and style of work composed within a very short period. It is a major artist in full command of his art who, in the diversity of *Season Songs, Gaudete, Cave Birds* and *Remains of Elmet*, still focuses consistently and intensely on his central, compelling themes.

Moortown not only reflects that variety of styles, but collects unpublished poems from stages of Hughes's development dating—in the poem 'Heatwave'—back to 1963. The book has four main sections. The first, from which the volume takes its title, is a verse journal of his experiences farming in Devon. These poems are more directly autobiographical than anything Hughes has published before and are the most remarkable achievement of the various styles represented in this volume.

The second part, 'Prometheus on His Crag', was written in 1971, while Hughes was working on *Orghast* in Persia, and published in limited edition in 1973. It belongs in a kind of hiatus between the abandonment of *Crow* and the astounding creativeness of more recent years. We have commented on the limitations of its style in Chapter 2. In the *Moortown* context it stands as a salutary and somewhat grim contrast to the expansiveness, of both style and spirit, of most of the other poems. It does make, however, tentative steps towards what, reading it on its first appearance, one could not have believed would follow. At the end of Poem 18 ('Even as the vulture buried its head', be it noted) a lizard says to Prometheus: 'Lucky, you are so lucky to be human!' And, in the very last lines of the sequence, Hughes achieves, in a delicately beautiful sentence, the kind of vision and cadence that we have subsequently come to take almost for granted: 'He treads/On the dusty peacock film where the world floats.'

The third part, 'Earth-numb', is the longest, consisting of a selection of poems mostly from the limited edition *Orts* and a number of short sequences and miscellaneous poems representing the styles of the *Wodwo* and *Crow* periods as well as later developments. If the variable quality of these poems suggests that Hughes is becoming less selective in making up his volumes, there are some outstanding successes, notably 'The stone', which we discussed in Chapter 4. The poignantly personal terms in which death is felt in 'The stone' exemplify one of the main strengths of this section of *Moortown*, and of Hughes's most recent work generally. This personal note is heard in some of the best of the 'Orts' group, such as 'Each new moment my eyes' and 'Speech out of shadow', and in the rather obscure legend of 'Seven dungeon songs'. It links, surprisingly, the diverse styles of these poems with the fine realistic autobiographical records found in 'Here is the Cathedral' and 'A knock at the door'. Indeed, the poems written from the point of view and experience of an individual tend to be the most successful in this section. 'Nightwind, a freedom' and 'Second birth', for example, come closer to the quality of 'The stone' than the abstract dialectics of 'Song of Long-sight' or the bald iconography of 'The wolf'. Even 'Tiger-psalm', which might appear to be a formal and obvious dialectic between natural and mechanistic killing, is lifted into the exaltation of psalm by the author's commitment to what he has called the tiger's 'sacred activity of life' (public reading at Leeds, 10 March 1979).

The most interesting, and perhaps most difficult, of the sequences in 'Earth-numb' is 'Seven dungeon songs', several of which have previously appeared in magazines with the general title 'Caprichos'. The sequence, which contains one of the finest poems in the book, narrates the murder and disintegration of the nature-goddess, an individual's frustrated attempt to achieve a reintegration in his own body, his debilitating perception of the earth as a prison, his un-answered longing for the earth itself to speak, and finally his recog-nition that the only adequate speech (which he still has not achieved) is that of his own body's earthliness. The opening poem, 'The wolf', is one of Hughes's most obscurely iconic, and some of the later poems in the sequence depend too much for their effect on repetitive accretion, but neither of these criticisms can be made of the marvellous second poem, which contains the essence of the sequence within itself.

> Dead, she became space-earth
> Broken to pieces.
> Plants nursed her death, unearthed her goodness.
>
> But her murderer, mad-innocent
> Sucked at her offspring, reckless of blood,
> Consecrating them in fire, muttering
> It is good to be God.
>
> He used familiar hands
> Incriminating many,

And he borrowed mouths, leaving names
Being himself nothing

But a tiger's sigh, a wolf's music
A song on a lonely road

What it is
Risen out of mud, fallen from space
That stares through a face.

The local density of poetic texture in, for example, the third line, is matched by the overall structure: the way the poem builds to the seeming finality of 'nothing', which is then so startlingly qualified, the echo of the opening line forcing the recognition that the resurrection of the goddess can and must be achieved within the 'murderer' himself. So often, as in the second half of this poem (and 'Walls' in *Remains of Elmet*), Hughes is at his best when he draws a long sentence through a number of lines: the pauses and windings of the sentence create a quasi-dramatic embodiment of the thought's development.

The final section of *Moortown*, 'Adam and the Sacred Nine', is closely related in theme to 'Seven dungeon songs'. It tells a story of Adam, reluctant to awake and arise, being called upon by nine birds—each living, like the Phoenix which summarizes them, 'in the blaze'—to follow their example of being fully alive. But Adam's problem is that of Wodwo, Crow, Lumb and the protagonist of *Cave Birds*: what does it mean to be fully himself? 'The song', an invocation which opens this lyrical sequence, summarizes the theme. The song 'did not want' air, sky, leaves or stones, nor the mouth, throat, lungs and veins 'from which it poured'. Though 'made of joy' it

Searched, even like a lament

For what did not exist

Pouring out over the empty grave
Of what was not yet born.

Ignorant of, or unwilling to acknowledge, its own sources, and consequently barred from the joy it is made of, it searches for some other, illusory source. If there is a strong sense of futility in these

final lines, we cannot forget that the spirit of creativity would be
dead without the search for 'what is not yet born'. The problem
hinges, like the single line itself, on whether 'what did not exist' is an
object of escape or discovery.

There is no such ambivalence in the second poem where Adam is
incapable of song and simply dreams escapes into contradictions of
his physical reality:

> Wrapped in peach-skin and bruise
> He dreamed the religion of the diamond body.

'Peach-skin' is as precise and suggestive as 'the religion of the
diamond body' with all its associations of a simple, durable but
non-human perfection that is raised to a religion by Adam's dream.
This single poem sums up much that Hughes was doing in *Crow*.
'His dream played with him, like a giant tabby.' Everything Adam
dreams contradicts what he is and this prevents him from developing what he is. It is only when Adam stands on the earth in the final
poem that such a process can begin.

This sequence of twelve poems was earlier published in limited
edition with five additional poems. Those which have been omitted
had a narrative function and elaborated on Adam's state. The two
poems which preceded the final one, 'The sole of a foot', had an
important qualifying role in relation to that poem. They are also
beautifully achieved fables of the encounter between man and
world, and it is a pity that Hughes omitted them from the *Moortown*
version of the sequence. First:

> Light
>
> Eased eyes open, showed leaves.
>
> Eyes, laughing and childish
> Ran among flowers of leaves
> And looked at light's bridge
> Which fled from leaf, upward, and back down to leaf.
>
> Eyes, uncertain
> Tested each semblance.
> Light seemed to smile.

Eyes ran to the limit
To the last leaf
To the least vein of the least flower-leaf.

Light smiled
And smiled and smiled.

Eyes
Darkened

Afraid suddenly
That this was all there was to it.

The lapse into disbelief in or dissatisfaction with the natural world brings the sequence full circle. But the last line is important for an understanding of Adam's eventual achievement. When, at the end of the sequence, he says to the rock, 'I was made/ For you' he is doing no more than accepting that 'this was all there was to it.' If there is any redemption or transcendence in the final poem it must be of a kind that can be restated in the terms of that line. This suggestion is taken further in the penultimate poem of the original sequence.

Bud-tipped twig

Touched nipple.
The tree recoiled, aloof, still wintry.

Feathery grass-plume touches
Stroked across nipple
And the grass fled, shrinking, queerly far off.

Brambles by chance clawed breast
Sprang off, and reached quietly elsewhere
Still green-tender, otherworldly.

Clouds tumbled their godly beds
Drawing a vast coldness
Over the breast.

The sea, preoccupied with moon and sun
With earth's centre, with its own substance and the laws
of waves

Made the breast feel lost.

Breast lifted its simple face
To the sun.
The first beggar.

Unable to see
Or to hear
Or to cry.

The clarity and poise of this poem, typical of the whole sequence, conveys a reassuring confidence in its vision, a celebration of this being all there is to it: no reciprocation of caress, no establishment of connection after touch. To accept the natural world is to accept that it retreats after touch and is simply itself. This is the world in which Adam must find his sense of himself and his connectedness—as 'the first beggar'.

We have stressed these two omitted poems because, in the sequence as it stood, they guarded against the danger of a sentimental or too easy sense of reciprocal connectedness in the final poem:

The sole of a foot

Pressed to world-rock, flat
Warm

With its human map
Tough-skinned, for this meeting
Comfortable

The first acquaintance of the rock-surface
Since it was star-blaze,
The first host, greeting it, gladdened

With even, gentle squeeze
Grateful
To the rock, saying

I am no wing
To tread emptiness.
I was made

For you.

248

That a description of a simple sensuous act can achieve the profound symbolic unity of this poem is surely a clear confirmation of Hughes's artistic maturity. The complete integration, from the opening of the poem, of the metaphysical and the personal is indicated by the easy use of both 'world-rock' and 'Warm'. As is so often the case in *Remains of Elmet* there is a complete unity between the vision of the poem and its language. The final statement of the poem is the human equivalent to the discovery of selfhood that concludes 'How Water Began to Play'; it is a personal expression of the symbolic marriage in *Cave Birds*; it is a resolution of the metaphysical tensions explored in *Gaudete*. Arising typically from direct contact with material reality this discovery is the elusive combination of what it is to be human (rather than bird, or indeed animal or water) in a state of joyful and humble connection with the world.

As *Remains of Elmet* suggests, it is farmers who forge this connection in a working relationship, and in the poems about his own farming in *Moortown* Hughes provides example after example of the practical meaning of 'The sole of a foot'. The spirit of celebration, humility and respect that underlies these poems derives in part from their personal significance. In 1978 these poems were published in limited edition as *Moortown Elegies*, and in a strong sense all the poems derive elegiac qualities from the writer's engagement with the life and death of one man, Jack Orchard, with whom he farmed at Moortown Farm. The writer's record of his attempt to start a frozen tractor therefore stands as a rather unusual but entirely appropriate elegy to one man's way of life, just as much as it also represents an archetypal trial between man and the elements:

> the seat claims my buttock-bones, bites
> With the space-cold of earth, which it has joined
> In one solid lump.
>
> ('Tractor')

The vivid immediacy yet universal vision of these poems recalls *Season Songs*, but in these poems the observer is also participant, which involves responsibility. This is the price of man's finding his place in the natural world and the consequence of his specifically human contribution. In a dramatically developed, poignant poem, 'Ravens', the writer explains to a three-year-old child that a lamb 'died being born. We should have been here, to help it.' In the final sentence of the poem Hughes reflects that this lamb was 'lucky' in making its 'first day of death' into a momentarily paradisal world. The emphasis on 'this one' paradoxically reminds the reader of other lambs born in other conditions, such as those described in 'February 17th':

> A lamb could not get born. Ice wind
> Out of a downpour dishclout sunrise. The mother
> Lay on the mudded slope. Harried, she got up
> And the blackish lump bobbed at her back-end
> Under her tail. After some hard galloping,
> Some manoeuvring, much flapping of the backward
> Lump head of the lamb looking out,
> I caught her with a rope. Laid her, head uphill
> And examined the lamb. A blood-ball swollen
> Tight in its black felt, its mouth gap
> Squashed crooked, tongue stuck out, black-purple,
> Strangled by its mother. I felt inside,
> Past the noose of mother-flesh, into the slippery
> Muscled tunnel, fingering for a hoof,
> Right back to the port-hole of the pelvis.
> But there was no hoof. He had stuck his head out too early
> And his feet could not follow. He should have
> Felt his way, tip-toe, his toes
> Tucked up under his nose
> For a safe landing. So I kneeled wrestling
> With her groans. No hand could squeeze past
> The lamb's neck into her interior
> To hook a knee. I roped that baby head
> And hauled till she cried out and tried
> To get up and I saw it was useless. I went
> Two miles for the injection and a razor.
> Sliced the lamb's throat-strings, levered with a knife
> Between the vertebrae and brought the head off.
> To stare at its mother, its pipes sitting in the mud
> With all earth for a body. Then pushed
> The neck-stump right back in, and as I pushed
> She pushed. She pushed crying and I pushed gasping.
> And the strength
> of the birth push and the push of my thumb
> Against that wobbly vertebra were deadlock,
> A to-fro futility. Till I forced
> A hand past and got a knee. Then like

Pulling myself to the ceiling with one finger
Hooked in a loop, timing my effort
To her birth push groans, I pulled against
The corpse that would not come. Till it came.
And after it the long, sudden, yolk-yellow
Parcel of life
In a smoking slither of oils and soups and syrups—
And the body lay born, beside the hacked-off head.

In this poem there is no division between man and animal, which was such a dominant theme in Hughes's early poems, and which often tended to be expressed to man's discredit. In this poem those divisions are resolved in practical action of such urgency and intensity that they are not an issue. Indeed the poem's rhythm of the repeated word 'push' builds towards a harnessing of the natural force of the birth push. The archetypal undercurrents of all this are rightly undeveloped, but undoubtedly contribute to the poem's depth of effect. Similarly the symbolic meeting-point of birth and death is hinted at only in an entirely literal description of the cut-off head of the lamb 'sitting in the mud/With all earth for a body'. Characteristically the language here presents not an imagined vision, as if from *Gaudete*, but a symbolic moment as it arises in everyday practical life.

Part of our response to the poem is the belief that the writer has had this experience, and in reading it we inwardly measure ourselves against the actions the poem describes. An important part of its effect is the reader's respect for the man who has undergone this trial. The writer's feelings, however, are never expressed; the poem is entirely focused on responses to necessity. These actions represent, in fact, not unusual qualities of character, but the necessities of a particular way of life, and our admiration of the poet's capacity to act leads to our admiration of the uniquely human engagement in the creative-destructive processes of nature that farmers undertake in their daily work.

In the final six poems that engagement is celebrated by specific reference to the life and death of Jack Orchard. Here is a human life that had the toughness, sureness, vitality and wholeness that Hughes had previously observed only in animals. 'A monument' evokes all those qualities in a poem which recalls the stubborn man erecting a fence in December rain in a thorny copse, 'using your life up'. The final phrase catches the tone of pathos and celebration that makes each of these six poems so moving. A simple description of Jack Orchard shearing a sheep also breaks new ground for Hughes. 'A memory' is a quite unironical description of a man 'mastering' an animal. In 'The Bull Moses', for example, Hughes's treatment of the bull's subjection focuses entirely on the mystery of the animal's own inner being. The role of man was small in that poem because the bull had consented to the imposition of the human ego—that inexplicable consent was the poem's theme. In 'A memory' there is no ego imposition, but an engagement that is unconcerned about the self, even at a physical level: 'Heedless of your own surfaces'. In this unromanticized heroic poem a cigarette is

> Preserving its pride of ash
> Through all your suddenly savage, suddenly gentle
> Masterings of the animal.

Here is a master-craftsman who is in total command of his own nature. He is not, like the men in 'Thrushes' for example, a victim of his potentialities, but his emotional character is expressed in the practical skill of his craft. This is an individual human image of the wholeness of self and relatedness with material reality which is felt towards in the symbolic images of *Crow, Gaudete* and *Cave Birds*.

These fine poems represent better than anything else what is obviously different in *Moortown* from what has gone before. It has been a long discipline of imaginative objectivity that has brought Hughes to the point where positive connections between man and nature can be expressed, and in directly personal terms. For us this sense of connection has always been one of the main criteria by which Hughes's work should be judged. Hughes's poetry has not been striving towards mystical transcendence or for some supposedly invulnerable stance. In it he is seeking a position of practical engagement with the world that is utterly honest, stripped of self-deceptions, humble and respectful but at home in the only world, that is our life and our death. Certainly such a search is not without its dangers, but what is remarkable in the development of the poetry of Ted Hughes is not only the small proportion of failures but the consistency of focus that runs through the varied forms of the successes. No doubt he will continue to surprise us, but we look forward to the developing presence in his work of the unimaginably hard-earned sense of the fitness, dignity and responsibility of being human expressed in 'The day he died'.

The day he died

Was the silkiest day of the young year,
The first reconnaissance of the real spring,
The first confidence of the sun.

That was yesterday. Last night, frost.
And as hard as any of all winter.
Mars and Saturn and the Moon dangling in a bunch
On the hard, littered sky.
Today is Valentine's day.

Earth toast-crisp. The snowdrops battered.
Thrushes spluttering. Pigeons gingerly
Rubbing their voices together, in stinging cold.
Crows creaking, and clumsily
Cracking loose.

The bright fields look dazed.
Their expression is changed.
They have been somewhere awful
And come back without him.

The trustful cattle, with frost on their backs,
Waiting for hay, waiting for warmth,
Stand in a new emptiness.

From now on the land
Will have to manage without him.
But it hesitates, in this slow realisation of light,
Childlike, too naked, in a frail sun,
With roots cut
And a great blank in its memory.

✂ Notes ✂

Chapter 2

1. This earlier version is published in *Antaeus*, no. 28, Winter 1977, p. 81.
2. If this seems to leave the conceptual too much out of account, perhaps the following passage from Mr Smith's book compensates:

   > Another close relationship existed between HOAN, 'light', and the forms of the verb 'to be'. 'You can't say "is" without saying "light",' Hughes observed. It was one of the clearest examples of his intention to create an *organic* language, in which abstractions could not breed more abstractions, but were always returned to the physical root. Or, to put it another way, all conceptual thought was a metaphor of what the body, first, had perceived. (p. 51)

   In historical languages too, of course, most conceptual words are constructed out of what were once concrete metaphors, and we can see the breeding of abstractions when changing use cuts a word off from any comprehensible connection with its root.
3. This reading is recorded on *Listening and Writing* (two talks from *Poetry in the Making*), BBC Records RESR 19M.
4. *The Poet Speaks*, no. 5, Argo PLP 1085.
5. 'Ghost Crabs' was introduced at a reading at Lancaster (1 May 1978) as being from a play: 'The idea was that the whole world was run by a kind of angel or demon, a rather terrible kind of angel, and this is just a part to describe it.'

Chapter 3

1. The story is given in the guide to Barnburgh Church and village, *The Cresacre Treasure*, by the Revd W. J. Parker, p. 14. Barnburgh is in

South Yorkshire, between Barnsley and Doncaster, a few miles from Mexborough where Hughes spent his later childhood and adolescence.

2. Quoted by J. M. Newton in his review of *Crow*, *Cambridge Quarterly*, vol. 5 no. 4, p. 383.

Chapter 4

1. The authenticity of Castaneda's books (to which we shall be referring again in later chapters) has been brought into question by Richard de
. Mille in his thoroughly researched book *Castaneda's Journey, The Power and the Allegory* (Capra Press, Calif., 1976; Abacus, London, 1978). This however is perhaps unimportant, since as Hughes wrote of Don Juan in his review of *A Separate Reality*, 'Everything he says goes to the bone' (*Observer Review*, 5 March 1972).

Chapter 5

1. In a manuscript now in the library of Liverpool University Hughes has written:

> Well, how fed up I am
> Of poetry and its concrete reinforced
> Pose stretched in public. I will
> Forgo all that henceforth
> I will renounce it and be rid of it
> And here see the last of it
> Henceforth according to Yeats go naked.

This is followed by a draft of 'Fern', one of the last poems to be published (in 1967) before the appearance of the *Crow* poems.

2. He describes this as one of the episodes in which Crow misunderstands and mismanages an encounter with his creator.

3. Or possibly an Americanism. The only other place where we have encountered it is in Faulkner's *As I Lay Dying*.

4. Not so simple, the reader might say who recognizes that the passage is a parody of the 'warp-spasm', the seizure which possesses Cúchulainn, the hero of the Irish epic *Táin Bó Cuailnge*, as a prelude to his superhuman feats of violence (see *The Táin*, translated by James Kinsella, pp. 150–3). We hope that this knowledge, to which Keith Sagar first drew attention, is not necessary to an understanding of the poem. For us it does not alter the effect of these lines in their context. If the knowledge has any effect it is rather to make the bizarre and terrifying occurrences

255

in *The Táin* more comprehensible by relating them to a familiar experience.

5. Our commentary on the poem's effect should be compared with Hughes's account in a letter to ourselves (October 1979) of his intention:

> What Crow is grappling with is not 'something dangerous' but what becomes—at the end of all his mistakes and errantry—his bride and his almost humanity. To every action, an equal but opposite reaction: in their alarming aspect, the transformation images are mirror-images of his method of interrogation. The hidden thing defends itself with these.
>
> The 'violence' of the poem, therefore, is limited to a purely psychological and even barely conscious event. It inheres in Crow's attitude to the hidden thing. And in the difference in electrical potential—in value potential—between his mentality and the nature of what he's trying to grasp—which is the difference between his ego-system and the spirit dimension of his inner link with his creator. The first cannot in any way cope with or know the second. For Crow to 'know' the second he will have to go through the annihilation of the first.
>
> The components of each image are: one aspect of the nature of the hidden thing, plus a mirror-image of Crow's own mood, plus an image of his motive, of his expectation, and of the incompatibility between his mentality and the hidden thing, plus a representation of the fleeting escape of the hidden thing, the momentariness of his glimpse of it and the strain of his effort to hold on to it. (The images are all from a series of dreams I once had, memorable to me for the shock they came with and the interpretation of them that presented itself—correctly I think.) The hidden thing is a simple existence, an actuality. But the defensive images it throws up are ... compound metaphors, instructive warnings in the form of hieroglyph symbols. As Crow persists, the proportions of the components in each image change, there is less of one thing and more of another. There is an advance, in other words. Crow's determination is itself an advancing thing.
>
> The deadlock can end in only two ways. Either Crow gives up or he breaks through to what he wants and is exploded by it—his culpable ego-machinery is exploded. That he explodes is positive. It is not an image of 'violence' but an image of breakthrough. If he had withdrawn, he would have remained fixed in his error. That he pushes to the point where he is annihilated means that now nothing remains for him but what has exploded him—his inner link with his creator, a thing of spiritfire ('he that loses his life shall find it' etc.). This is Crow's greatest step forward. But he regresses, and has to make it again and again, before his gain is finally consolidated in his union with his bride.

256

6. When reading from *Crow*, Hughes gives a more detailed explanatory account of the narrative behind 'Lovesong' than for any part of the story apart from Crow's creation. At a late stage in his adventures Crow encounters a hag, who is an accumulation of all the monstrous elements in all the female figures he has met. She forces him to carry her across a river, asking him questions about the nature of love as he does so. They are dilemma questions, questions with no answer, so each time Crow tries a series of answers. The more wrong his answers are, the heavier she becomes, and his head is forced down into the water. When this happens he corrects himself and she becomes a little lighter. So each line of these poems is a fresh start, a new attempt at an answer. The earlier questions in the sequence demand harsh and dark answers, but as he progresses across the river the questions and answers become brighter and joyful. 'Lovesong' is Crow's attempt to answer the first of these questions. When he reaches the farther bank the hag jumps off his back, turns into a beautiful woman and disappears. As well as 'Lovesong' and 'Bride and groom' Hughes has used this story to elucidate 'The Lovepet' (American *Crow* and *Moortown*).

7. In the same context as Trickster we should also mention the 'Spirit Mercurius' of the alchemists, whom Jung in his *Alchemical Studies* describes as 'child of chaos' (p. 228) and says that he 'consists of all conceivable opposites' (p. 237). He quotes a poem in which Mercurius says, 'To a black crow am I kin' (p. 229). The following are extracts from Jung's commentary.

> In comparison with the purity and unity of the Christ-symbol, Mercurius-lapis is ambiguous, dark, paradoxical, and thoroughly pagan. It therefore represents a part of the psyche which was certainly not moulded by Christianity and can on no account be expressed by the symbol 'Christ'. On the contrary, as we have seen, in many ways it points to the devil, who is known at times to disguise himself as an angel of light. The lapis formulates an aspect of the self which stands apart, bound to nature and at odds with the Christian spirit. It represents all those things which have been eliminated from the Christian model. But since they possess living reality, they cannot express themselves otherwise than in dark Hermetic symbols. The paradoxical nature of Mercurius reflects an important aspect of the self—the fact, namely, that it is essentially a *complexio oppositorum*, and indeed can be nothing else if it is to represent any kind of totality. . . .
>
> So clear and definite is the Christ figure that whatever differs from him must appear not only inferior but perverse and vile . . . . As a result, a tension of opposites such as had never occurred before in the whole history of Christianity beginning with the Creation arose between Christ and the Antichrist, as Satan or the fallen angel. At the

time of Job, Satan is still found among the sons of God. . . . It looks as if the super-abundance of light on one side had produced an all the blacker darkness on the other. One can also see that the uncommonly great diffusion of black substance makes a sinless being almost impossible. A loving belief in such a being naturally involves cleansing one's own house of black filth. But the filth must be dumped somewhere, and no matter where the dump lies it will plague even the best of all possible worlds with a bad smell.

(*Alchemical Studies*, pp. 241–3)

8. The affinity with primitive mythology can be seen again if we compare the following, from a Bantu creation myth:

In the beginning, in the dark, there was nothing but water. And Bumba was alone.

One day Bumba was in terrible pain. He retched and strained and vomited up the sun. After that light spread over everything. The heat of the sun dried up the water until the black edges of the world began to show. Black sandbanks and reefs could be seen. But there were no living things.

Bumba vomited up the moon and then the stars, and after that the night had its light also.

Still Bumba was in pain. He strained and nine living creatures came forth; the leopard named Koy Bumba, and Pongo Bumba the crested eagle, the crocodile, Gonda Bumba, and one little fish named Yo; next, old Kono Bumba, the tortoise, and Tsetse, the lightning, swift, deadly, beautiful like the leopard, then the white heron, Nyanyi Bumba, also one beetle, and the goat named Budi.

(Mircea Eliade, *From Primitives to Zen*, p. 91)

Chapter 6

1. This is actually a misquotation. Burnet's translation reads: 'For if it were not to Dionysos that they made a procession and sang the shameful phallic hymns, they would be acting most shamelessly. But Hades is the same as Dionysos, in whose honour they go mad and keep the feast of the wine-vat' (Fragment 127 in *Early Greek Philosophy*). Whether deliberate or not, Hughes's shift of emphasis from Dionysos to Hades is surely significant.

2. This episode closely resembles the *taurobolium*, a bull sacrifice practised by, among others, the Romans, in the cult of the Great Mother of the Gods.

The person dedicating the sacrifice lay in a pit with a perforated board placed over the pit's opening. A bull was slaughtered above him, and the person in the pit bathed in the blood streaming down. Thus the ceremony, perhaps influenced by Christianity, gradually took on the elements of moral purification.　　　　(*Encyclopaedia Britannica*)

NOTES

3. Keith Sagar suggests (*Art of Ted Hughes*, 2nd edition, p. 201) that this episode is a flashback: that 'Lumb' is the original vicar and the double a premonition of the changeling. This, though it involves some narrative obscurity, is fairly plausible and not inconsistent with the main suggestions of our commentary.
4. According to Kerényi, on the evidence of the name 'Nysan Meadow', on which the rape of Persephone occurred, of an archaic vase showing Persephone with Dionysos, and of Demeter's refusal of wine, it can be deduced that 'the wine god in his quality of Lord of the Underworld was the girl's ravisher' (*Eleusis*, pp. 34–41).
5. In her thesis on the Double in Dostoevsky, Sylvia Plath makes the following comments:

> In such situations [i.e. such as Jekyll and Hyde and Dorian Gray], where the Double symbolizes the evil or repressed elements in man's nature ... man's instinct to avoid or ignore the unpleasant aspects of his character turns into an active terror when he is faced by his Double, which resurrects those very parts of his personality which he sought to escape. The confrontation of the Double in these instances usually results in a duel which ends in insanity or death for the original hero. (p. 3)

> In folk superstition the Double appears frequently as an omen of doom. (p. 7)

> [Quoting Freud, 'The Uncanny']: 'From having been an assurance of immortality, (the Double) becomes the ghastly harbinger of death.' (p. 18)

6. A more extended comparison with *The God of Glass* is made in Neil Roberts's review of *Gaudete* (*Delta*, 57).

Chapter 7

1. In letters to ourselves (October 1978 and October 1979) Ted Hughes wrote:

After the First Fright is crude—at one point I replaced it—but I put it back. Keith Sagar urged me not to drop it, and he's right, it has a kind of intactness—it states its case in a way I haven't been able to improve. And it has a place in the pattern. The subject here—that no doubt had some influence on the tone and style of the piece—is the crude and degenerate state of the mutual understandings between what is desirable and required, and what is inescapably and blindly undergone. 'Civilisation' and 'Sanity' are variable terms, according to what is desirable and required. What is 'desirable' and 'required' to what is truly suffered? In Cave paintings, there exist many stencil outlines of hands lacking fingers, one, two or more. These are widespread. And in various surviving primitive societies, one of the 'requirements' of mourning, is that the mourner loses a finger. It is evidently a spontaneous instinctive 'requirement'—at the time of bereavement. One would hesitate to call it 'civilised' or 'sane', but where it exists, as a custom, it is a required and (by everybody else in the society) desirable thing to do. It is part of the coherent, balanced, successfully adapted system by which those societies manage life and their world.

In the same way, the 'cross-shaped cut' is, or was, required and desirable in Japanese society in certain circumstances. Part of the fascination of Hara-kiri is our recognition of what it implies—an ultimate confrontation of the real pain of pain, a deliberate, controlled translation of psychological pain into physical pain, the absolute acceptance of pain on its own terms. In that sense, it is an act not only of absolute courage, but of absolute honesty. It is *the* symbolic act of the acceptance of the *reality* of what hurts. It is part of the reverence—in that case not short of worship—for the actuality of inner experience.

Without this explanation, perhaps those textual details are obscure—I intended them to work on their own, and yet, in my mind, be properly in place, not merely arbitrary. The point of the poem is that the real language of pain is clear—its declaration to the 'I' in the poem is immediate and complete, totally understood. But at the same time (perhaps this too influences the tone and style of the piece) it is a language that excludes concepts and words.

2. Hughes has written to us that the basic idea of *Cave Birds* is 'the psychological crime, punishment and compensation of Socrates', and that at one point it was subtitled

> The Death of Socrates and his Resurrection in Egypt—with some idea of suggesting that aspect of it which is a critique of sorts of the Socratic abstraction and its consequences through Christianity to us. His resurrection in Egypt, in that case, would imply his correction, his re-absorption into the magical-religious archaic source of intellectual life in the East Mediterranean, and his re-emergence as a Horus—beloved child and spouse of the Goddess.

(The falcon was sacred to Horus and the hieroglyph of his name.) Hughes originally intended to include in *Cave Birds* the poem 'Actaeon' (published in *Moortown*), which was itself originally subtitled 'based on the death of Socrates'. We have given this information in a note rather than the main text of our chapter because, in Hughes's own words, 'Better if the poem operates without historical confinements or scholarly-pedantic baggage.'

260

❧ Bibliographical Appendix ❧

The following are some points we have noticed in our work, which may be of interest to readers.

1. The version of 'The Jaguar' published in *Poetry from Cambridge 1952–54* is substantially different from the version collected in *The Hawk in the Rain*. In particular, the final stanza has been completely changed, but Hughes later incorporated one line, 'Swivelling the ball of his heel on the polished spot', into 'Second Glance at a Jaguar'.

2. 'Scene Without an Act', published in *Granta*, 12 May 1956, is a much longer version of 'Parlour Piece' (*The Hawk in the Rain*) and its last line resurfaces, slightly altered, as the last line of 'Thrushes' (*Lupercal*):

> You had learned why the gestures of these lovers keep
> Nonchalance and enigma, had you guessed
> In what flaming red gulf their hearts lie lost,
> Under what black wilderness of waters weep.

3. 'On Westminster Bridge', published in *Poetry* (Chicago), vol. 103 no. 3, December 1963, has the lines

> Let us all go down to exult
> Under the haddock's thumb, rejoice
> Through the warped mouth of the flounder, let
> us labour with God on the beaches!

which appear with alterations in *Critical Quarterly*, vol. 8 no. 4, Winter 1966, in a poem entitled 'Public Speech'. This poem was collected in *Wodwo* under the title 'Karma', but was dropped from *Selected Poems 1957–1967*, when these lines were further incorporated into the expanded version of 'Stations'.

4. 'Warm Moors', published in *Critical Quarterly*, vol. 8 no. 1, Spring 1966, has these lines:

261

This is the way the lark climbs into the sun—

Till your eye's gossamer snaps and your hearing
   floats back widely to earth.

After which the sky lies blank open
Without wings, and the earth is a folded clod.
Only the sun goes silently and endlessly on with
   the lark's song.

The last four lines reappear in 'Skylarks' (*Wodwo*).

5. *Journal of Creative Behaviour*, vol. 1 no. 3, July 1967, has 'Three Legends' of the creation of Crow. The first of these is 'Black was the without eye', with which *Crow* begins. The other two, 'How deeply the stone slept' and 'Black had swallowed the sun', are uncollected. These were among the very first *Crow* poems to be published.

6. 'Crow's Song of Himself' is incorporated into a longer poem, 'The Space-Egg was Sailing', published in *New Poems 1970–1* the year after the first edition of *Crow*.

7. The library of the University of Liverpool has the manuscripts of eight out of at least nine poems, several of them collected in *Crow*, which seem at one stage to have been conceived as a sequence of 'Bedtime Stories'. The published titles of the poems are: 'Song of Woe', 'Lovesong', 'A Bedtime Story', 'Criminal Ballad', 'Crow's Account of the Battle', 'Crow's Elephant Totem Song', 'Existential Song', 'Anecdote'. Even the poems from this group that are collected in *Crow* do not name him except in their titles.

8. In the broadcast version of *Cave Birds* there were two poems subsequently omitted from the Faber text: 'What is the legal position? You are one gargantuan debt' and 'Your mother's bones wanted to speak'. What these poems have in common is a much more explicitly and aggressively accusing tone than any in the Faber text. Also two poems, 'The plaintiff' and 'A riddle', have been revised almost beyond recognition from the broadcast versions, and the first-mentioned of these was also much more accusing in the earlier version. Altogether nineteen of the poems are more or less the same as the broadcast versions and nine are significantly altered. In only one case, 'In these fading moments', a drastically revised version appeared subsequently to the broadcast (as 'He called', *London Magazine*, April/May 1976) but the Faber text reverted to the original version. The following poems were published in the Scolar Press edition, in this order: 'The knight', 'The baptist', 'A flayed crow in the hall of judgement', 'The gatekeeper', 'A green mother', 'I meet you for the audit' (first version of 'A riddle'), 'The scapegoat', 'The guide', 'Walking bare', 'The owl flower'.

9. The following poems in *Moortown* have formerly been published as Crow poems: 'The Lovepet' (in the American edition of *Crow*), 'Life is Trying to be Life' (as 'Crow Rambles' in *Crow* limited edition), 'Prospero and Sycorax' (as 'Crow's Song about Prospero and Sycorax' in *Crow* limited edition) and 'Tiger-psalm' (as 'Crow's Table Talk' in *Crow Wakes*). The 'Orts' section of *Moortown* includes thirteen of the sixty-three poems in the Rainbow Press volume *Orts*. This section of *Moortown* also contains several poems not in *Orts*. The poem 'Actaeon' was originally intended as part of *Cave Birds*.

✧ Bibliography ✧

Keith Sagar's *The Art of Ted Hughes* (reprint of 2nd edition) has a comprehensive bibliography up to 1980, to which we are indebted. Rather than reproduce Sagar's work, we have aimed to provide a selective listing of material that we think will be of particular interest to readers. We have added separate entries for some poems which are collected only in limited editions but are also more easily available in periodicals.

I Books and pamphlets by Hughes

The Hawk in the Rain (40 poems), Faber, London, 1957; Harper and Brothers, New York, 1957.

Lupercal (41 poems), Faber, London, 1960; Harper and Brothers, New York, 1960.

Selected Poems by Thom Gunn and Ted Hughes (24 Hughes poems from *Hawk in the Rain* and *Lupercal*), Faber, London, 1962.

Recklings (31 poems), 150 signed copies, Turret Books, London, 1966.

The Burning of the Brothel (poem), 300 copies, 75 signed, Turret Books, London, 1966.

Wodwo (40 poems, 5 stories and a play), Faber, London, 1967; Harper and Row, New York, 1967, omits 'Logos', adds 'Root, Stem, Leaf' and 'Scapegoats and Rabies'.

Crow, From the Life and Songs of the Crow (60 poems), Faber, London, 1970; 2nd edition with 7 additional poems, 1972; limited edition, 400 signed, illustrated by Leonard Baskin, with 3 additional poems, 1973; Harper and Row, New York, 1971, as 2nd Faber edition with 'The Lovepet' in place of 'Crowcolour'.

A Few Crows (contains 'Carnival', not published elsewhere), illustrated by Reiner Burger, 75 signed copies, Rougemont Press, Exeter, 1970.

264

A Crow Hymn (poem), 100 copies, 26 signed, Sceptre Press, Frensham, Surrey, 1970.

Crow Wakes (12 poems), 200 copies, Poet and Printer, London, 1971.

Poems: Ruth Fainlight, Ted Hughes, Alan Sillitoe (6 Hughes poems), 300 signed copies, Rainbow Press, London, 1971.

Eat Crow (radio play), 150 signed copies, Rainbow Press, London, 1971.

Selected Poems 1957–1967 (68 poems from *Hawk in the Rain*, *Lupercal* and *Wodwo*, including 2 poems not in Faber *Wodwo* and major emendations to several *Wodwo* poems), Faber, London, 1972; Harper and Row, New York, 1973, illustrated by Leonard Baskin, omits 'Kafka'.

In the Little Girl's Angel Gaze (poem), a broadsheet designed by Ralph Steadman, 50 signed copies, Steam Press, London, 1972.

The Story of Vasco (opera in three acts, music by Gordon Crosse, libretto based on an English version by Ted Hughes of the play *L'Histoire de Vasco* by Georges Schehadé), OUP, London, 1974.

Eclipse (poem), 250 copies, 50 signed, Sceptre Press, Knotting, Beds., 1976.

Gaudete (narrative poem with Epilogue of 45 short poems), Faber, London, 1977; Harper and Row, New York, 1977, has longer Argument, as does Faber paperback edition, 1979. Two further extended versions of the Argument have been published, in the Ilkley Literature Festival Programme, May 1975, and in the programme for a National Theatre Platform Performance, 18 July 1977. Only the Harper and Row and Faber paperback versions are identical.

Chiasmadon (poem), with etching by Claire Van Vliet, 185 signed copies, Janus Press, West Burke, Vermont, for Charles Seluzicki, Baltimore, 1977. Collected in *Moortown* as 'Photostomias'.

Orts (63 poems), 200 signed copies, Rainbow Press, London, 1978.

Cave Birds, An Alchemical Cave Drama (28 poems), with drawings by Leonard Baskin, Faber, London, 1978; Viking Press, New York, 1978; 10 poems with facsimiles of early drafts, and drawings by Leonard Baskin, 100 signed copies, Scolar Press, London, 1975; 'The Interrogator' with facsimile and drawing, Scolar Press, 1975.

A Solstice (poem), 350 copies, Sceptre Press, Knotting, Beds., 1978.

Remains of Elmet, A Pennine Sequence with photographs by Fay Godwin (64 poems), Faber, London, 1979; Harper and Row, New York, 1979; Rainbow Press edition, 1979, includes one extra poem, 'Wycoller Hall'; 'Sunstruck' published separately as a pamphlet (300 copies, 100 signed) by Sceptre Press, Knotting, Beds., 1977.

Moortown (125 poems), Faber, London, 1979; *Prometheus on His Crag* published, with some textual differences, by Rainbow Press (160 signed copies), London, 1973; *Moortown Elegies* (175 signed copies), Rainbow Press, 1978; *Adam and the Sacred Nine*, with five extra poems (200 signed copies), Rainbow Press, 1979; *Four Tales Told By An Idiot* (150 copies, 50 signed), Sceptre Press, Knotting, Beds., 1979; 'Pan' and 'Night arrival of seatrout' published as broadsheets, 30 signed copies, Morrigu Press, distributed by Rainbow Press, 1979. Some poems in this volume have also appeared in *Recklings*, the American and limited editions of *Crow*, *Crow Wakes*, *Season Songs*, *Orts* and *Moon-Bells*. American edition, Harper and Row, 1979, includes 'Bride and groom lie hidden for three days' and omits 'The Lovepet'.

Brooktrout (poem), 60 signed copies, illustrated by Ted Hughes, Morrigu Press, North Tawton, Devon, 1979.

The Threshold (story), 100 signed copies, illustrated by Ralph Steadman, published by Ralph Steadman at the Steam Press, London, 1979.

In the black chapel (poem), poster with drawing by Leonard Baskin, published on the occasion of the exhibition 'Illustrations to Ted Hughes Poems' at the Victoria and Albert Museum, 12 September–28 October 1979.

Wolverine (poem), 75 signed copies, illustrated by Ted Hughes, Morrigu Press, North Tawton, Devon, 1979.

II Magazine appearances of poems not collected in trade editions

'Wild West': *Don and Dearne*, Mexborough Secondary School, June 1946; *Scotsman*, 14 Sept. 1968; *Young Winter's Tales*, Macmillan, London, 1970, pp. 82–3.

'The Little Boys and the Seasons': *Granta*, 8 June 1954 (under pseudonym: Daniel Hearing); *Accent*, Spring 1957; *Poetry from Cambridge 1952–54*, ed. Karl Miller, Fantasy Press, 1955, pp. 27–8; quoted in full by Karl Miller, *New York Review of Books*, vol. XXI no. 3, 7 Mar. 1974.

'Scene Without an Act': *Granta*, 12 May 1956 (with illustration by 'M.N.').

'Bawdry Embraced': *Poetry* (Chicago), vol. 88 no. 5, Aug. 1956, pp. 12–14 (dated 'August 1956'); *Gemini*, 5, Spring 1958; *Recklings*.

'Quest': *The Grapevine*, University of Durham Institute of Education, Feb. 1958; quoted in full by Keith Sagar, *The Art of Ted Hughes* (2nd edition), p. 228.

'Shells': *New Yorker*, 1 Aug. 1959; *London Magazine*, vol. 8 no. 3, March 1961, pp. 19–20.

'Gulls Aloft', 'Snails': *Christian Science Monitor*, 15 Dec. 1959.

'A Fable': *TLS*, 9 Sept. 1960; *Mademoiselle*, Mar. 1961.

'Lines to a Newborn Baby': *Texas Quarterly*, vol. 3 no. 4, Winter 1960, pp. 214–15.

'For Frieda in her First Months': *Western Daily Press*, 22 Feb. 1961;

Sewanee Review, vol. 71 no. 1, Jan. 1963 (retitled 'To F. R. at Six Months').

'Last Lines', 'Flanders, 1960', 'Toll of Air Raids': *Observer*, 16 Apr. 1961; *Recklings* (titles emended to 'Flanders' and 'Toll'); 'Flanders' and 'Last Lines' also in *Sewanee Review*, vol. 17 no. 1, Jan. 1963; 'Flanders' also in *Spectator*, 26 May 1961.

'Fishing at Dawn': *New Statesman*, 26 May 1961; *Recklings*.

'The Lake': *New Yorker*, 21 Oct. 1961; *London Magazine*, vol. 3 no. 4, July 1963; *The Faber Book of Twentieth Century Verse*, Faber, London, 1965.

'Two Poems for a Verse Play': 'The Captain's Speech' and 'The Gibbons': *Texas Quarterly*, vol. 4 no. 3, Autumn 1961.

'Tutorial': *New Statesman*, 2 Nov. 1962, p. 628; *Northern Review*, vol. 1 no. 1 (entitled 'Two'), 1965; *Recklings* (emended).

'The Road to Easington': *English Poetry Now, Critical Quarterly Supplement 3*, 1962; *New Lines II*, ed. Robert Conquest, Macmillan, London, 1963, pp. 58–60.

'Poem to Robert Graves Perhaps', 'On Westminster Bridge', 'After Lorca', 'Era of Giant Lizards', 'Small Hours': *Poetry* (Chicago), vol. 103 no. 3, Dec. 1963, pp. 152–6; 'After Lorca' also in *New Poetry 1964, Critical Quarterly Supplement 5*, 1964.

'Bad News Good!': *Agenda*, Dec./Jan. 1963/4, p. 16.

'Stealing Trout on a May Morning': *New Yorker*, 21 Mar. 1964, p. 44; *Books, Poems, Plays*, BBC, Summer 1965; *Recklings* (emended version); *All Around the Year* by Michael Morpurgo, John Murray, London, 1979, pp. 138–40.

'Dice': '1. Torture Chamber, 2. Eclipse of Moon-man, 3. Fiesta, 4. Statue of Atalanta, 5. Porpoises at Brighton, 6. Guinness (also in *Recklings*), 7. Durst, 8. Upper Code': *Critical Quarterly*, vol. 6 no. 2, Summer 1964, p. 153.

'Fallen Eve': *Agenda*, vol. 4 no. 1, Apr.–May 1965; *Recklings*.

'Trees': *New Yorker*, 17 July 1965, p. 30; *Recklings*.

'Carol' (To the tune 'Once in Royal David's City'): *Sunday Times Review*, 19 Dec. 1965, p. 29.

'Gibraltar', 'A Colonial': *New Statesman*, 8 Apr. 1966, p. 504; 'A Colonial' also in *Recklings*.

'Warm Moors': *Critical Quarterly*, vol. 8 no. 1, Spring 1966.

'The Last Migration': *The Animal Anthology*, ed. Diana Spearman, 1966. Hughes wrote the poem especially for the anthology, the royalties of which were donated to the Fauna Preservation Society. See also 'Irish Elk'.

'Birdsong': *London Magazine*, vol. 6 no. 6, Sept. 1966, pp. 62–4.

'Beech Tree': *A Tribute to Austin Clarke*, Dolman Press (OUP), London, 1966, p. 16; *Poetry Review*, Autumn 1966; *Recklings*.

'The Toughest', 'Public Bar T.V.': *Paris Review*, 40, Winter–Spring 1967;

Recklings. 'Public Bar T.V.' is a different poem from the one with the same title collected in *Wodwo*.

'Small Events', 'Thaw': *New Yorker*, 18 Mar. 1967, p. 48 (also version of 'Fern' substantially different from the one in *Wodwo*); *Recklings*.

'Three Legends': *Journal of Creative Behaviour*, vol. 1 no. 3, July 1967 (includes the first of 'Two Legends' in *Crow* and two uncollected poems).

'The Brother's Dream': *Poetry 1900–1965*, ed. George Macbeth, Longman with Faber, London, 1967, pp. 326–9.

'T.V. On': *Listener*, 23 Sept. 1967.

'Crowquill': *Poetry Gala*, 1968, p. 7.

'The New World': '1. It's not long you'll be straddling the rocket, 2. When the star was on her face, 3. A star stands on her forehead, 4. I said goodbye to earth, 5. The street was empty and stone, 6. Where did we go?': *Three Choirs Festival* programme, Aug.–Sept. 1972, pp. 69–70. Set by Gordon Crosse in 1968–9. Text accompanies record Argo ZRG 788. No. 4 also in *Gaudete*. No. 6 quoted in full by Sagar, *The Art of Ted Hughes* (2nd edition), p. 140.

'Song of Woe': *Critical Quarterly*, vol. 12 no. 2, Summer 1970; quoted in full by Sagar, *The Art of Ted Hughes* (2nd edition), pp. 136–7.

'A Lucky Folly': *Workshop*, 10, 1970.

'Existential Song', 'Song Against the White Owl': *London Magazine*, vol. 10 no. 4, July/Aug. 1970; *Corgi Modern Poets in Focus*, 1; *New Poems 1971–2*, a P.E.N. anthology, Hutchinson, London, 1972; 'Song Against the White Owl' also in *Crow Wakes*; 'Existential Song' quoted in full by Sagar, *The Art of Ted Hughes* (2nd edition), pp. 132–3.

'The Space-Egg was Sailing': *New Poems 1970–1*, a P.E.N. anthology, Hutchinson, London, 1971. Incorporates 'Crow's Song of Himself'.

'Crow's Courtship': *Vogue*, 15 Apr. 1971, p. 81; *Critical Quarterly*, vol. 13 no. 3, Autumn 1971; *New Poems 1972–3*, a P.E.N. anthology, Hutchinson, London, 1973; *Poems: Ruth Fainlight, Ted Hughes, Alan Sillitoe*; limited edition of *Crow*.

'Genesis of Evil': *Vogue*, 15 Apr. 1971, p. 81; *Critical Quarterly*, vol. 13 no. 3, Autumn 1971; *Poetry 1972, Critical Quarterly Supplement*; *New Poems 1972–3*, a P.E.N. anthology, Hutchinson, London, 1973.

'An Alchemy': *Poems for Shakespeare*, 2, ed. Graham Fawcett, Globe Playhouse Trust Publications, 1973, pp. 13–16.

'Welcombe', 'Exits': *Bananas*, I, Jan.–Feb. 1975.

'The Lamentable History of the Human Calf': *New Departures*, 7/8, 10/11, 1975.

'Light', 'Air', 'Skin': *Granta '76*, April 1976, p. 14; 'Light' in Rainbow Press *Adam and the Sacred Nine*; 'Air' and 'Skin' in *Orts*.

'The fallen oak sleeps under the bog', 'You have come down from the clouds': *Boston University Journal*, vol. 24 no. 3, 1976, p. 34; *Orts*.

'Let that one shrink into place', 'Stilled at his drink', 'The bulging oak is not as old', 'Why do you take such nervy shape': *Listener*, 20 Mar. 1975, p. 375. Described as 'part of a new sequence called "Lumb's Remains"'; all are in *Orts*, none in *Gaudete*.

'Eye went out to hunt you': *Aquarius* 9, Jan. 1977, p. 45; *Orts*.

'Whiteness': *Hand and Eye*, An Anthology for Sacheverell Sitwell, ed. Geoffrey Elborn (175 copies), The Tragara Press, Edinburgh, 1977; *Saturday Night Reader*, ed. Emma Tennant, W. H. Allen, 1979.

'After the Grim Diagnosis': *Poetry Supplement*, ed. Colin Falck, Poetry Book Society, Christmas 1977.

'Who lives in my skin with me?', 'If you doubt this face': *Mars*, I, 1977 (from *Caprichos*).

'Unknown Warrior': *New Poems 1977–78*, a P.E.N. anthology of contemporary poetry, ed. Gavin Ewart, Hutchinson, London, 1977.

'Wycoller Hall': *Antaeus*, 30/31, Spring 1978, pp. 99–100; Rainbow Press *Remains of Elmet*.

'Tiger': *London Magazine*, vol. 18 no. 2, May 1978, p. 31.

'A Nation's a Soul': quatrain for the Silver Jubilee, carved in the paving-stones of Queen Square, London WC1; printed in *TLS*, 23 June 1978, p. 704.

'A Solstice': *A Solstice*, limited edition, Sceptre Press, Knotting, Beds., 1978; *All Around the Year* by Michael Morpurgo, John Murray, London, 1979, pp. 60–64.

'The foal has landed': *Critical Quarterly*, vol. 20 no. 3, Autumn 1978, pp. 7–8; *All Around the Year* by Michael Morpurgo, John Murray, London, 1979, pp. 12–13 (as 'Foal').

'Irish Elk': *Listener*, 18 Jan. 1979, p. 121 (a rewritten section of 'The Last Migration').

'A Dove': *Listener*, 15 Mar. 1979, p. 381; *Ploughshares* (Cambridge, Mass.), vol. 6 no. 1, ed. Seamus Heaney, 1980.

'Barley': *All Around the Year* by Michael Morpurgo, John Murray, London, 1979, pp. 12–13.

'The Rose': *Poetry London/Apple*, 1, October 1979.

'Salmon Taking Times', 'You Hated Spain': *Poetry Book Society Poetry Supplement*, ed. Douglas Dunn, 1979; 'You Hated Spain' also in *Ploughshares* (Cambridge, Mass.), vol. 6 no. 1, ed. Seamus Heaney, 1980.

'Woodpecker': Morrigu Press broadsheet, North Tawton, Devon, 1979; *TLS*, 14 Dec. 1979.

'Puma': Morrigu Press broadsheet, North Tawton, Devon, 1979; *Listener*, 20/27 Dec. 1979.

'The Iron Wolf': Morrigu Press broadsheet, North Tawton, Devon, 1979; *Listener*, 28 Feb. 1980, p. 281.

'Unfinished Mystery', 'The Earthenware Head': *London Review of Books*, 21 Feb. 1980, p. 4.

'Nightjar': *London Review of Books*, 15 May 1980, p. 8.

'Lily', 'Do not pick up the telephone': *Ploughshares* (Cambridge, Mass.), vol. 6 no. 1, ed. Seamus Heaney, 1980.

'The Snow-Shoe Hare': *Listener*, 23 Sept. 1980, p. 413.

'Eagle', 'Low Water': *London Review of Books*, 2–16 Oct. 1980, p. 16; 'Eagle' also a Morrigu Press broadsheet, North Tawton, Devon, 1980.

'Fort': *A Garland of Poems for Leonard Clark*, compiled by R. L. Cook, The Lomond Press, Kinnesswood with the Enitharmon Press, London, August 1980.

'September Salmon', 'The Merry Mink', 'Last Act', 'The Moorhen': *Quarto* 11, October 1980.

'The Arctic Fox': *Listener*, 6 Nov. 1980, p. 622.

'The Word River': *New Departures* 12, 26 Sept. 1980.

III Uncollected stories

'Bartholemew Pygge Esq.': *Granta*, 4 May 1957.

'O'Kelly's Angel': *Granta*, 18 May 1957.

'The Caning': *Texas Quarterly*, vol. 3 no. 4, Winter 1960.

'Miss Mambrett and the Wet Cellar': *Texas Quarterly*, vol. 4 no. 3, Autumn 1961.

'The Head': *Bananas*, 11, Summer 1978, pp. 38–42; *The Saturday Night Reader*, ed. Emma Tennant, W. H. Allen, London, 1979.

IV Essays, reviews, interviews and other prose pieces

'Ted Hughes Writes': *Poetry Book Society Bulletin*, 15, 1957; reprinted in *Worlds*, ed. Geoffrey Summerfield, Penguin, Harmondsworth, 1974.

Review of *Weekend in Dinlock* by Clancy Segal: *Nation*, 2 July 1960.

Review of *Living Free* by Joy Adamson and other books: *New Statesman*, 10 Nov. 1961.

'Context': *London Magazine*, vol. 1 no. 11, Feb. 1962, pp. 44–5.

Review of *The Nerve of Some Animals* by Robert Froman and *Man and Dolphin* by J. C. Lilly: *New Statesman*, 23 Mar. 1962.

'Leonard Baskin': programme for an exhibition at the Royal Society of Painters in Water-Colours, London, May 1962.

Review of *Primitive Song* by C. M. Bowra: *Listener*, 3 May 1962.

Review of *One Fish Two Fish Red Fish Blue Fish* by Dr Seuss, *The Cat's Opera* by Eilis Dillon and *The Otter's Tale* by Gavin Maxwell: *New Statesman*, 18 May 1962.

'The Poetry of Keith Douglas': *Listener*, 21 June 1962, pp. 1069–71. Different from Introduction to *Selected Poems* of Douglas.

Review of *Imitations* by Robert Lowell, *Listener*, 2 Aug. 1962.

Review of *Rule and Energy* by John Press: *New Statesman*, 9 Aug. 1963.

Review of *Vagrancy* by Philip O'Connor: *New Statesman*, 6 Sept. 1963.

Review of *Emily Dickinson's Poetry* by Charles R. Anderson: *Listener*, 12 Sept. 1963.

'The Rock' (a radio talk about his childhood in the Calder Valley): *Listener*, 19 Sept. 1963; *Writers on Themselves*, BBC, London, 1964; *Worlds*, ed. Geoffrey Summerfield, Penguin, Harmondsworth, 1974.

Introduction to *Selected Poems* of Keith Douglas, Faber, London, 1965.

'Patrick White's *Voss*': *Listener*, 6 Feb. 1964, pp. 229–30.

Review of *Myth and Religion of the North* by E. O. G. Turbeville-Petre: *Listener*, 19 Mar. 1964.

Review of *Astrology* by Louis MacNeice and *Ghost and Divining Rod* by T. C. Lethbridge: *New Statesman*, 2 Oct. 1964, p. 500.

Review of *Shamanism* by Mircea Eliade and *The Sufis* by Idries Shah: *Listener*, 29 Oct. 1964, pp. 677–8.

Review of *Mysterious Senses* by Vitus Dröscher: *New Statesman*, 27 Nov. 1964, pp. 838–40.

'Sylvia Plath': *Poetry Book Society Bulletin*, 44, 1965.

'Desk Poet', interview with John Horder: *Guardian*, 23 Mar. 1965.

Review of *The Faber Book of Ballads*, ed. Matthew Hodgart: *Guardian*, 14 May 1965, p. 11.

Review of *Men Who March Away, Poems of the First World War*, ed. I. M. Parsons: *Listener*, 5 Aug. 1965.

Review of *The Selected Letters of Dylan Thomas*, ed. Constantine Fitzgibbon: *New Statesman*, 25 Nov. 1966, p. 783.

Introduction to *A Choice of Emily Dickinson's Verse*, Faber, London, 1968.

Introduction to *Selected Poems* of Vasko Popa, Penguin, Harmondsworth, 1969, and to *Collected Poems 1943–1976* (a slightly expanded version of the first Introduction), Carcanet, Manchester, 1977.

'The Chronological Order of Sylvia Plath's Poems': *The Art of Sylvia Plath*, ed. Charles Newman, Faber, London, 1970.

'Myth and Education': *Children's Literature in Education*, 1, 1970, pp. 55–70; extensively revised version in *Writers, Critics and Children*, ed. Geoffrey Fox, Agathon Press, Heinemann Educational, London, 1976; revised version reprinted in *TES*, 2 Sept. 1977, pp. 11–13.

Review of *The Environmental Revolution* by Max Nicholson: *Spectator*, 21 March 1970; expanded version in *Your Environment*, 3, Summer 1970, pp. 81–3.

'Ted Hughes's *Crow*': *Listener*, 30 July 1970.

Introduction and Note to *A Choice of Shakespeare's Verse*, Faber, London, 1971.

'Ted Hughes and Crow', an interview with Egbert Faas: *London Magazine*, vol. 10 no. 10, Jan. 1971. pp. 5–20.

271

'Sylvia Plath's *Crossing the Water*: Some Reflections': *Critical Quarterly*, vol. 13 no. 2, 1971, pp. 165–72.

Interview with Tom Stoppard reported in 'Orghast': *TLS*, 1 Oct. 1971, p. 1174.

Letters in *TLS*, 19 Nov. 1971, and *Observer*, 21 Nov. 1971, about Alvarez's *The Savage God*.

Article by Hughes included in 'Orghast: Talking without words', *Vogue*, Dec. 1971.

'The Birth of Sogis' (part of *Orghast*) and long sections of the Tom Stoppard interview in 'The Persepolis Follies of 1971' by Geoffrey Reeves, *Performance*, Dec. 1971, pp. 47–70.

Letter in *Sunday Times*, 23 Jan. 1972, replying to Christopher Ricks's review of *A Choice of Shakespeare's Verse*.

Review of *A Separate Reality* by Carlos Castaneda: *Observer*, 5 Mar. 1972.

'Children plant trees for tomorrow': letter in *TES*, 17 Nov. 1972, p. 2.

Notes in *Worlds*, ed. Geoffrey Summerfield, Penguin, Harmondsworth, 1974—contains 'The Rock', text of contribution to *Poetry Book Society Bulletin*, 15, and author's notes on several poems.

Introduction to *Children as Writers*, 2, Heinemann, London, 1975.

Notes on *Cave Birds* and *Gaudete*, including extended Argument of *Gaudete*, Ilkley Literature Festival Programme, May 1975.

Introduction to *Selected Poems* of Janos Pilinszky, Carcanet, Manchester, 1976.

'A conversation with Ted Hughes about the Arvon Foundation': Arvon Press, Hebden Bridge, West Yorks., 1976.

'Janos Pilinszky': *Critical Quarterly*, vol. 18 no. 2, pp. 75–86 (different from Introduction to Pilinszky's *Selected Poems*).

Introduction to *Johnny Panic and the Bible of Dreams* by Sylvia Plath, Faber, London, 1977. Revised, shorter version in 2nd edition, 1979.

Introduction to *Amen* by Yehuda Amichai, OUP, Oxford, 1977.

'A Memorial Address' (delivered at St Martin-in-the-Fields): *Henry Williamson: The Man, The Writings: A Symposium*, T. J. Press, Padstow, Cornwall, 1980, pp. 159–65. Published as *Henry Williamson* by Rainbow Press (200 signed copies), London, 1979.

Introduction to *The Reef and other poems* by Keith Sagar, Proem Pamphlets. Ilkley, 1980.

Comment on Poetry International, poetry festivals and the reading aloud of poetry: *New Departures* 12, 26 Sept. 1980 (one page).

V Works for children

Meet My Folks! (12 poems) illustrated by George Adamson, Faber, London, 1961; illustrated by Mila Lazarevitch, Bobbs-Merrill, New

York, 1973 (2 poems omitted and 4 added); Puffin, Harmondsworth, 1977 (1 poem omitted, 2 poems and 4 drawings added).

How the Whale Became and other stories (11 stories) illustrated by George Adamson, Faber, London, 1963; illustrated by Rick Schreiter, Athenaeum, New York, 1964.

The Earth-Owl and Other Moon-People (23 poems) illustrated by R. A. Brandt, Faber, London, 1963. All but one of these poems are also in *Moon-Whales*.

Nessie the Mannerless Monster (a narrative poem) illustrated by Gerald Rose, Faber, London, 1964; *Nessie the Monster*, illustrated by Jan Pyk, Bobbs-Merrill, New York, 1974.

Poetry in the Making (an anthology of poems and programmes from *Listening and Writing*), Faber, London, 1967; as *Poetry Is*, Doubleday, New York, 1970.

The Iron Man (A Story in Five Nights) illustrated by George Adamson, Faber, London, 1968; as *The Iron Giant*, illustrated by Robert Nadler, Harper and Row, New York, 1968; adapted for children learning to read, illustrated by Colin Smithson, Penguin, Harmondsworth, 1973.

The Demon of Adachigahara (A Cantata for junior choir, narrator, and instruments, with optional mime, based on a Japanese folk-tale) by Gordon Crosse, words by Ted Hughes, OUP, London, n.d. (1969).

The Coming of the Kings and other plays ('The Coming of the Kings', 'The Tiger's Bones', 'Beauty and the Beast', 'Sean, the Fool, the Devil and the Cats'), Faber, London, 1970.

The Tiger's Bones (as *The Coming of the Kings* with 'Orpheus' added) illustrated by Alan E. Cober, Viking Press, New York, 1974.

Season Songs (28 poems), Faber, London, 1976; American edition with illustrations by Leonard Baskin, Viking Press, New York, 1975 (lacks 5 poems in English edition; has one, 'The Defenders', not in English edition); *Spring, Summer, Autumn, Winter*, 140 signed copies, Rainbow Press, London, 1974, has one poem, 'Hunting the Summer', not in either edition of *Season Songs*.

Earth-Moon (31 poems) illustrated by the author, 226 signed copies, Rainbow Press, London, 1976. All contained in *Moon-Whales*.

Moon-Whales (54 poems) illustrated by Leonard Baskin, Viking Press, New York, 1976. Contains all the poems in *Earth-Moon*, and all except 'Moon-Transport' from *The Earth-Owl*.

Moon-Bells and other poems (22 poems), Chatto and Windus, London, 1978. Some poems also in *Recklings*, *Crow Wakes*, *Earth-Moon*, *Moon-Whales* and *Moortown*.

Under the North Star: At the time of our going to press, Faber and Viking Press plan to publish, early in 1981, a volume of 22 poems, with illustrations by Leonard Baskin. It is expected to include the following poems mentioned elsewhere in our bibliography: 'The Wolverine', 'The Snow-

273

Shoe Hare', 'Woodpecker', 'Brooktrout', 'The Arctic Fox', 'Puma', 'The Iron Wolf' and 'Eagle'.

VI Works translated by Ted Hughes

Seneca's Oedipus adapted by Ted Hughes, Faber, London, 1969; illustrated by Reginald Pollack, Doubleday, New York, 1972.

Amichai, Yehuda: *Selected Poems*, Penguin, Harmondsworth, 1971 (from the Hebrew with Assia Gutmann and Harold Schimmel);
Amen, Harper and Row, New York, 1977, OUP, Oxford, 1978 (from the Hebrew with the author), introduction by Ted Hughes;
Time, OUP, Oxford, 1979 (from the Hebrew by the author with Ted Hughes).
Pilinszky, Janos: *Selected Poems*, Carcanet, Manchester, 1976 (from the Hungarian with Janos Csokits), introduction by Ted Hughes.

VII Works edited by Ted Hughes (see also IV)

New Poems, Hutchinson, London, 1962, a P.E.N. anthology, with Patricia Beer and Vernon Scannell.
Five American Poets, Faber, London, 1963, with Thom Gunn.
Modern Poetry in Translation, nos. 1–10 (1965–71), with Daniel Weissbort.

VIII Recordings

Listening and Writing, BBC Records RESR 19M, 1971. Two talks which are published in *Poetry in the Making*: 'Capturing Animals' and 'Learning to Think'. These contain readings by Hughes of 'The Thought-Fox', 'Pike', 'View of a Pig' and 'Wodwo'.
Poets Reading, no. 5, Jupiter JEP OC27. Recorded Spring 1962. Hughes reads 'The Thought-Fox', 'Soliloquy of a Misanthrope', 'Mayday on Holderness' and 'Pibroch'.
The Poet Speaks, no. 5, Argo PLP 1085. Recorded 29 Aug. 1963. After a brief introduction Hughes reads 'Her Husband', 'Bowled Over', 'Still Life', 'Wodwo', 'Mountains', 'The Warriors of the North', 'Gog', 'Out' and 'Full Moon and Little Frieda (longer than published version).
Jupiter Anthology of 20th Century English Poetry, Part III, Jupiter JUR OOA8. Recorded 1963. Hughes reads 'The Hawk in the Rain' and 'Hawk Roosting'.

Crow, Claddagh CCT9–10, 1973. Hughes reads all the poems in the first English edition of *Crow* with the exception of 'Robin Song' and 'Crow Improvises'. Brief account of background to poems on sleeve.

The New World by Gordon Crosse, sung by Meriel and Peter Dickinson, Argo ZRG 788, 1975. Includes text of poems.

The Poetry and Voice of Ted Hughes, Caedmon TC 1535 (distributed in UK and Europe by Teakfield), 1977. Hughes reads 'The Thought-Fox', 'The Jaguar', 'Wind', 'Six Young Men', 'Mayday on Holderness', 'The Retired Colonel', 'View of a Pig', 'Sunstroke', 'Pike', 'An Otter', 'Hawk Roosting', 'Icecrust and Snowflake', 'Sheep I', 'His Legs Ran About', twelve poems from the Epilogue of *Gaudete* and 'Bride and Groom'.

Ted Hughes and R. S. Thomas, The Critical Forum, Norwich Tapes Ltd, Markfield House, Caldbec Hill, Battle, Sussex, 1978. Hughes reads and discusses six poems from *Moortown*.

IX Manuscripts in public collections

1. Liverpool University Library has been making a systematic collection of all Hughes's work, including limited editions. The manuscript collection includes interesting unpublished material from the *Wodwo* period (see Note 1 to Chapter 5), together with some early versions of published and unpublished Crow poems, an unpublished play, 'The Demon', performed in a programme of 'Plays for Easter' at the Orchard Theatre, Barnstaple, March 1970, and three early television scenarios, each one page of typescript.

2. The British Library Department of Manuscripts collection of Hughes manuscripts is fully listed in *The Arts Council Collection of Modern Literary Manuscripts 1963–1972* by Jenny Stratford, Turret Books, London, 1974, pp. 61–2. This collection consists of drafts of published and unpublished poems from the *Wodwo* period, fragments of BBC scripts, 'Air' (broadcast 2 Oct. 1961) and 'Difficulties of a Bridegroom' (broadcast 21 Jan. 1963), and of the unpublished play 'The Calm'.

3. Exeter University Library has the manuscript of *Cave Birds*.

X Criticism

Abbs, Peter, 'The Revival of the Mythopoeic Imagination—a study of R. S. Thomas and Ted Hughes', *Poetry Wales*, vol. 10 no. 4, 1975, pp. 10–27.

Adams, John, 'Dark Rainbow: Reflections on Ted Hughes' and a 'postscript', *The Signal Approach to Children's Books*, ed. Nancy Chambers, Kestrel Books, Penguin, Harmondsworth, 1980.

BIBLIOGRAPHY

Alvarez, A., Introduction to *The New Poetry*, Penguin, Harmondsworth, 1962.

Bedient, Calvin, *Eight Contemporary Poets*, OUP, London, 1974.

Bold, Alan, *Thom Gunn and Ted Hughes*, Oliver and Boyd, Edinburgh, 1976.

Bradshaw, Graham, 'Ted Hughes's Crow—Trickster-hero or trickster-poet?', *The Fool and the Trickster, A Festschrift for Enid Welsford*, ed. Paul V. A. Williams, Boydell Press, Ipswich, 1979.

Dunn, Douglas, Review of *Gaudete*, *Encounter*, 50, Jan. 1978, pp. 78–83.

Eagleton, Terry, Review of *Gaudete*, *Stand*, vol. 19, no. 2, 1978, pp. 78–9.

Faas, Ekbert, *Ted Hughes: The Unaccommodated Universe*, Black Sparrow Press, Santa Barbara, 1980. Reprints Faas's *London Magazine* interview, 'Ted Hughes and *Crow*'; includes a new interview about *Gaudete* and a large selection from Hughes's critical prose.

Gifford, Terry, 'A Return to "The Wound" by Ted Hughes', *Kingfisher*, vol. 1, no. 2/3, 1978, pp. 46–53.

Grubb, Frederick, *A Vision of Reality: a study of liberalism in twentieth-century verse*, Chatto, London, 1965.

Heaney, Seamus, 'Deep as England', review of *Selected Poems*, *Hibernia*, 1 Dec. 1972, p. 13;
'Now and in England' (Hughes, Geoffrey Hill and Philip Larkin), *Critical Inquiry*, vol. 3 no. 3, Spring 1977, pp. 471–88; reprinted in *Preoccupations*, Faber, 1980.
Interview with John Haffenden, *London Magazine*, vol. 19 no. 3, June 1979: comments on Hughes, pp. 27–8.

Holbrook, David, 'From "Vitalism" to a Dead Crow: Ted Hughes's Failure of Confidence' in *Lost Bearings in English Poetry*, Vision Press, London, 1977.

Kramer, Lawrence, 'The Wodwo Watches the Water Clock', *Contemporary Literature*, vol. 18 no. 3, 1977, pp. 319–42.

Law, Pamela, 'Poetry as Ritual: Ted Hughes', *Sydney Studies in English*, 2, 1976/77, pp. 72–82.

Lewis, P. E., 'The New Pedantry and "Hawk Roosting"', *Stand*, vol. 8 no. 1, 1966.

Libby, Anthony, 'Fire and Light, Four Poets to the End and Beyond' (Hughes, Robert Bly, James Dickey and W. S. Merwin), *Iowa Review*, Spring 1973, pp. 111–26;
'God's Lioness and the Priest of Sycorax: Plath and Hughes', *Contemporary Literature*, vol. 15 no. 3, Summer 1974, pp. 386–405.

Liberthson, Daniel, 'The Quest for Being: Theodore Roethke, W. S. Merwin and Ted Hughes', Ph.D. thesis, State University of New York at Buffalo, 1976.

Lodge, David, '*Crow* and the Cartoons', *Critical Quarterly*, vol. 13 no. 1, Spring 1971, pp. 37–42 and 68; reprinted in *Poetry Dimension*, 1, ed.

276

Jeremy Robson, Abacus, London, 1973, pp. 30–9.

May, Derwent, 'Ted Hughes' in *The Survival of Poetry*, ed. Martin Dodsworth, Faber, London, 1970.

Miller, Karl, 'Fear and Fang', *New York Review of Books*, vol. 21 no. 3, 7 Mar. 1974.

Morse, Brian, 'Poetry, Children and Ted Hughes', *The Signal Approach to Children's Books*, ed. Nancy Chambers, Kestrel Books, Penguin, Harmondsworth, 1980.

Newton, J. M., 'Mr Hughes's Poetry', *Delta*, 25, Winter 1961, pp. 6–12;
'Ted Hughes's Metaphysical Poems', *Cambridge Quarterly*, vol. 2 no. 4, Autumn 1967, pp. 395–402;
'Some Notes on Ted Hughes's *Crow*', *Cambridge Quarterly*, vol. 5 no. 4, 1971, pp. 376–82;
'No longer "through the pipes of Greece"?' (review of *Gaudete*), *Cambridge Quarterly*, vol. 7 no. 4, 1977, pp. 335–45.

Porter, David, 'Beasts/Shamans/Baskin: The Contemporary Aesthetics of Ted Hughes', *Boston University Journal*, vol. 22 no. 3, Fall 1974, pp. 13–25;
'Ted Hughes', *American Poetry Review*, vol. 4 no. 5, 1975.

Raban, Jonathan, *The Society of the Poem* (Chapters 2 and 9), Harrap, London, 1971.

Rawson, Claud, 'Ted Hughes: A Reappraisal', *Essays in Criticism*, vol. 15 no. 1, Jan. 1965, pp. 77–94;
'The Flight of the Black Bird' (review of *The Art of Ted Hughes* by Keith Sagar), *TLS*, 19 Mar. 1976, pp. 324–5.

Ries, Lawrence R., *Wolf Masks: Violence in Contemporary Poetry*, Kennikat Press, Port Washington, New York, 1977.

Roberts, Neil, 'The Spirit of Crow', *Delta*, 50, Spring 1972, pp. 1–15;
'What was my error?' (review of *Gaudete*), *Delta*, 57, 1977, pp. 1–8.

Robinson, Ian, and Sims, David, 'Ted Hughes's *Crow*', *Human World*, 9, Nov. 1972, pp. 31–40.

Rosenthal, M. L., *The New Poets*, OUP, New York, 1967.

Sagar, Keith, *Ted Hughes*, Longman for the British Council, 1972;
The Art of Ted Hughes, CUP, Cambridge, 1975; 2nd edition, enlarged, 1978;
An Exhibition in Honour of Ted Hughes, Ilkley Festival, 1975.

Schmidt, Michael, *An Introduction to Fifty Modern British Poets*, Pan, London, 1979.

Schmidt, Michael, and Lindop, Grevel (eds.), *British Poetry since 1960*, Carcanet, Oxford, 1972.

Strauss, P. E., 'The Poetry of Ted Hughes', *Theoria* (South Africa), 38, 1972, pp. 45–63.

Thurley, Geoffrey, 'Beyond Positive Values: Ted Hughes', in *The Ironic Harvest*, Arnold, London, 1974, pp. 163–89.

277

Trilling, Ossia, 'Playing With Words at Persepolis', *Theatre Quarterly*, vol. 2 no. 5, Jan.–Mar. 1972, pp. 33–40. (Critical response to the performance of *Orghast*, including three paragraphs of Hughes's comments at a press conference.)

Uroff, Margaret D., *Sylvia Plath and Ted Hughes*, University of Illinois, 1979.

Walder, Dennis, *Ted Hughes, Sylvia Plath* (A/306/29), Open University Press, Milton Keynes, 1976.

Wood, Michael, 'We All Hate Home: English Poetry since World War II', *Contemporary Literature*, vol. 18 no.3, 1977, pp. 305–18.

XI General

Armstrong, E. A., *The Folklore of Birds*, Collins, London, 1958.

Brodsky, A. T., Danesewich, R., and Johnson, N. (eds.), *Stones, Bones and Skin: Ritual and Shamanic Art*, The Society for Art Publications, Toronto, 1977.

Burnet, John, *Early Greek Philosophy*, Adam and Charles Black, London, 1908.

Campbell, Joseph, *The Hero With a Thousand Faces*, Pantheon, New York, 1949;
The Masks of God: Primitive Mythology, Secker and Warburg, London, 1960.

Castaneda, Carlos, *A Separate Reality* (1971), Penguin, Harmondsworth, 1973;
Journey to Ixtlan (1973), Penguin, Harmondsworth, 1974.

Dodds, E. R., *The Greeks and the Irrational*, Univ. of California, 1951.

Eliade, Mircea, *Patterns in Comparative Religion*, London and New York, 1958;
Shamanism, Routledge, London, 1964;
From Primitives to Zen, Collins, London, 1967.

Euripides, *The Bacchae and Other Plays*, translated by Philip Vellacott, Penguin, Harmondsworth, 1954.

Farid ud-din Attar, *The Conference of the Birds*, translated by C. S. Nott, Samuel Weiser, New York, 1969.

Frazer, James George, *The Golden Bough* (abridged edition), Macmillan, London, 1922.

Geertz, Clifford, 'Religion as a Cultural System', in Michael Banton (ed.), *Anthropological Approaches to the Study of Religion*, Tavistock, London, 1966.

Graves, Robert, *The Greek Myths*, Penguin, Harmondsworth, 1955, revised edition 1960;
The White Goddess, Faber, London, 1961.

Harner, Michael J. (ed.), *Hallucinogens and Shamanism*, OUP, New York, 1973.

Harrison, Jane, *Themis: A Study of the Social Origins of Greek Mythology*, CUP, London, 1912.

Heaney, Seamus, *Death of a Naturalist*, Faber, London, 1966;
North, Faber, London, 1975.

Heilpern, John, *Conference of the Birds* (an account of Peter Brook's African venture), Faber, London, 1977.

Herbert, Zbigniew, *Selected Poems*, translated by Czeslaw Milosz and Peter Dale Scott with an introduction by A. Alvarez, Penguin, Harmondsworth, 1968;
Selected Poems, translated with an introduction and notes by John and Bogdana Carpenter, OUP, Oxford, 1977.

Holub, Miroslav, *Selected Poems*, translated by Ian Milner and George Theiner, with an introduction by A. Alvarez, Penguin, Harmondsworth, 1967.

Jung, C. G., 'Answer to Job' (*Collected Works*, vol. 11: *Psychology and Religion*, Routledge, London, 1958, 1963);
Alchemical Studies (*Collected Works*, vol. 13), Routledge, London, 1967.

Jung, C. G., and Kerényi, C., *Introduction to a Science of Mythology*, translated by R. F. C. Hull, London, 1951.

Kerényi, C., *Eleusis*, translated by Ralph Mannheim, Routledge, London, 1967.

Kroll, Judith, *Chapters in a Mythology: the Poetry of Sylvia Plath*, Harper and Row, New York, 1976.

Lawrence, D. H., *Phoenix*, Heinemann, London, 1936.

Lévi-Strauss, Claude, 'The Sorcerer and His Magic', 'The Effectiveness of Symbols', 'The Structural Study of Myth': Chapters 9–11 of *Structural Anthropology*, translated by Claire Jacobson and Brooke Grundfest Schoepf, Penguin, Harmondsworth, 1968 (translation first published 1963).

Malinowski, Bronislaw, *Myth in Primitive Psychology*, Kegan Paul, London, 1926.

Morgan, Edwin, *East European Poets*, Open University Twentieth-Century Poetry Unit 32, Open University Press, Milton Keynes, 1976.

New Larousse Encyclopaedia of Mythology, Hamlyn, 1968.

Plath, Sylvia, *The Colossus*, Heinemann, London, 1960, Faber, London, 1967;
Ariel, Faber, London, 1965;
Winter Trees, Faber, London, 1971;
Crossing the Water, Faber, London, 1971;
Letters Home, ed. Aurelia Schober Plath, Faber, London, 1975;

Johnny Panic and the Bible of Dreams, with an introduction by Ted Hughes, Faber, London, 1977;
'The Magic Mirror: a study of the Double in two of Dostoyevsky's novels', Dissertation for Special Honours English, Smith College, 1955 (photocopy in Cambridge University Library).

Popa, Vasko, *Selected Poems*, translated by Anne Pennington with an introduction by Ted Hughes, Penguin, Harmondsworth, 1969;
Earth Erect, translated by Anne Pennington, Anvil Press in association with Routledge, London, 1973;
Collected Poems 1943–1976, translated by Anne Pennington with an introduction by Ted Hughes, Carcanet, Manchester, 1978 (incorporates all the poems in the other two volumes).

Radin, Paul, *The World of Primitive Man*, New York, 1953;
The Trickster, Routledge, London, 1956;
Primitive Man as Philosopher, Dover, New York, Constable, London, 1957.

Redgrove, Peter, *Sons of My Skin, Selected Poems 1954–1974*, chosen and introduced by Marie Peel, Routledge, London, 1975;
From Every Chink of the Ark and other new poems, Routledge, London, 1977;
The God of Glass, A Morality, Routledge, London, 1979.

Shah, Idries, *The Sufis*, W. H. Allen, London, 1964.

Sharkey, John, *Celtic Mysteries*, Thames and Hudson, London, 1975.

Smith, A. C. H., *Orghast at Persepolis*, Eyre Methuen, London, 1972.

Táin, The, translated by Thomas Kinsella, OUP, London, 1970.

Tibetan Book of the Dead, compiled and edited by W. Y. Evans-Wentz, OUP, London, 1960 (1927).

Watts, Alan, *The Way of Zen*, Penguin, Harmondsworth, 1962 (1957).

Widengren, Geo, *Mani and Manichaeism*, translated by Charles Kessler, Weidenfeld and Nicolson, London, 1961.

❧ Indexes ❧

I Works by Ted Hughes

The following abbreviations are used to indicate the volumes in which poems are most readily to be found: *ASN*: Rainbow Press *Adam and the Sacred Nine*; *C*: *Crow*; *CB*: *Cave Birds*; *CW*: *Crow Wakes*; *G*: *Gaudete*; *HR*: *The Hawk in the Rain*; *L*: *Lupercal*; *M*: *Moortown*; *MB*: *Moon-Bells*; *R*: *Recklings*; *RE*: *Remains of Elmet*; *SP*: *Selected Poems 1957–67*; *SS*: *Season Songs*; *W*: *Wodwo*. Most poems collected only in limited editions have also been published in magazines etc. This information is given in Section II of the Bibliography. Page numbers in italics refer to detailed discussion.

II General